PSYCHOBILLY

KIMBERLY KATTARI

PSYCHOBILLY

Subcultural Survival

TEMPLE UNIVERSITY PRESS

Philadelphia • *Rome* • *Tokyo*

TEMPLE UNIVERSITY PRESS
Philadelphia, Pennsylvania 19122
tupress.temple.edu

Library of Congress Cataloging-in-Publication Data

Names: Kattari, Kimberly, 1980– author.
Title: Psychobilly : subcultural survival / Kimberly Kattari.
Description: Philadelphia : Temple University Press, 2020. | Includes bibliographical
  references and index. |
Identifiers: LCCN 2019034796 (print) | LCCN 2019034797 (ebook) |
  ISBN 9781439918616 (pdf) | ISBN 9781439918593 (cloth) |
  ISBN 9781439918609 (paperback)
Subjects: LCSH: Psychobilly music—Social aspects. | Subculture.
Classification: LCC ML3918.P79 (ebook) | LCC ML3918.P79 K37 2020 (print) |
  DDC 781.66—dc23
LC record available at https://lccn.loc.gov/2019034796

♾ The paper used in this publication meets the requirements of the American National
Standard for Information Sciences—Permanence of Paper for Printed Library Materials,
ANSI Z39.48-1992

Printed in the United States of America

9 8 7 6 5 4 3 2 1

CONTENTS

ACKNOWLEDGMENTS

This book is the result of more than ten years of exploration into psychobilly. In 2007, after writing my master's thesis on reggaeton and Latinx identity, I was working at a preschool in Austin, Texas, while I considered various potential topics for my doctoral studies. Dave, the father of one of the children in my class, was an avid music fan, and we often talked about the punk, metal, and rock bands we enjoyed. One day, when he mentioned a psychobilly band that would be performing at a local venue, he was surprised to find that—although I was from Southern California, the epicenter of the psychobilly scene—I had never heard of the band or even the genre. I was so fascinated by what I saw and heard the night I attended the concert (see the discussion in the Introduction to this book) that I knew I had found the genre that would become the focus of my doctoral studies. I cannot thank Dave enough for introducing me to the scene and for helping me to understand its subculture.

My doctoral dissertation, "Psychobilly: Imagining and Realizing a 'Culture of Survival' through Mutant Rockabilly" (Kattari 2011), was the starting point for this book. I revised that work extensively to include the overall development of the genre and to explore key issues in the subculture in chronological order. I reframed, restructured, and revised each chapter, taking into account the extensive ethnographic research I carried out after the completion of my doctoral studies, and included a new Introduction and a new Afterword. I am deeply grateful to all those who provided input on my work and commented on drafts of the dissertation and the manuscript, particularly my professors and fellow students at the University of Texas at Austin and my colleagues at Texas A&M University: Robin Moore, Sonia Seeman, Veit Erlmann, Karl Miller, Martha Menchaca, Penne Restad, Sidra Lawrence, Melanie Morgan, Kathryn Metz, Krista Kateneva, Ryan McCormack, Justin Patch, Daniel Sharp, James Ball III, Emily McManus, Jayson Beaster-Jones, Leonardo Cardoso, Andrés Amado, and Jamie Freedman. My deepest appreciation goes to fellow academic and psychobilly fan Nathan Katz for his expertise and feedback. I am indebted to all the staff at Temple University Press (especially Sara Cohen, Sarah Munroe, and Joan Vidal), as well as the anonymous readers of the manuscript; I thank them for their insight, patience, support, and wisdom.

I am happy to have this opportunity to thank the University of Texas at Austin for fellowships and research grants during my graduate studies that supported my initial ethnographic fieldwork and writing. I am also grateful for the financial research assistance provided by Texas A&M University through the Department of Performance Studies, the College of Liberal Arts, and the Melbern G. Glasscock Center for Humanities Research.

I thank all the psychobillies and rockabillies who took the time to share their passion for this music and trusted me with their reflections on the subculture. I will forever remember not only our conversations but also the beers, laughs, and gigs we shared. Knowing that psychobilly has, at times, been stigmatized and misrepresented in the press and social media, I strove to listen attentively, to fully hear what those within the subculture had to say. I did my utmost to represent the scene in ways that stay true to their experience and convey what they love so much about it. I hope this book gives readers a sense of why it is so meaningful to those who are a part of it. I offer my deepest appreciation to each and every one of the hundreds of psychobillies and rockabillies who contributed to this book. I especially thank those who consented to interviews, allowed their lyrics and artwork to be reproduced in this book, and helped me learn about the subculture through numerous discussions, event invitations, and adventures. They include Karling Abbeygate, Eric Alvarado, Danny Arechiga, Stu Arkoff, Lee Barnett, Dirk Behlau, Frank Benavidez, Brett Black, Sarah Blackwood, Zteben Blarg, Jonny Bowler, Craig Brackenridge, Spencer Burns, Remy Casillas, Dylan Cavaliere, Nick Centino, Cherry Red Records, Victor Czerniak (aka Rockin' Vic), Ungie Davila, Deke Dickerson, Norm Elliott, Tawney Estrella, Simon Farrell, Rob Fatal, Jeremie Fletcher, Kris Fotino, Mike "Frye," Dave Gambler, Dusty Grave, Jacob Gutierrez, Melane Gutierrez, David Guzman, Jason Hammond, Chuck Harvey, Danny B. Harvey, Pete and Connor Hillary, Tom Ingram, James Irvine, Reb Kennedy, Tommy Koffin, Shelby Legnon, Paul

"Hodge" Leigh, Sarah "Betty Elle" Leinen, David Levee, Thomas Lorioux, Brian Lux, Tony "T-Mac" Macías, Gary "Sinner" Marsh, Gaz Marson, Aaron Martinez, Al Martinez, Gator McMurder, Frank Mendez, Emilio Menze, Kim Nekroman, Robert "Nix" Nixon, Johnny O'Prez, Xavier Ortiz, Randy Padrón, Adriana Pérez Palacios, Mark Pennington, "Phat Elvis," Destin Pledger, Duck Plunkett, Tony "Slash" Red-Horse, Orla Reed, Oscar Reyes, Orlando Rios, Mark Robertson, Paul Roman, Robert Rose, Ricky "Lobo" Salazar, Daniel Sanchez, Jen Schevers, Ramon Sitoci, Mauri SixSickSix, Jessica Stemen, Elvis Suissa, Alex Tapia, Revillie Trenary, Alex "Bear" Vandaley, Carlos Fernando Varela (aka Sol Rac), Jorge Vargas, Vic Victor, Del Villareal, Brando Von Badsville, Chip Waite, Eric "E-Ball" Walls, Rockin' Ronnie Weiser, Steve Whitehouse, Robert Williams (Big Sandy), Roy Williams, Sydney Williams, Alan Wilson, and Steve Young. I am grateful to all the bands I interviewed, including 13 Black Koffins, 56 Killers, Astro Zombies, Becky & the Blacktones, The Caravans, The Chop Tops, Cold Blue Rebels, The Creepshow, Gamblers Mark, Hotrod Hillbillies, Klax, Koffin Kats, Mariachis del Infierno, Moonlight Trio, The Mutilators, The Quakes, The Quaranteds, The Rocketz, The Sharks, Stellar Corpses, Surfin' Wombatz, The Surf Rats, and Three Bad Jacks. I owe special thanks to Crow Phantom for creating the cover design for this book. And I thank Dick Lucas for being so generous and friendly when I was a young punk; I owe my interest in subcultures to him.

Finally, I could not have brought this project to fruition without the support of my family and friends. I thank Emily for her keen eye, thoughtful commentary, and unfailingly kind words. My brothers, Dean and Dave, taught me to question authority and to stand up for what I believe in. My parents, Jan and John, nurtured my growth into the ethnomusicologist I have become by fostering my curiosity, my love of research, and my interest in learning about diverse lives and cultures. I express my gratitude to Joshua and Tabby for making it through the "Captain Partykill" time and teaching me how to love life even when I was stressed about the book. Without the unwavering love and encouragement of Brandon, my partner throughout the book production process, I could not have completed this work. I thank him for standing by my side throughout this journey; for putting up with the anxiety and the sleepless nights it caused; for pushing (or even bribing) me, when necessary, to continue; and most of all, for showing me how to live and love.

PSYCHOBILLY

Subcultural Participation as a Survival Strategy

I was jumping to those rocking tunes, bopping on my feet
Then I heard those jungle rhythms, those crazy beats
Whey hey, well what can I say?
I got 1-2-3-4 psychobilly DNA
The only drug I needed was this music through my brain
Voodoo rhythms pump me up, drive me insane
Whey hey, well what can I say?
I got 1-2-3-4 psychobilly DNA
Now all these years later I'm changed beyond repair
Because I'm a psychobilly and I don't care
Whey hey, well what can I say?
I got 1-2-3-4 psychobilly DNA

—**NORM AND THE NIGHTMAREZ**, "Psychobilly DNA,"
Psychobilly D.N.A., 2016

A s my eyes adjusted to the dim light in the small club in Austin, Texas, I took in unfamiliar sights and sounds. This, I was told by my friend who had invited me, was the psychobilly subculture. I saw that participants had fused a 1950s aesthetic with punk elements. Men's heads were shaved on the sides, as with Mohawk haircuts, but rather than sticking up into pointed liberty spikes, their hair had been combed forward into one flat-topped, triangular wedge that jutted out and up from their foreheads.

Some women had the same haircut, while others had their hair styled in curls and bangs like those seen on vintage pinup illustrations. Leather jackets, cuffed blue jeans, tight-fitting capris, polka-dot dresses, animal prints, kitten heels, and pompadours reminded me of the movie *Grease*, but the patches, buttons, metal studs, Dr. Martens boots,[1] and dyed hair colors gave everything a punk twist. Bats, skulls, and zombies adorned clothes, accessories, and skin.

When the headliner, Nekromantix, came onstage, I saw a performer covered head to toe in tattoos furiously slapping a custom-designed upright bass that looked like a black coffin (see Figure I.1). He had a tattoo of the coffin bass on his neck. He poured Jägermeister on the neck of his instrument and licked it off while using his tongue to fret his bass, eliciting whoops and hollers from the crowd, who approved of the showy display. A catchy, pop-inflected melody accompanied lyrics about his girlfriend (or ghoulfriend?) getting horny in a hearse outside a cemetery, but other songs featured more shouting and growling. During a solo section, he opened his eyes wide and rolled his pupils upward as if possessed and then straddled his bass on the floor while continuing to play it at a frenetic pace with his feet and hands.

I started to feel like a sixteen-year-old punk again, registering that visceral feeling that came from abandoning myself to the noise and speed of the music. Old habits resurfaced as I found myself bracing against the bodies that slammed up against me. But the bodies in this "wrecking pit" moved differently from those in the punk circle pits of my youth. Instead of following one another in a counterclockwise direction, some staggered around slowly with their arms raised in front of them like Frankenstein's monster; some threw hooks and jabs at others while they stomped around randomly; and a few stood in the middle of the chaos, letting their bodies rebound off others. The music, too, was different from what I used to hear at punk shows. The slapping bass, the clean and crisp Gretsch guitar solos, and the shuffling beat all signified rockabilly. But the aggressive energy, intense vocals, breakneck speed, and deliberately shocking attitude reminded me of punk. True to its name, the music seemed to be a "psychotic" mutation of rockabilly.

That night I discovered that an underground subculture that I knew nothing about had been thriving in my own backyard. As an ethnomusicologist specializing in popular music, I was surprised by this. I had been a graduate student teaching assistant for a history of rock class for years but had no idea that there was a style that brought together elements of rockabilly, punk, heavy metal, new wave, and shock rock. Why had I not run across this before? An acquaintance had told me about this show, and I bombarded him with questions afterward. Where had this fusion of so many different elements started? Why were the participants interested in 1950s

Figure I.1. Kim Nekroman of Nekromantix performing with his coffin bass. (*Photo by the author.*)

music and fashion? Did they adopt other lifestyle habits one might associate with a "retro" interest in the 1950s? How did people find out about this subculture, which is not featured on the radio or performed at popular music festivals? Were the lyrics usually like the ones I had heard that night, full of references to monsters, necrophilia, murderers, and insanity? Why did the music feel worlds apart from the gore of death metal or the gloom of goth, even when the singer was fantasizing about killing the cheerleader who called him a freak? Why were these seemingly macabre lyrics underscored by a finger-snappingly pop music sound? On my drive home I thought about *Subculture: The Meaning of Style*, Dick Hebdige's classic study of punks and mods, which I had read in one of my graduate seminars. Would that book provide a useful model for understanding how psychobilly fans "make sense of the world" through their stylistic play with signifying elements of rockabilly, punk, and horror (1979, 113)?

Psychobilly 101

I explore the development of psychobilly in greater detail in the next chapter. Here I provide just a bit of cultural and historical context to situate the theoretical framework I employ in this book. Psychobilly developed in England in the early 1980s, born out of a frustration with the clichés of the already subcultural and ideologically rebellious rock 'n' roll, rockabilly, and punk scenes. Bands such as The Meteors, The Sharks, and Guana Batz wanted to shake up rockabilly, playing it faster, louder, and more aggressively than ever before—like punk. They found the themes that characterized 1950s music and its contemporary revival—pink-pegged pants, Cadillacs, blue suede shoes, going dancing on a Saturday night—outdated and irrelevant to working-class kids growing up in the economic recession of 1980s London. But they were not interested in adopting punk's insistence on critiquing the British monarchy or drawing attention to the socioeconomic disparities that characterized their lives. Brandishing a "no politics, no religion" slogan, they injected their revved-up rockabilly with themes borrowed from horror and science fiction while also celebrating silliness, camp, and cheese. The subculture grew mostly through word of mouth but also through rare references in alternative music media to the development of "psycho rockabilly." Fans of rockabilly, punk, skinhead, garage/trash, goth, mod, and new wave came together to witness the development of a new subculture.

They liked that the wild energy and the fast tempo made them feel a little crazy, especially when they threw themselves around in the chaotic frenzy of the wrecking pit and drank some "snakebite."[2] Fans of cheesy horror movies enjoyed lyrics about breaking out of a mental institution, becoming a zombie, or killing a girlfriend's dad. Songs could also give them a good laugh, such as King Kurt's ridiculously goofy "Banana Banana" (1984), replete with all the double entendres one can imagine. They were entertained by shocking and silly performances onstage, whether an act involved fake blood running down from the performer's mouth or a giant wheel spinning attendees who were strapped on after they had consumed vast quantities of alcohol. Given their lack of funds during England's economic recession, fans appreciated that the fashion reappropriated objects that were easy for them to acquire or make: denim jeans they bleached themselves, secondhand jackets, work boots, and cheap hair spray.

They met others who shared both their unconventional interest in this obscure and eclectic style and their lack of interest in mainstream[3] trends. Through the performative and stylistic elements of the subculture, including its signature fashion, music, and practices, psychobillies resisted normative expectations and refused complacency. They enjoyed a release and escape from the obligations, frustrations, and challenges that characterized their working-class lives. They had fun, drank excessively (as much as they could afford), threw their bodies into the wrecking pit, took every opportunity to "go mental" (go wild, act crazy), and sometimes topped this all off at the end of the night by hooking up with someone or fighting someone from another subculture outside the club. Psychobilly has since spread across the world, thriving in relatively small and geographically scattered but spectacularly distinct and enthusiastic underground pockets.

The Significance of Subcultural Identity and Participation

Over the course of ten years of ethnographic fieldwork, I came to appreciate how identification with this small subculture informs many aspects of my interlocutors' lives. Many of them "look" psychobilly most of the time; their distinctive tattoos, hair, makeup, clothes, and other stylistic signifiers identify them as psychobillies whether they are at work, home, school, or a show. Others do not feel the need to express their appreciation for psychobilly music through their sartorial choices or do not have the luxury of doing so because of restrictions on their appearance in work or social environments, but they are nevertheless committed to their subcultural identity. Many of them indicated that the majority of their friends are psychobillies, both because they organize their social lives around subcultural events and because they have more in common with other psychobillies than with non-psychobillies. While there are inevitably varying degrees to which people's lives are informed by their interest in psychobilly, the majority of my interlocutors identified themselves by saying, "I am a psychobilly" rather than "I listen to psychobilly." For example, one musician expressed the totality of his identification with the subculture by saying, "I'm not a musician who plays psychobilly. I'm a psychobilly who plays music." Likewise, in the song that opens this chapter, Norm Elliott of Norm and the Nightmarez identifies himself as a psychobilly; the "jungle rhythms" he listens to have even changed his DNA.

Through my research I attempted to understand why the psychobilly subculture both affects and reflects participants' lives and identities so strongly. What is it about psychobilly that attracts them? How does it represent who they are and what they care about? Why is the subculture such a meaningful part of their lives? What is it "doing" for them? One fan's response was particularly revealing: "Psychobilly is the only place where I feel like *me*." That fan, Pammy, did not say, "Psychobilly is the only *music* I listen to that makes me feel like me." Rather, she chose to define psychobilly as a "place" in both imagined and real senses; she was trying to convey how her every engagement with psychobilly—whether listening to music on her own, going to the supermarket dressed in her psychobilly clothes, attending a show with friends, or participating in an online Facebook group dedicated to the subculture—allowed her to access an alternative world where she could express herself freely and completely. Her response also suggested that she did *not* feel that she could express her true self in non-psychobilly contexts. This feeling of alienation outside of the subculture was a recurring topic in my conversations with psychobillies. My interlocutors had in common a tendency to identify themselves as different from "the norm" and uninterested in "the mainstream," their most common ways of referring to an ambiguous and vague "Other" against which they defined themselves. Their language at times suggested that they chose to identify themselves as nonnormative and differentiate themselves from "the mainstream," deciding to reject values, trends, jobs, behaviors, leisure activities, music, expectations, and aspirations they associated with "normal" and "boring" people. However, many psychobillies also told me about ways they have been marginalized, excluded, and stigmatized by others because of their race, gender, sexuality, class, body image, style, behavior, values, or interests. And some felt that their race, class, gender, or geographic location automatically placed them at a social and structural disadvantage. Sometimes we discussed whether distancing themselves from "the norm" was a self-defensive response to having already been excluded from social and economic opportunities for "typical" success.

Regardless of whether they felt that they had elected not to "buy into" dominant norms or that structural inequalities and discriminatory practices had prevented them from having the opportunity to do so in the first place, it became clear that most of my interlocutors self-identified as "different" from what they considered to be "normal." They rejected what Mark Slobin has called "the superculture": "the usual, the accepted, the statistically lopsided, the commercially successful, the statutory, the regulated, the most visible" (1993, 29). For them, psychobilly is a subcultural arena that celebrates rebellion and nonconformity and offers them an escape from the expectations, disappointments, and challenges that characterize their lived experience outside of the subculture. In both the physical and virtual spaces of the subculture, they belong; they find other "sick freaks" (as they affectionately call one another) who see difference from the "mainstream" as a virtue, and together they perform a refusal to become "boring squares." They use their bodies in ways that are normally frowned on or prohibited: they throw their weight around in the violent and chaotic wrecking pit, where they might even crack a rib or lose a tooth (or worse); overindulge in alcohol; tattoo and pierce their skin to excess; style and dye their hair in unconventional ways; cultivate an alternative style of clothing (anti-fashion); and leave evidence of their revelry through vomit, sweat, blood, and spilled beer. They break taboos through their bodies and practices and then imagine breaking even greater taboos as they sing along with choruses about killing the cheerleader or having sex with a corpse in a graveyard. Most important, they survive, preserving their countercultural identities and practices despite hegemonic attempts to repress them, exclude them from opportunities for success, police their behavior, and subdue them. They take the quality of their lives into their own hands by finding a way to have a hell of a good time while helping each other get through hard times.

Subcultural Theory

I have always been interested in subcultures: subgroups of people who, while they are part of the larger society, express their "difference" from "the rest" in some way. As Ross Haenfler notes: "Many of us find subcultures incredibly fascinating. Circus freaks, sexual swingers, and extreme skateboarders can seem exciting or unsettling, and body modifiers who tattoo their entire bodies or implant horns on their heads are interesting and exotic" (2016, 3). Many academics who study subcultures do so because we have identified as "different" ourselves and have participated in subcultural scenes (e.g., Hodkinson 2002; Muggleton 2000; Purcell 2003; Haenfler 2006; Kahn-Harris 2007). My first love was heavy metal, which I picked up from my older brothers, and then came grunge in the early 1990s. I was becoming more aware of my difference from the "cool" kids at school, and I embraced and cultivated my nonnormativity. As I would learn decades later when reading subcultural theory, I was not the only subcultural kid who felt a sense of superiority about my dissimilarity from the "mainstream." "They are all sheep; they are all just brainwashed by popular culture," I thought at the time. Then there was that fateful moment when I learned that Kurt Cobain had taken his own life, and I wept copiously for a man I had never met, a man I felt had articulated the anxieties and frustrations of my adolescence so precisely on those cassette tapes I wore out on my Walkman (with critical hindsight, was I a sheep, too?). And then, when one of my brother's friends introduced me to punk, I found my subculture. Rather than prohibiting me from attending shows as a fifteen-year-old, my parents drove me all over Southern California, patiently waiting at a Denny's for hours while I jumped and bashed around in sweaty circle pits at all-ages punk clubs. In these tiny, dingy, glorious venues, I chanted my heart out with my heroes, such as Dick Lucas from Citizen Fish and The Subhumans, feeling waves of overwhelming pleasure and a sense of similarity with the other "misfits" there:

> *All of us playing the waiting game in a state of mutual desperation.*
> *No use saying, "Well, I can't complain" if you want to change a*
> *situation.*
> *Imagine what the change could be if what was thought so constantly*
> *was said, not kept locked up inside our heads.*
> —CITIZEN FISH, "Can't Complain," *Millennia Madness*, 1995

More than ten years later, I found myself at the Nekromantix show described previously and felt an immediate sense of recognition. I noticed that the fashion, music, and behaviors I saw there reflected shared practices and aesthetic values—even while there was room for individual interpretation—and that the sonic and visual culture expressed a spirit of nonnormativity. I also registered the familiar sense of community, of like-mindedness, among a group of "outcasts" or "weirdos" who identified with one another instead of with "the mainstream." These characteristics are representative of many theoretical definitions of subculture (but not all, for there are many perspectives).[4] Ross Haenfler, for instance, defines subculture as "a relatively diffuse social network having a shared identity, distinctive meanings around certain ideas, practices, and objects, and a sense of marginalization from or resistance to a perceived 'conventional' culture" (2016, 3). The last item in Haenfler's definition underscores how subculturalists[5] may resist "dominant" culture, *choosing* to express themselves in nonnormative ways, but also how they may be marginalized from "mainstream" culture by others, stigmatized (Goffman 1963) or labeled (Becker 1963) as deviating from hegemonic expectations, or even criminalized as "folk devils" that threaten the norms of society (Stanley Cohen 1972).

Haenfler uses "scare quotes" around the word "conventional" to describe culture, as I have around "dominant" and "mainstream," to draw attention to the constructed and imaginary nature of such labels. Scholars have rightly observed that there is no intrinsically existing, stable, monolithic "mainstream," no neat and clear polarization between "the dominant culture" and "the subculture" in any given society. In an early critique of this binary, Paul Willis stated: "There has not been a vigorous analysis of the status of the culture a sub-culture is supposed to be 'sub' to. The notion implies a relative positioning which seemed to give an altogether misleading sense of absoluteness and dominance of the main culture" (1972, xlv–xlvi). As Willis suggests, the distinction between "us" and "them" is always and already an act of construction, framed from the perspective of whoever is distinguishing themself from someone or something else (Clarke [1981] 1990; Thornton 1996; Muggleton 2000).[6] Accordingly, my interest is not to establish what dominant culture is, but rather to understand how psychobillies identify and perform themselves as alternative to what they *perceive to be* dominant values, music, style, and practices (see, e.g., Baron 1989; Leblanc 1999; MacDonald 2001; Haenfler 2014; Hannerz 2015).[7] As J. Patrick Williams points out, as amorphous as the mainstream might be in reality, distinguishing oneself against it is "powerfully linked to notions of selfhood and identity, as well as to social behavior" (2011, 10).[8]

I thus situate this work within a discipline of subcultural studies that attempts to understand how and why subculturalists collectively identify and express themselves as different from (what they perceive to be) the mainstream.[9] Key to the development of subcultural theory were scholars from the Chicago School and Birmingham's Centre for Contemporary Cultural Studies (CCCS), who theorized that subcultures represent attempts by marginalized members of society to solve or deal with certain problems by expressing values, styles, and practices that counter dominant norms. Chicago School sociologists analyzed local gangs and street culture as responses to social, economic, and cultural struggles with urban life; they argued that members of these "deviant" groups adopted alternative norms and codes of conduct to attain the status, wealth, and sense of belonging they were unable to achieve through conventional means (A. Cohen 1955; Merton 1957). The CCCS was concerned with postwar structural changes throughout Britain that encouraged the "middle-classing" of society and consumerism even while the working class faced heightened unemployment, educational disadvantage, low-paying, routinized jobs, and the breakdown of communities as a result of urban redevelopment and relocation; Teddy Boy, mod, rocker, skinhead, and punk styles were seen as collective working-class responses to these changes and challenges, resisting hegemonic culture through their spectacular style (Hall and Jefferson 1976; P. Willis 1977; Hebdige 1979). These "classical subcultures," as Dylan Clark observes, "were understood to be groups of youths who practiced a wide array of social dissent through shared behavioral, musical, and costume orientations" (2003, 223).

Toward the end of the twentieth century, the rise of clubbing and raving prompted some scholars to question the CCCS's vision of subcultures as collective, unified, working-class manifestations of resistance to hegemonic culture. "Post-subcultural"[10] scholars argued that changes associated with postmodernity have made group affiliations and participants' identities much more fleeting, fragmented, multiple, and partial (Bennett 1999; Muggleton 2000; Muggleton and Weinzierl 2003). They suggested that an individual's leisure choices and aesthetic preferences were not determined automatically by a particular socioeconomic experience but were freely and actively chosen from a variety of options (Bennett 1999) and that youth crafted a unique and hyperindividualized sense of themselves rather than committing to a group identity (Muggleton 2000). Consumers could shop in what Ted Polhemus calls the "Supermarket of Style,"[11] putting on and taking off different styles and identities at will, regardless of their structural positionality: "We now inhabit a Supermarket of Style where, like tins of soup lined up on endless shelves, we can choose between more than fifty different styletribes. Jumbling geography as well as history, British Punk circa 1976 sits on the shelf next to 1950s American Beatnik or late Jamaican Ragga. You name it, we've got it. You too can be an anarchic Punk, a bohemian Beatnik or a bad ass Raggamuffin. If only for a day" (1997, 150).

For post-subculturalists, postmodernism had spelled the "death" of the classical subculture.[12] To convey the transitory and individualistic ways people float between different group affiliations in the postmodern context, post-subculturalists developed new terms, such as "club cultures" (Thornton 1996; Redhead, Wynne, and O'Connor 1997), "tribes" (Maffesoli 1996) and "neo-tribes" (Bennett 1999), "postmodern subculture" (Muggleton 2000), "scenes" (Sara Cohen 1991; Straw 1991; Shank 1994; Stahl 2003), and "lifestyles" (Shields 1992; Chaney 1996; Miles 2000). Post-subculturalists have been criticized for denying the continued existence of collective identities and practices and for ignoring how structural disadvantages (e.g., those having to do with race, class, gender, and sexuality) can impact one's choice of leisure activities and access to them (see Blackman 2005; Hesmondhalgh 2005; Shildrick and MacDonald 2006).[13]

Since the turn of the twentieth century, scholars have debated the strengths and weaknesses of subcultural and post-subcultural theory.[14] I find much of value in post-subcultural theory and recognize many of the criticisms of the CCCS, but I also see the applicability of broad aspects of traditional subcultural theory (see, e.g., Hodkinson 2002, 2016; Blackman 2005; Shildrick and MacDonald 2006; Williams 2011). As Hodkinson points out, a "polarised understanding of the subcultures debate" has perpetuated an "inflexible" and "an unnecessarily narrow and CCCS-driven conception of what subculture might infer"—namely, an insistence on structural determinism, an affirmation of the complete fixity of youth groups, and the inability to "accommodate even the smallest measure of individual diversity" (2016, 630–632). This, he argues, "underestimates the complex, multifaceted history of subcultural theory";[15] "leaves us with a caricature that few of its adherents would recognize"; and mischaracterizes contemporary subcultural theorists as necessarily defending all aspects of CCCS theory (632). He concludes that the perceived incompatibility of "subcultural" and "post-subcultural" scholarship has served to "mask substantial areas of possible common ground" (630), and he encourages "a continuing focus on the importance and operation of distinct youth cultural communities and a developing emphasis on the context in which they operate" (635). Indeed, my goal is not to defend every aspect of the CCCS's theory but rather to draw on different subcultural and post-subcultural approaches to convey to the reader the creative and complex ways psychobillies engage in a community of like-minded individuals to mediate and improve their daily lived experience.

The Survival of Subcultures

As indicated by its title, this book demonstrates that classical subcultures are not dead. While I do not deny that many groups organized around a common leisure interest may be "post-subcultural," characterized by heterogeneity, temporary and partial affiliations, little or no "group mindedness," and no specific intention to express nonmainstream norms, these traits do not describe the psychobilly community I researched. As explored throughout this book, psychobilly is distinguished by a high degree of what Paul Hodkinson (2002) calls "subcultural substance": the expression of consistent and distinct values and tastes, collective identification as different from an Other, committed involvement over long periods of time and throughout everyday life, and relative autonomy from non-subcultural networks. While post-subculturalists such as Steven Miles suggest that "rapid social, cultural and structural change" has resulted not in "the form of a deep-rooted sense of sameness, but in a flexible, mutable and diverse sense of identity" (2000, 158), I find that psychobilly demonstrates the continued longing of marginalized youth for a concrete and clear group identity manifested through a unified style and ideology that have changed little over thirty years.

At the same time, I do not suggest that the psychobilly scene is completely homogeneous, bounded, or stable. In fact, contemporary scholars have pointed out that Chicago and CCCS theorists acknowledged the diversity of values and identities within subcultural groups and were not as dogmatic about stylistic homogeneity as some post-subcultural scholars have suggested (see, e.g., Hesmondhalgh 2005; Blackman 2005; Shildrick and MacDonald 2006; Greener and Hollands 2006; Hodkinson 2016). It is unrealistic to expect total sameness among the participants of any group. I privilege here the diverse definitions of "psychobilly" and "psychobilly-ness"; the spectrum of values found within psychobilly; the variety of reasons people participate in it and the relative degree to which they do so; the diversity of their backgrounds; the multiple ways they express themselves through music, fashion, and practices; and the changeable nature of all these factors.

Moreover, because psychobilly values nonconformity, one might wonder if it can have any stylistic or ideological consistency. As psychobilly fan Pammy put it, "When your fans are rebellious at heart and hate labels, chaos ensues." Many psychobillies, like many punks, "proclaim there should be 'no rules,' that individualism should rule the day," as Ross Haenfler notes (2016, 43). However, as he points out, "maintaining some sort of boundaries or, dare I say, rules are perhaps essential to subculture. Otherwise, anything goes and it becomes impossible to determine an 'us' and a 'them'" (43). Despite the inevitable plurality found within psychobilly, particular aesthetics, values, and behaviors collectively distinguish the subculture. Moreover, I agree with Hodkinson that plurality can coexist meaningfully with collective identity and style: "Abandoning substantive attempts to make sense of the workings and significance of such collective affiliations at the first sight of individual difference makes little sense when we could, instead, seek to understand the ways individual specificities and ephemeralities coexist with aspects of stability and community that can influence and shape young lives" (2016, 636).

This study of psychobilly joins contemporary scholarship in demonstrating that "spectacular" subcultures have in fact survived into the twenty-first century and that their participants still perform collective ideologies and practices that distinguish them from what they consider dominant or mainstream culture, while recognizing that a relative degree of internal diversity and fluidity exists within such groups (see, e.g., Kruse 1993; MacDonald 2001; Hodkinson 2002; Purcell 2003; Greener and Hollands 2006; Haenfler 2006, 2016; Goodlad and Bibby 2007; Williams 2011; Williams and Hannerz 2014; Hannerz 2015).

Survival through Subculture

My real interest is not *that* spectacular subcultures or "subcultures of substance" (Hodkinson 2002) still exist, but rather that they exist *because* people still meaningfully and actively construct and participate in them. Subcultures are still incredibly important to how many people live their lives. This is my main focus throughout this book: exploring how active engagement in the subculture allows psychobillies to negotiate and improve their lived experience, one generally characterized by socioeconomic marginalization from and/or frustration with mainstream culture. They find therein some "solution" to some "problem," as the Chicago School and the CCCS suggested, but I do not claim that they all look to the subculture to solve the same problem or that their stylistic choices are automatic, homogeneous, and universal responses to social or structural changes. I argue that their interest in the subculture is motivated by a variety of structural and social experiences, a consideration that some early post-subcultural theorists failed to underscore.[16] Thus I join contemporary subcultural scholars who address the diverse ways in which social and material processes impact subcultural identities and participation (see, e.g., MacDonald 2001; Hollands 2002; Böse 2003; Nayak 2003; Pilkington 2004; Blackman 2005, 2014; Shildrick 2006; Shildrick and MacDonald 2006; Williams 2011). The anxieties psychobillies seek to address through their subcultural participation are multiple, as are their strategies for alleviating them. This study highlights subcultural participants' agency in creatively generating their own ways to improve their lived experience.

The CCCS was preoccupied with how the working class manifested a "collective response to the material and situated experience of their class" (Clarke et al. 1976, 47). Indeed, psychobillies often seek release from economic marginalization. Most of my interlocutors self-identified as working class and characterized the subculture as a whole that way. Unemployment, low-paying jobs, unfulfilling work, poverty, temporary labor, and slim opportunities for economic and educational advancement were common concerns. But their interest in the subculture was not *predetermined* by their class position, as the CCCS implied; moreover, their frustrations were not always or only economic. Their sense of marginalization from society can be related to other structural, social, and personal experiences, as other scholars have shown (e.g., Pilkington 2004; Blackman 2005; Hesmondhalgh 2005; Halnon 2006a; Greener and Hollands 2006; Kahn-Harris 2007; P. Greene 2011; Hodkinson 2016). My interlocutors described examples of racial or ethnic discrimination, sexism, homophobia, body shaming, and other forms of social stigmatization and structural inequality. Many felt they just did not fit in—or *want* to fit in—with mainstream society and were frustrated by rules, expectations, and authority figures that threatened to repress their individuality, nonconformity, and preferred lifestyle. Others specifically rebelled against what they considered to be "mainstream" music, "seeking escape from the superficial world of corporate-sponsored music," as Karen Halnon found in her study of shock metal participants (2006a, 202). Some were looking for a way to cope with personal matters, for instance frustration with family, friends, coworkers, and classmates, while others sought relief from emotional and mental health struggles, such as post-traumatic stress disorder after returning from overseas military service. Moreover, Paul Greene observed that metal fans in Nepal "raged against a machine that was distinctly local" (2011, 111); given the global development of the psychobilly subculture, I do not assume that psychobillies in Europe and the United States rebel against the same things that those in other countries do. In short, participants may be drawn to psychobilly to "solve" a variety of different structural, social, and personal "problems" or frustrations.

They find in the subculture multiple and diverse "solutions," and I do not presume that every psychobilly derives satisfaction from participation in exactly the same way(s) or for the same reason(s). I engage with contemporary ethnographic studies that recognize the plurality of solutions that subculturalists find by "creating a counter-world with its own rules and values that give meaning to their existence" (Schröter 2004, 54).[17] Many achieve relief from frustration by engaging in transgressive or shocking behavior that is not permitted elsewhere. As Keith Kahn-Harris argues in his study of extreme metal, participation in transgressive behavior can help disempowered individuals experience a satisfying sense of control over their own lives: "Transgression is one way of surviving the fraught experience of modernity. It is one of the few sources of almost unrestricted agency in modernity. While modernity disempowers individuals within alienating systems and structures, transgression allows individuals to feel utterly in control, utterly 'sovereign' (Bataille 1993) over their being through practices that resist instrumental rationality" (Kahn-Harris 2007, 158). As this book explores, transgressive practices provide subculturalists with different types of pleasure, particularly as they liberate themselves not only from society's restrictions but also from conventional norms of self-control over their own bodies (Bakhtin [1936] 1984; Frith 1981; Fiske 1989; Weinstein 2000; Kahn-Harris 2007). I also consider how the community provides a number of benefits that help subculturalists manage and survive external challenges, particularly through the circulation of economic capital and the socio-emotional bonds they develop with each other. The subculture provides psychobillies with opportunities to transgress societal regulations and constraints, express nonnormative identities, meet like-minded people, share economic resources, support one another emotionally and socially, have fun, and feel empowered as they stake out their own way to live.

One of my interlocutors described psychobilly as a "culture of survival." He explained, "Just like psychobilly keeps rockabilly alive, psychobilly keeps us alive." He could have been referring to the social, emotional, and economic resources that members of the subculture share to help each other literally survive hard times, but he went on to explain how participating in the subculture makes him *feel* alive. He has fun at shows, viscerally experiencing the ecstasy of the music, the wrecking, and the alcohol, all while feeling the joy of belonging to a group of like-minded, nonnormative individuals. He can express his true self, indulging in the things *he* values, as his frustrations melt away. Participating in psychobilly helps him survive daily challenges and make the most out of his life despite outside attempts to suppress and oppress him. I thus see psychobillies' performance of alternative, nonnormative practices, values, and aesthetics as meaningful and diverse self-expressions of distinction from the mainstream (as they perceive it) and as responses and "survival solutions" to various experiences of structural or social marginality or stigmatization. This book provides further documentation that subcultures of substance still exist because they are important vehicles through which marginalized members of society actively create ways to survive and enact sovereignty over their own lives.

The Survival of Resistance

A recurring debate within subcultural studies concerns the potential for subcultural "resistance" to hegemonic culture. Even while CCCS scholars romanticized the working class's "heroic" resistance against dominant society through stylistic subversion, they ultimately suggested that this resistance was only "imaginary" because subculturalists could not fundamentally change the systemic structure that subordinated them (Clarke et al. 1976, 47–48). Moreover, Hebdige suggested that subcultural styles lose their resistant potential, however symbolic, once they are appropriated and sold back to the public as a commodity (1979, 92–99). Some postsubculturalists have an even bleaker view of the possibility for resistance, suggesting that "subcultures are just another form of depoliticized play in the postmodern pleasuredome" in which participants are looking for "a hedonistic escape into a Blitz Culture fantasy characterized by political indifference" (Muggleton 1997, 200). After surveying subcultural and postsubcultural perspectives, Shane Greene observes: "This is what most of the theorizing of subculture has left us with. . . . Subcultures routinely express structural antagonisms but do not breed a *real* revolutionary consciousness powerful enough to *really* fuck the system, provoking *real* systemic ruptures that result in *real* historical change" (2012, 581).

Greene argues that an understanding of subcultural resistance requires a redefinition of "real" resistance. It cannot only mean a revolution that completely topples the current system:

The insight is to imagine and identify in material-political practice other possible framings of the underground experience without giving in to the impulse to believe in an Enlightened Marxist idea of revolution as some sort of total systemic rupture. Stop placing so much fucking faith in the idea that liberation lies only on the other side of absolute destruction followed by total revolutionary renewal. Stop dreaming of completely fucking over the system. Learn to *under-fuck* the system in your daily material practices. This is a task to which underground punks have long dedicated themselves. (2012, 581)

He asserts that punks in Peru have "under-fucked the system" by adopting a do-it-yourself (DIY) philosophy that disturbs the means through which the culture industry typically asserts and maintains its control. He also demonstrates that underground punks have held and expressed diverse political ideologies (and have faced dire consequences for doing so), revealing alternative visions for society that correspond to neither the status quo of the state nor the agenda of the Marxist revolutionaries. He thus argues that "under-fucking the system implies a series of refusals" that disrupt "systemic forms of power" (584).

Many contemporary scholars agree that everyday subcultural expressions and practices resist the totalizing control of hegemonic culture and may be expressed on micro or macro, covert or overt, and individual or collective levels (Williams and Hannerz 2014). Ross Haenfler, for example, echoes Shane Greene, noting that "meaningful resistance does not always have to be *revolutionary*, in the sense of radically altering the social order"; "countering hegemonic ideas (or *frames*) perpetuated by powerful people and institutions is a significant act of resistance" (Haenfler 2014, 44). He argues that by creating, fostering, and expressing alternative values and identities, "subculturalists of all sorts question the perceived hegemony of dominant groups and mass culture" (Haenfler 2016, 20). In his study of straightedge, for example, Haenfler considers how participants challenge normative assumptions about alcohol and drug use, not by engaging in direct action designed to change legislation but rather through leading by example and making visible their conscious rejection of mainstream behaviors and values (2006). Similarly, while some post-subculturalists have dismissed any political potential in electronic dance music (EDM) culture (e.g., Redhead 1993; Thornton 1996; Reynolds 1997), others have suggested that clubbers' construction of an alternative vision of society that values PLUR (peace, love, unity, and respect) is an explicit refusal of dominant values and lifestyles (Greener and Hollands 2006; Wilson 2006; Riley, Griffin, and Morey 2010; Dimou and Ilan 2018). Borrowing from Maffesoli's (1996) idea that neo-tribalists enact a "politics of survival" through sociality and pleasure, some have framed clubbers' performance of alternative values as a sort of "everyday politics" that offers participants sovereignty over their own lives even when they do not articulate a specific political agenda (Riley, Griffin, and Morey 2010; Dimou and Ilan 2018).

By "finding ways to think about resistance that neither inappropriately cast youth as heroic cultural revolutionaries nor reduce participants' experiences to ineffectual consumerism" (Haenfler 2014, 50), scholars have forged a middle ground between traditional subcultural theory and post-subcultural theory that allows us to consider how subculturalists disrupt the absolute power of hegemony. Like EDM clubbers, psychobillies do not frame their performative expression of difference from the mainstream as an explicitly political statement of "resistance." They also do not want "their way" of living to become "the way" for everyone. Yet by "refusing to uncritically follow the rules" and "intentionally break[ing] with the mainstream" (Williams and Hannerz 2014), psychobillies "create moments in which to live out their own values, creating temporary pockets of sovereignty over their own existence" (Riley, Griffin, and Morey 2010, 348; see also Greener and Hollands 2006; Dimou & Ilan 2018). Building on Shane Greene's theory (2012), I see this as "under-fucking the system"; despite hegemonic attempts to regulate their individuality and marginalize them socially and economically, psychobillies refuse to passively accept the status quo.

When Gramsci articulated his theory of hegemony, he noted that it depended on the "spontaneous consent given by the great masses of the population to the general direction imposed on social life by the dominant fundamental group" (1971, 12). He recognized the possibility that one might "work out one's own conception of the world consciously and critically . . . to choose one's own sphere of activity, to participate actively in making the history of the world" (58). This book considers how psychobillies actively make their own world. They defiantly enact a "politics of survival" by finding pleasure and excitement within their own community, where they can freely express their true selves; engage in practices, styles, and values that are deemed unacceptable elsewhere; and take matters into their own hands to improve their lived experience in substantive ways. For psychobillies such as Pammy, finding a "space" to express one's true self is incredibly meaningful and represents a resistant act of self-expression in defiance of normative expectations.

Finally, I apply performativity theory to the framing of subcultural resistance. In *Gender Trouble: Feminism and the Subversion of Identity*, Judith Butler suggests that gender is not "given" but rather constructed through "the repeated stylization of the body, a set of repeated acts within a highly rigid regulatory frame" ([1990] 2007, 45). There is nothing "natural" about male or female identities; gender is "real only to the extent that it is performed" (527). In other words, we imitate, naturalize, and (re)inforce hegemonic ideas about how we expect men and women to behave. Using Michel Foucault's idea that "discourse transmits and produces power; it reinforces it, but also undermines and exposes it, renders it fragile and makes it possible to thwart" (1978, 101), Butler argues that it is possible to "trouble" gender expectations by performing alternatives. Drag, for example, parodies our assumptions about the naturalness of gender and draws attention to the very constructedness of those ideas (Butler [1990] 2007). Thus, if discourse and repeated performances shape our ideas about what we think to be true, then it follows that we can question those ideas through new discourse and performative acts and create the possibility of alternative ideas and identities. Accordingly, I interpret subcultural performances as ways of "troubling" normative expectations and highlighting the constructedness of them. By refusing to behave, dress, and live their lives in the ways that discourse and authority have reinforced to be the "right" way, psychobillies "make noise" (Hebdige 1979; Wong 2004) and "under-fuck the system" (S. Greene 2012), not only making visible subculture's potential to resist hegemonic control but also drawing attention to the arbitrariness of norms. I situate this work, then, within academic discourse that understands subcultural practice not as "imaginary" and ultimately futile resistance, as the CCCS concluded, nor as individually motivated hedonistic consumption, as some post-subculturalists have suggested, but rather as evidence of the active ways subculturalists enact their agency, refusing to be passive pawns in the hegemonic game of life. While not articulating a political agenda, psychobillies nevertheless construct and perform alternative ways of being that illustrate the possibilities for subverting hegemony and winning sovereignty over their own lives: surviving the way they want to.

Dialogic and Polyvocal Ethnography

I am aware that I have just attributed "resistance" to a subculture whose participants have reminded me over and over again is apolitical. But I only do this after having thoroughly discussed different perspectives on resistance and subcultural practice with psychobillies. Throughout my fieldwork and writing process, I took to heart the critiques leveled against the CCCS for not engaging directly with subcultural participants and for not taking their perspectives and lived experience into account.[18] In his classic text *Subculture: The Meaning of Style*, Hebdige admitted that "it is highly unlikely that the members of any of the subcultures described in this book would recognize themselves reflected here" (1979, 139). This was the case for David Muggleton, a punk who struggled to read the book and "was left feeling that it had absolutely nothing to say about my life as I had once experienced it" (2000,

2). Having reread the book after earning a degree in sociology and cultural studies, he "now knew exactly what it meant, and *still* found that it had very little to say about my life!" (2). I also recognize that my own background, my involvement in punk as a teenager (which was always "political" for me), and my intellectual leanings inform my instinct to read resistance into subcultural performance, and I am aware of Sarah Thornton's warning about this tendency. She noted that many subcultural theorists "were diverted by the task of puncturing and contesting dominant ideologies," perhaps in part because "their biases have tended to agree with the anti-mass society discourses of the youth cultures they study," leading to conclusions that "both over-politicized youthful leisure and at the same time ignored the subtle relations of power at play within it" (Thornton 2005, 185).

I heed these critiques, and like many post-Birmingham scholars (Thornton 1996; Muggleton 2000; Blackman 2005), I use an approach that "privilege(s) the subjective meanings of subculturalists" (Muggleton 2000, 9). I am particularly influenced by Harris Berger's methodological use of "critical phenomenology" in *Metal, Rock, and Jazz: Perception and the Phenomenology of Musical Experience* (1999). In "Phenomenology and the Ethnography of Popular Music: Ethnomusicology at the Juncture of Cultural Studies and Folklore" (2008), he explains that participant observation and preliminary interviews were his first steps in understanding the relationship between heavy metal music and what it meant to the musicians who performed it. He then engaged his interlocutors in critical dialogue, discussing with them what previous scholars had suggested about heavy metal and its meanings: "Respecting my research participants enough to engage them in a critical dialogue paid off, and the metalheads' responses offered a realm of ethnographic insights" (74). Subcultural and popular music scholars' interest since the 1990s in accounting for the subjective meanings of their research participants corresponds with the development of polyvocal ethnographies around the same time (Abu-Lughod 1990; Minh-ha 1989). Influenced by Third Wave feminist and queer theory, these works drew attention to the problematic ways researchers had traditionally excluded or misrepresented the voices of some of their research subjects, particularly women. This prompted scholars to more seriously consider and represent heterogeneous perspectives and to regard each viewpoint as equally valid.

I believe that gaining an understanding of meaning within psychobilly requires a dialogic engagement with my research participants, and my analyses are informed by conversations with psychobillies wherein we considered a range of phenomenological interpretations. I often went back to my interlocutors after the initial interviews to ask more questions and probe deeper into the meanings they had attributed to certain practices, styles, and signifiers. Furthermore, in my intention to write a polyvocal ethnography, I represent heterogeneous perspectives I encountered during my fieldwork. I privilege psychobillies' own interpretations by sometimes quoting them at length and offering more than one individual's perspective on a topic. By allowing psychobillies to "speak for themselves" throughout this book and to do so in multiple ways, I strive to demonstrate the plurality of meaning and experience within the subculture. I hope this work represents their many voices, recognizes their creative expressive practices, and reminds us of the diverse ways people meaningfully engage with a subculture to shape their lived experience.

Fieldwork

The interpretations and analyses presented in this book reflect more than ten years of ethnomusicological fieldwork in psychobilly (and rockabilly) contexts, with the majority of the fieldwork having been conducted between 2007 and 2017. In "Ethnography and Popular Music Studies" (1993), Sara Cohen encourages a dialogue between ethnomusicology and popular music studies. She faults scholars from popular music studies and cultural studies for referring to their work as "ethnography" even when "it is usually not ethnography in the anthropological sense": "Many studies rely upon pre-formulated questionnaires, surveys, autobiographies or unstructured interviews which study people outside their usual social, spatial and temporal context. Their discourse is consequently disconnected from their day-to-day activities, relationships and experience (and obviously, what people say they do often differs from what they actually do, or from what they think they do)" (1993, 127).[19] She hopes that ethnomusicologists can offer a more holistic understanding of "the study of music as social practice" (136).

My graduate school training in ethnographic fieldwork provided me with an understanding of contemporary anthropological and ethnomusicological methods, which include conducting formal interviews, establishing rapport with interlocutors,[20] and practicing participant observation (see Myers 1992; Nettl 2005). The latter encompasses a wide range of activities designed to engage intimately with members of a community—within psychobilly contexts, as Cohen encouraged—in order to understand deeply their music and the practices and ideologies associated with it. Accordingly, I attended events throughout the United States and abroad, listened to the music and lyrics (both by myself and with psychobillies, and both at shows and elsewhere), followed online discussion groups, and drank lots of Lone Stars and Pabst Blue Ribbons with psychobillies as we talked late into the night (or rather, early into the morning). Throughout my fieldwork, my intention was to understand what psychobilly meant and did for those who loved and lived it, uncovering the substantive ways in which their subcultural participation shaped their experiences and identities.

I interviewed ninety-six people in sixty-seven interviews (some interviews included several members of a band or friends who wanted to be interviewed together). I preferred to conduct interviews in person, as I found it easier that way to establish rapport, explore insightful conversational avenues, and ask for further clarification when needed (forty-nine interviews were done this way). When conducting an in-person interview was not possible due to geographic distance, a conversation by phone was the next best option (eight were done this way). If the only way to secure an interview was through email, as was often the case with musicians who had busy schedules while touring, I used this as a last resort (ten were done this way). All but twenty-four interviewees lived in the United States. All but fifteen were male, a fact I discuss in Chapter 4. Interview participants ranged in age from eighteen to sixty-five; the majority in the United States were in their twenties and thirties at the time of the interview, while the majority from England and Ireland were in their forties and fifties.[21] I interviewed those who played a central role in the production and distribution of subcultural goods and services—musicians (some from extremely popular bands and others from less well-known ones), music producers, writers, graphic artists, event promoters, and deejays—as well as people I met at shows who identified (only) as fans. They were exterminators, bartenders, mortuary assistants, graphic artists, carpet cleaners, mechanics, furniture movers, retail workers, teachers, undergraduate and graduate students, and unemployed individuals. "Snowball sampling" (Biernacki and Waldorf 1981) helped me gain access to other interlocutors, as interviewees suggested others I should talk to and helped put me in touch with them, but I also introduced myself to "random" people at shows.

Though I had prepared a series of questions (see Appendix), interviews inevitably became conversational, and we never progressed directly through my list in Q&A fashion. We explored tangents, redirected, and followed more tangents. We considered questions and topics that interviewees brought up, producing wonderful insights about subjects I might not have considered or asked about (Baron 1989; Berger 2008). Interviewees explained how they discovered the genre, why they liked it, what their lives were like, what they thought of other music, what jobs they had (or didn't have, in the frequent case of unemployment), what bands they liked and hated, what things were going on in the subculture or in society that they agreed with or didn't, what horror movies they liked, their favorite gigs, their interest or noninterest in vintage culture, and so forth. Conversations reflected an individual's particular interests; some might talk at length about technical elements of the music, others might be more excited to discuss car culture or fashion, and yet others were more interested in the social aspects of the subculture. Interviews generally lasted about two hours[22] and usually took place at a bar or restaurant of the interviewee's choice or at a venue before or after a show.

When quotations from interlocutors appear without a cited attribution, they come from author-conducted interviews. I have included excerpts from interviews without editing. I have not "cleaned up" the language by eliminating repeated words or fillers (such as "like"). I have used an em dash (—) when a speaker did not finish a phrase or idea, paused as if searching for words, or was interrupted by something or someone (usually me through crosstalk). A colon and quotation marks indicate when a speaker switched intonation in order to designate internal dialogue (e.g., And then I thought: "Wow, I really want to party tonight."), while a comma and quotation marks indicate paraphrasing of dialogue that was spoken aloud by the interviewee or someone else (e.g., And then I told her, "Let's go party tonight!"). Given that conversations tended to explore tangents, I have indicated with an ellipsis (. . .) portions of the conversation omitted because they do not apply to the topic being analyzed.[23] I have changed participants' names to obscure their identities. The exception to this is when the topic at hand refers to the interviewee's involvement in a particular band or when an interviewee asked to be identified by their real name rather than a pseudonym. In all cases, interviewees understood the purpose of my research and that it would be published, and they consented to the inclusion of interview material in this book.[24]

In addition to conducting formal interviews, I engaged in participant observation, including attendance at hundreds of shows, festivals, car meets, and other social activities associated with the subculture, and I recorded ethnographic observations at 166 events. I took notes on the aural elements of the music, the lyrics, what performers said and did, the props they used, interactions between performers and audience members, what the sound "guy" did (the employee was almost always male), the social dynamics and demographics of the crowd, the fashion, the wrecking pit, the songs the deejay played, moments of conflict and moments of pleasure, how people drank, conversations I heard and had in the restroom, what the event flyers looked like, and so forth. Like any ethnomusicologist, my understanding of the subculture was shaped as much by informal conversations and "deep hanging out" (Geertz 1973) with psychobillies as it was by formal interviews. Many of the psychobillies I came to know best were those I met "naturally" at shows rather than those I specifically sought out for interviews. I often stayed in touch with my interlocutors, seeing them regularly at events and communicating with them through social media. I contacted them again when working through questions I had about my analyses, inspired by the critical phenomenology of Berger's approach (1999, 2008).

I collected data at multiple research sites (Fine 2003). I began my research while a graduate student in Austin at the University of Texas during a thriving era of Texas psychobilly (especially from about 2007 to 2009), attending events throughout the state but particularly in Houston, Austin, and San Antonio. I often visited Southern California, where I am from and where the psychobilly scene in America is arguably the strongest; I spent one full year there (2009–2010) and two summers traveling up and down the state between San Diego and San Francisco. I attended psychobilly and rockabilly festivals (multiday festivals called "weekenders") in Nevada, California, Texas, and Spain. I also sought out events during personal trips. In fact, one of my first psychobilly shows took place on a memorable night during a family vacation when I dragged my brother to a bar in Nokia, Finland. While my brother enjoyed drunken conversations with Finnish psychobillies about dynamite fishing, I took diligent notes on the performance by the band Vulture Club.

Finally, this book is really the product of having the opportunity to travel to Europe in 2015 to compare the experiences of my American interlocutors with those of European participants. In England and Ireland I interviewed musicians and fans who had played an instrumental role in the development of psychobilly there in the 1980s, and in Pineda de Mar, Spain, I attended the Psychobilly Meeting International Summer Festival (henceforth referred to as "Pineda," following psychobilly usage), a well-established weekender that gave me the opportunity to meet subculturalists from all over the world. Without this international fieldwork experience, I would have felt less qualified to characterize the European history of the genre and its contemporary global dimensions.

Online technologies became more available over the course of ten years of ethnographic research. MySpace provided a useful method for contacting bands in 2007; later, Facebook offered a fantastic way to stay in touch with interlocutors and arrange interviews with nonlocal bands. I paid close attention to online discussion groups on Facebook. (Psychobilly Worldwide is the largest, with more than sixteen thousand members at the time of writing.) Sometimes I messaged those members who frequently shared astute observations about the subculture, and a few agreed to answer interview questions by phone or email. While developing the major interpretations and analyses I share in this book, I concentrated on the information I had acquired through formal and informal conversations, for this was the most dialogic data, representing give and take between me and my interlocutors.

However, online comments on discussion boards have the advantage of (generally) being worded concisely and carefully, having been thought out in advance, edited, and constructed to make a particular point. As a result, I have sometimes used comments from online groups in this ethnography instead of excerpts from interviews to support a particular discussion. I have done this always and only because they express an interpretation I found to be true in my conversations with psychobillies, communicated more effectively than on-the-spot, in-person speech tends to be.

Reflexive Ethnography

The ways I chose to translate my fieldwork experiences and analyses into this text concern issues of representation and ethnography. I intend this to be a dialogic and polyvocal ethnography that represents a multiplicity of perspectives encountered during my research, but I am also influenced by reflexive ethnographic styles. Early anthropological ethnographies attempted to "objectively" communicate an analysis without regard to the researcher or his presence in the field (he, again, for it was usually a male). Reflexive ethnographies, on the other hand, represented the researcher and their field experience in the text (Sara Cohen 1993).[25] The publication of *Writing Culture: The Poetics and Politics of Ethnography* (Clifford and Marcus 1986) marked a critical turn that encouraged scholars to reflect on the subjective nature of the ethnographic process. As Barz and Cooley note: "Ethnographers attempt reflexively to understand their positions in the culture being studied and to represent these positions in ethnographies, including their epistemological stances, their relations to the cultural practices and individuals studied, and their relationships to their own cultural practices. Reflexive ethnography is keenly aware of experience and of the personal context of experience" (2008, 20). Thus, as Michael Taussig suggests, in reflexive ethnographies "the anthropologist is inevitably part of the reality analyzed" (2006, viii).

I recognize that my fieldwork, and the analyses I drew from it, were informed by the fact that I do not identify as a psychobilly. Many subcultural scholars identify as members of the groups they examine or participated in them to some extent prior to doing research (e.g., Bennett 2000; Hodkinson 2002; Muggleton 2000; Purcell 2003; Haenfler 2006; Kahn-Harris 2007; Anderson 2009). I had not encountered the subculture before attending the event described at the beginning of this Introduction that led to the development of my research project. While I enjoy psychobilly music and spent ten years participating in the subculture for my research, it is not my primary musical taste, and I do not identify myself "as a psychobilly" as most of my interlocutors did. Thus, this is not an autoethnography or insider ethnography, for I do not draw on "insider knowledge" (Hodkinson 2002) or a "known status as both a complete member and researcher" (Anderson 2009, 183). On the contrary, I am sensitive to how my fieldwork was shaped by the ways psychobillies understood and perceived me to be an outsider. I performed this identity, introducing myself to psychobillies (and especially to musicians I sought to interview) not as a "fan" but as an academic researcher. I dressed in ways that were appropriate within the subculture—typically wearing black capris, jeans, or a skirt with a tank top and either heels or Converse sneakers, depending on how comfortable I wanted to be—but this was not unlike how I might have dressed if attending a non-psychobilly event. I have never had a psychobilly wedge quiff, which would have required shaving the sides of my head (though I sometimes styled my hair into a feminine rockabilly style with a small pompadour), and while I have "half-sleeve" tattoos on my arms, they are not like the tattoos one normally finds in the subculture. Thus my style communicated to others that while I might enjoy psychobilly, I was quite clearly not someone who identified as a "card-carrying" member of the subculture.

The transparency of my outsiderness and my academic intentions inevitably shaped the ways that psychobillies engaged with me. As Kai Fikentscher observes in his ethnographic analysis of underground dance music (2000), academic research can be perceived as antithetical to the values of a subculture. The theories of academia seem far removed from the everyday frustrations and pleasures most psychobillies experience, and my research struck some members of the community as self-indulgent, patronizing, elitist, or irrelevant. I understood why some seemed suspicious or resentful of my presence: I was intruding into a time and space that they looked forward to, when they could relax among their peers and escape reminders of the outside world. I represented elite structures that some of them associated with their own socioeconomic marginalization, and I seemingly enjoyed privileges and opportunities that they had never felt were within their reach (something we talked about often).[26] Their skepticism also derived in part from how psychobilly has been maligned and misrepresented in some newspapers, magazines, online articles, and news reports on television. Many members of the community carefully guard their words and behaviors around outsiders, justifiably concerned about how interviews will be used and with what intentions. This is not to suggest that psychobillies completely distanced themselves from me or disapproved of my academic interest in the subculture. On the contrary, many were enthusiastic that someone was sincerely and seriously committed to understanding the community ("Finally!," many of them said), and they wanted to contribute to the accurate portrayal of their subculture. However, I want to acknowledge from the outset the inherent issues at play when documenting a subculture that is suspicious of casual "tourists" and point out that my representation of the community is shaped and informed not only by the uneasy tension between academia and subcultural values but also by the ways psychobillies perceived and engaged with me as a researcher.

Throughout the research and writing process, I considered how various aspects of my identity and subjectivity affected the fieldwork experience and informed my analysis: my age, race, nationality, educational level, class, language, values, behaviors (particularly my tendency toward introversion), sex, gender, and sexuality, and more important, how I performed all these identities. I self-consciously leave myself in this text in some places. I reflect on times when my subjectivity affected my fieldwork and analyses—for instance, in Chapter 4, where I explore my observations and experiences as a woman researcher within the subculture. My intention is for these reflections to come across not as "self-indulgent" and "confessional" but rather as "ethnographically relevant" (Barz and Cooley 2008, 20). In the end, I hope this work translates my fieldwork and analytical interpretations alongside what I have learned from psychobillies, and that members of the subculture find herein a vibrant description of their community that reflects the important role it plays in their lives.

Chapter Outline

This book is intended to introduce the reader to the core aspects of the subculture while also presenting its development historically. I have organized each chapter around a significant "watershed" moment that provides a gateway through which to explore a characteristic aspect of the subculture, such as its music, carnivalesque performances, horror-influenced lyrics, gender politics, and social and economic dimensions. I am aware that my presentation of general trends in the historical development of psychobilly is necessarily generalized and simplified and by no means exhaustive, and that any understanding and representation of history is subjective and incomplete (Cavicchi 2011). There inevitably will be exceptions to the general observations I make; precursors to those whom I highlight as influential; and people, places, and events I have had to leave out of this book. My intention is not to provide a detailed history[27] but rather to explore how psychobillies' participation in the subculture represents a response to feelings and experiences of socioeconomic marginalization as they express their nonnormativity, transgress hegemonic values and behaviors, and construct ways to improve the quality of their lived experience. I have tried to represent the creative ways psychobillies survive in a challenging world and how subcultural participation represents a "meaningful cultural experience" (Anderson 2009) and "innovative social practice" (Kahn-Harris 2007).

Chapter 1 describes how the genre emerged from a belief among some of England's working-class youth that the rebellious spirit of rock 'n' roll, rockabilly, and punk had disintegrated and that those styles had become clichés of themselves. By strategically combining particular elements of each and adding influences drawn from horror and science fiction movies and shock rock performances, early psychobillies expressed their rebellious identity politics and their experiences of difference from not only hegemonic values but also other subcultural styles. Outlining the "first wave" of psychobilly's development, which began around 1980, I explore why some youth were attracted to this new sound and style and its playful revival of rebellion against normativity. This analysis demonstrates how "retro" cultural artifacts were drawn on and resignified in meaningful ways situated in the present rather than representing a reactionary and nostalgic longing for the past.

Excluded from the rock 'n' roll and rockabilly circuits, psychobilly bands gravitated toward alternative venues in London such as the Klub Foot. Here, between 1982 and 1988 the U.K. psychobilly community defined the subculture's unique performances, behaviors, and style. Chapter 2 considers the carnivalesque elements that distinguished the expressive culture at the Klub Foot and continue to characterize the scene today. I argue that the creation of an alternative world, a "world turned upside down," in these performative contexts defies social restrictions and bodily control, breaks taboos, and subverts normative expectations. In these spaces, participants express their refusal of hegemonic culture and construct a countercultural utopia where they can have fun in their own way, improving the quality of their lived experience.

After the Klub Foot was demolished in 1988, psychobilly entered what many of my interlocutors refer to as the "dark ages" of the 1990s in the United Kingdom. The genre continued to survive on mainland Europe as the "second wave" of development accentuated its macabre obsession with monsters, murderers, and madness. Chapter 3 explores how psychobillies' fascination with these subjects expresses their identification with "misunderstood" or psychologically tortured characters who, like them, resist behavioral expectations and normative values. Listeners imagine reversing hegemonic power dynamics, living vicariously through songs about murdering one's parents or returning as a zombie to eat the brains of a former girlfriend. Not intended to be taken seriously, these fantasies invent an alternative world for subculturalists to imagine, a carnivalesque free-for-all, a momentary escape from their disempowered reality.

While women have participated in psychobilly since its inception, they were generally absent from the stage until the mid-2000s, or the "third wave" of subcultural development. Chapter 4 explores the dynamics of gender and sexuality in this subculture. I consider whether images and songs that fantasize about the sexual domination and objectification of women have perpetuated the peripheralization of women from the stage. But I also examine how women have actively constructed their own ideas about gender and sexuality, contesting stereotypical representations of women by asserting their agency and expressing their own sense of empowerment. Interviews with active female fans and musicians reveal the complexity of this issue and contribute to a polyvocal account that complicates a homogeneous representation of women's experience in this subculture.

Chapter 5 begins with an ethnographic description of an annual festival in Spain at which members of the international community meet to support bands and strengthen their social relationships. While a few major cities have a psychobilly scene large enough to support local and touring acts every weekend, today many psychobillies must travel out of town to festivals or concerts to socialize with others who share their identity and interests. The increase in international festivals corresponds with the accessibility of the Internet over the last couple of decades, a tool many psychobillies use to develop virtual relationships with other subculturalists around the globe, which often develop into face-to-face encounters at weekenders. This chapter highlights how these relationships and global flows of communication provide socio-emotional and economic resources that help psychobillies negotiate and improve their lives.

Lack of interest in mainstream tastes and markets continues to be an important reason that people identify with psychobilly, as discussed previously in this Introduction. They want their music to remain "underground," hard to find, and different, just as they themselves continue to identify as nonnormative. Accordingly, psychobillies very clearly define the parameters of their subculture. The Afterword explores issues of gatekeeping, highlighting debates about what constitutes "real" or "pure" psychobilly fashion and music. The "first wave" of the genre was self-consciously diverse, explicitly responding to the clichés that characterized the stagnant rocker, rockabilly, and punk scenes at the time by embracing a range of influences and an "anything goes" attitude. However, the subculture subsequently developed its own set of clichés and expected sounds, behaviors, and fashion. I am interested in the tension between a perspective that espouses innovation, experimentation, and rebellion on the one hand, yet seeks to establish, preserve, and protect the defining characteristics of the psychobilly on the other. When a subculture is founded on a desire to resist norms and expectations, what happens when it develops its own norms and expectations, and what happens when the latter are questioned or resisted from within? Will the subculture continue to exist only as a simulacrum of itself, endlessly imitating itself (even though this would be antithetical to its original ethos), or can it evolve and adapt without losing its identity, purpose, and meaning? In other words, how will the subculture survive, and can it continue to be an important vehicle through which its participants survive?

THE DEVELOPMENT OF PSYCHOBILLY

Carrying on the Nonconformist Legacy
of Rockabilly and Punk

All of a sudden, there was a strange sound
What's that? We all looked around
To hear that crazy phantom rocker sound

—THE SHARKS, "Phantom Rockers," *Phantom Rockers*, 1983

As subcultural theorist Ross Haenfler points out, "Rather than popping up out of nowhere, new subcultures often emerge from the ashes of the old, recycling some aspects of previous scenes and replacing others" (2016, 97). Indeed, psychobilly was developed by former Teds, rockabillies, and punks who felt that those subcultures had stagnated. They were frustrated by an overreliance on clichés, the homogenization of sound and style, and the loss of the rebellious spirit that had originally motivated each of those subcultures. Transgressing established aesthetic limitations and cultural norms, they combined musical, sartorial, and ideological elements of rock 'n' roll, rockabilly, Teddy Boy, punk, new wave, shock rock, hard rock, and neo-rockabilly with an interest in horror and science fiction to create what was known variously as "mutant rockabilly," "punkabilly," "punk hillbilly," "psycho rockabilly," "psychebilly," and eventually "psychobilly." They sought to revive rockabilly's raw sound, DIY philosophy, nonconformist approach, and uninhibited performance style while reflecting contemporary influences and experiences by borrowing from the "Loud Fast Rules!"[1] attitude of punk and the horror-themed theatricality of shock rockers.

This chapter explores the origins of psychobilly in England in the early 1980s, contextualizing its significance to those rebellious teens and young adults who participated in the first wave of its development. I draw on the recollections of my interlocutors, historical accounts and interviews published in print and online, and reviews in alternative music magazines. These descriptions of the period reveal that most first-wave psychobillies shared a passion for 1950s rockabilly, particularly its "wild" and "raw" sound; its use of the upright bass (slap bass); and the countercultural lives, identities, values, and performances of the musicians who created it. Like the original rockabillies, first-wave psychobillies were nonconformists at heart. Accordingly, they became frustrated with the imitative nature of the rock 'n' roll and rockabilly revivals of the 1970s. They were driven by a constant desire to experiment, refusing to be straitjacketed by the restrictive limits of those scenes. At the same time that they were growing increasingly frustrated with the limitations of contemporary rock 'n' roll and rockabilly, they were influenced by the nonconformist sounds and culture of punk. They recognized how rockabilly and punk both celebrated a working-class sensibility and a rebellious ethos. They hybridized the two subcultural styles sonically, sartorially, and ideologically to signify their own economic marginalization and resistance to hegemonic culture. Because their performances reflected diverse influences, first-wave psychobilly bands such as The Meteors and The Sharks were rejected by the Teddy Boy and rockabilly communities and found audiences in alternative clubs that openly embraced a new nontraditional and controversial style. This chapter traces how the rebellious antimainstream and nonconformist identities and interests of first-wavers influenced both their discovery and their rejection of (and by) the rock 'n' roll and rockabilly subcultures of the 1970s, leading to the development of neo-rockabilly and then psychobilly.

The representation here of psychobilly's origins demonstrates how musicians actively selected from previous and contemporary cultural influences to express themselves uniquely and precisely, like the bricoleur punks described in Dick Hebdige's *Subculture: The Meaning of Style* (1979). Psychobilly is not a nostalgic subculture that looks backward, longingly, reactively, toward the past. Rather, an understanding of first-wavers' lack of interest in "authentically" reconstructing 1950s rockabilly underscores how psychobilly musicians borrowed from the popular culture of the past while generating something new. This provides a counterargument to those postmodernists who consider retro-influenced styles evidence of culturally regressive addictions with the past that suppress innovation and creativity, a "false" sense of history, and depthless and empty pastiche of popular culture.

Rock 'n' Roll: From Rebellious Teds to a Mainstream Retro Revival (Early to Mid-1970s)

To understand how and why some people were drawn to psychobilly when it emerged, it is necessary to explore what type of music they were listening to before that time. As youth in the early to mid-1970s, most of them were drawn to rock 'n' roll artists who had been commercially successful in the 1950s: Chuck Berry, Bill Haley, Little Richard, Gene Vincent, Fats Domino, Roy Orbison, Buddy Holly, Elvis Presley, Jerry Lee Lewis, Johnny Burnette, and Carl Perkins. Many of my interlocutors were exposed to this music through their parents, as neo-rockabilly and psychobilly bassist Steve Whitehouse (a member of The Sharks, Frenzy, and The Blue Cats) recalled:

> Steve: When I was a kid, I started collecting vinyl when I was five years old because my dad was into Bill Haley, mainly, and Gene Vincent, and my mum was into Elvis. More of the sort of not-so-underground artists of the time.
>
> Kim: More mainstream.
>
> Steve: Yeah, she's into all that, the ones who did more love songs, like Elvis did and all that kind of thing. Anyway, it was wafting around the house, the music, and of course you get into it. Then to my dad, I said, "Oh, I love the cover on the Bill Haley album, the 'R-O-C-K Rock' one." I said, "I love that. Can I have that?" "Here, you can have that. That's the start of your record collection." That was it. Right from the start, I always wondered what that k-dink, k-dink, k-dink, k-dink noise was—
>
> Kim:—that click?
>
> Steve: Yeah, which was obviously Marshall [Lytle] playing the bass on Bill Haley's stuff and Bill Black on the Elvis stuff, and whatever, so I was really interested to find out what that was. Then on the front cover—Dad said, "Well, that's the bass." I said, "Wow, that's so cool," so I stood up on the bass [amplifier] and the sound was amazing. We had a pretty good stereo for the '70s in the house, and you could feel the bass, as well as just hear the slap. I thought: "That's just cool, when I'm older, I'm going to do that." I knew then that I wanted to play one of those.
>
> Kim: That was as a kid still?
>
> Steve: That was still when I was like five, six, seven years old.

Like Steve, most of my interviewees preferred the music of the past when they were young, listening to records that were originally produced about a decade before their births, instead of contemporary mainstream genres such as disco, Top 40 pop, glam rock, and progressive rock. In fact, its non-mainstream status and its difference from contemporary music were part of that music's allure:

> Jerry Chatabox: "The music and singing [of Elvis Presley and Buddy Holly] sounded so raw and powerful and urgent, nothing like the ridiculous manufactured glam rock in the charts." (Chatabox 2011, 10)
>
> P. Paul Fenech: "I hung around with a bunch of people at school and we just didn't want to be into disco and things like that so the obvious path was to go into rock 'n' roll, which meant to be a Teddy Boy." (Decay 2004)

While their classmates considered rock 'n' roll old-fashioned, my interlocutors were fascinated with the music their parents had listened to when *they* were teenagers, and they enthusiastically rooted through their parents' record collections and closets.

Signifying their passion for 1950s music, these "rocker" teens adopted elements of Teddy Boy fashion, the neo-Edwardian post–World War II style that came to be associated with rock 'n' roll by the late 1950s.[2] They wore crepe-soled suede shoes (known as "brothel creepers")[3] and velvet-trimmed drape suits, and they molded their hair into a pompadour in the front while combing the sides to form a "duck's arse" in the back (Polhemus 1994; Baddeley 2015). Cultivating a Teddy Boy look in the early to mid-1970s aesthetically marked them as nonconformists who were uninterested in mainstream trends. Pillaging old clothes from their parents' closets and secondhand shops, their "anachronistic dress" (McRobbie 1988) represented "anti-fashion," "styles of dress that are explicitly contrary to fashions of the day, worn to symbolize rebellion and signal belonging" (Fischer 2015, 48).[4]

Classmates who shared an affinity for rock 'n' roll naturally formed close bonds with each other, a necessary strategy given the outcast and "uncool" status that came with liking the music and fashion of the not-so-distant past. Alan Wilson, singer and guitarist of early psychobilly band The Sharks, remembered the excitement of discovering that one of his classmates also listened to rock 'n' roll:

> I had to do a school project for music class, and so I decided to do it about Buddy Holly. I was about eleven or twelve at the time, and so this would be '72 or something. Looking back, Buddy Holly hadn't been dead that long, really [thirteen years]. Now it seems like two

lifetimes ago, but it actually was comparatively recent. Anyway, I was quite new to the school, and so I didn't really know many of the kids there. And I did this project about Buddy Holly, and at the time, rock 'n' roll music wasn't in the charts. We didn't call it rockabilly then. It was just rock 'n' roll. Nobody really liked it. It was very sort of forgotten about. To my amazement, another kid got up and did his project on Eddie Cochran! So then instantly we became close straight away. We were the only two kids in one thousand people at school that knew and liked rock 'n' roll. . . . No one cared but us.

Fellow Sharks member Steve Whitehouse recalled a similar experience:

There were only two of us in the school who were into rock 'n' roll. . . . He didn't know me and I didn't know him to start with, and then we were turning up at school and getting told off for wearing the college jackets and having our hair all quiffed up, because I had my first quiff when I was eleven, what was called a D.A., duck's arse. My mum said, "Oh, you can't go to school with it like that." So when I'd get to school, I'd go to the boy's toilets and then do it. I'd have hairspray in my bag. And then I'd get in trouble for it. He was doing the same thing, and so we became mates.

While youth like Alan and Steve were in the minority at their schools, older Teds had been keeping rock 'n' roll alive since the 1950s and were desperate to see live performances by rock 'n' roll's pioneers. When Bill Haley performed at the Royal Albert Hall in May 1968, long after he assumed his career was over, he was so frightened by the wildly overenthusiastic Teds that he refused to come onstage for an encore (Guffey 2006, 100–101). Haley's outstanding reception triggered a rock 'n' roll revival in the 1970s, as stars who had long ago lost their popularity in the United States found a hungry audience of Teds in the United Kingdom. This provided an opportunity for young fans of rock 'n' roll, those who were not alive during its heyday, to dive headlong into the vintage music they loved. Alan, for instance, remembered seeing Roy Orbison, Bill Haley, Carl Perkins, Bo Diddley, Jerry Lee Lewis, and others on their "comeback" tours when he was fourteen and fifteen years old. In addition, new bands emerged who covered and imitated 1950s rock 'n' roll, inspiring Alan to form his own group: "I suddenly realized you didn't have to be born twenty years before to be able to play rock 'n' roll music."

The rock 'n' roll revival proved lucrative, and various entrepreneurs seized the opportunity to make money off nostalgic memorabilia and Teddy

Boy consumer goods. Malcolm McLaren, who later became the enterprising manager of the Sex Pistols, opened a shop called Let It Rock with fashion designer Vivienne Westwood in King's Road in Chelsea. Their experimental boutique designs, based on retro fashion, became popular with punks. Teds, who "were adamant in their quest for authentic re-creations of their own '50s past," were "increasingly dismayed to find drainpipe trousers sold next to latex gear, and drape jackets held together with safety pins" (Guffey 2006, 104–105). Clashes between punks and Teds were frequently highlighted in the press, reminding some of the "moral panics" caused by the media's sensationalized reports of violence between the mods and the rockers a decade earlier (Stanley Cohen 1972). But while Teds had been vilified by the press in the 1950s and 1960s and characterized as violent criminals, now "the prevalent media view saw the Teds as comforting time-travellers from an altogether saner and safer era" (Polhemus 1994, 37). Through its 1970s mainstreaming, rock 'n' roll came to represent "nostalgia for the good old days" (Guffey 2006, 112) as "black leather jackets, sock hops and *Happy Days* helped to convert a wide audience to the retro revival, translating Ted rebelliousness into Howdy Doody innocence" (105). Compared to the "drug-taking Hippies and the aggressive Skinheads," Teds now seemed innocent enough (Polhemus 1994, 37). As Dick Hebdige had warned, the Teds' subcultural style had been incorporated into mainstream culture and exploited through commodification, defusing the "symbolic challenges" to hegemonic society that it had once represented (1979, 96). As the 1970s revival became a vehicle through which quaint nostalgia for an imagined innocent past was engineered, rock 'n' roll's association with rebelliousness was effectively weakened. Moreover, as rock 'n' roll became a mainstream leisure activity, bands became more derivative and narrowed their repertoire to cover the most popular songs, catering to their audience's expectations and preferences. Some rock 'n' roll fans, however, were not happy with the consequences of the mainstreaming process; they grew weary of hearing the same sound and songs over and over again, and they were frustrated that "the piss had been taken out of rock 'n' roll," as one first-wave psychobilly told me.

The Rockabilly Revival: Discovering Forgotten Wild-Sounding Tracks and Reviving the Upright Bass (Mid-1970s)

Nigel Lewis, the original bassist for the pioneering psychobilly band The Meteors, remembers the day he heard something other than the predictable rock 'n' roll that had come to characterize the revival:

> In the summer of 1975, aged fourteen, I went to the Lyceum Ballroom in London where they had regular Rock n Roll [*sic*] shows, I was expecting to hear Chuck Berry, Bill Haley, etc. As I walked into the ballroom I heard—and was blown away totally by—what I now know was "One Hand Loose" by Charlie Feathers. I had entered a new world, very different from the one I had just left which was full of hippies and teenyboppers and people who would never know what I now knew. I probably wanted to start a band right then. (Lewis 2010)

The song he heard was an original rockabilly tune from 1956. Rock 'n' roll was a broad category that included different styles of rhythm and blues–based music during the mid-1950s; one particular type of rock 'n' roll retroactively became known as rockabilly.[5] Born and bred in the American South, rockabilly was typically associated with working-class white artists who played rhythm and blues in a distinctly country and western way, usually featuring a stripped-down combo of upright bass, rhythm guitar, and electric guitar. The rockabilly sound was most famously engineered by producer Sam Phillips and his early recordings of Elvis Presley in Sun Studios in Memphis, Tennessee. Inspired by Presley's music, particularly by his rags-to-riches success, many performers replicated his raw, hillbilly-inflected style of rock 'n' roll from approximately 1954 to 1958. While many of these tracks never saw the light of day, the rock 'n' roll revival in England provided an audience that was interested in "rediscovering" this vintage music. As rockabilly revival musician and journalist Max Décharné puts it: "The US had given the world rockabilly, but Europe—in particular Britain, Germany, France and Holland—got hold of the patient when it had been left for dead and applied a serious jolt to its system, bringing it back from the brink of oblivion" (2010, 272). Several labels released forgotten, no-hit rockabilly tracks from their vaults, exposing British youth to records that had previously been unavailable outside of the United States.

My interlocutors, who were frustrated with the way the mainstream revival had diluted and sanitized rock 'n' roll, were attracted to the less-mainstream rockabilly that was re-released at this time. To them, rockabilly represented a more unadulterated liberation from normative codes of behavior, the music of the true rebels of that mythological "golden era." Patrick Mullen describes rockabilly as a genre that privileged "rebellion against societal controls, excess, hedonism, and a sense of community among outsiders" (1984, 79). In "Hillbilly Hipsters of the 1950s," Mullen notes that rockabilly songs expressed countercultural values: "Rockabillies seem to resent any restraint in their pursuit of a good time, and a good time meant drinking, fighting, dancing, and womanizing. . . . Rockabilly songs are declaration of adolescent excess urging everyone to drink faster, fight harder, and dance longer, often to the point of destroying property or themselves" (86). My interlocutors identified with the wild behavior expressed in song lyrics and represented by the performers who sang them. O'Prez, for instance, recalled: "I liked rockabillies like Gene Vincent. Back then I was reading books about him, how he shot Gary Glitter, and I thought: 'This is the guy for me.' It was the whole bad boy thing, romanticized, the loner down at the pool hall. And I'm thinking: 'I'm fifteen, this is me.'" Moreover, those white Southern performers defied conventional ideas about music, race, sexuality, and class by embracing controversial rhythm and blues styles, moving their bodies in ways that shocked conservative audiences, and ignoring discourse that suggested they could not achieve anything because of their poor upbringing. The first-wave psychobillies I interviewed related to those subversive rockabillies of the 1950s, for they too defied authoritarian restrictions on their movements and appearance and identified as working class. As Levi told me, "Rockabilly has to do with being a rebel and an outsider, and being OK with that, and embracing it."

Many of my interlocutors also loved obscure rockabilly music because they perceived something in it that they said they did not find in more mainstream styles. Some felt that the context of rockabilly's origins resulted in a "wild," "pure," and "raw" sound that contrasted with commercial pop and rock 'n' roll. For instance, Alan Wilson felt that the "desperation" of the performers' attempts to achieve Elvis's success lent rockabilly an intense energy and excitement that he didn't hear or feel in other types of music:

> If you can imagine those people, they were dirt poor and they're probably picking cotton in the blazing heat. Along comes this guy Elvis—this is my version anyway—along comes Elvis and he shakes about a little bit and makes a fortune. And suddenly everyone thinks: "I want to do that, I don't wanna pick cotton, I wanna do what he's doing." In them days, you had to be good to get in a recording studio. So if someone got the chance to go to a recording studio, what are they going to do? They're gonna go crazy, they're gonna say, "Look at me, this is my twenty minutes to prove that I wanna be like Elvis." So you can almost smell the desperation in them records. So I think that Elvis was like a shining star, and it made other things come up and I think those other things have got a charm of their own. So they gave it balls out, 110 percent. And you can hear it in the recordings, they're really desperate for that, like, "Please sign me." Some of these

records were so great and the excitement in those recordings was just amazing.

For rockabilly event promoter Jerry Chatabox, rockabilly artists were inherently more earnest and naturally talented than contemporary performers:

> These 1950s "country rock," or rockabilly, tracks sounded very different from the mass-produced hits of their era, and we could not get enough of them. It was a stripped-down sound, just the bare essentials, often just a singer, a bass and a guitar. Drums were not always necessary, the upright bass (or bull fiddle) being slapped to produce the note and an added click, which was often the whole rhythm section. These records had a raw, exciting sound, often having been recorded in one take, with any mistakes left in. It was a fantastically "pure" music, sung from the heart with real emotion. Singers and musicians had to be truly talented, as there was no remixing or electronic gimmickry to help make them sound better. (2011, 11–12)

These reflections express a nostalgia that locates "authenticity" in the past rather than the present and further signifies how young British rockabilly fans expressed their lack of interest in the contemporary mainstream by romanticizing the sonic and cultural qualities of an alternative sound.

Driven to re-create that "raw" 1950s sound, rockabilly musicians in the 1970s revived the upright bass that was so fundamental to the original style. Alan remembered vividly how excited he was to finally see a band use the instrument that musicians had played in the 1950s:

> Everybody was using an electric bass [during the rock 'n' roll revival]. My first band, we had an electric bass. That was a very British version of rock 'n' roll and rockabilly. Then one of the revival bands—The Flying Saucers—suddenly had a double bass. I distinctly remember the guy, Pete Pritchard, had the double bass on the floor— he was playing electric bass all night, and then for one song he picked up the double bass and the audience went crazy because it was a novelty. I remember not so much the sound. I didn't think it sounded great, to be honest. But it was the fact that when he picked it up, everyone went crazy. So I thought: "There's something in it." And that's really how I got into rockabilly.

Many of my interlocutors shared Alan's excitement about the upright bass. They were fascinated by the novelty of it and the way it drove crowds wild, as Alan suggested, but they also valued its historical authenticity. Only by using upright bass could they try to replicate the slap style of bass playing that was featured in the original rockabilly recordings of the 1950s, the sound that had so fascinated Steve Whitehouse when he listened to his dad's Bill Haley records. In this sense, the rockabilly revival of the mid-1970s corresponds to Tamara Livingston's model of musical revivals: "Revivalists position themselves in *opposition* to aspects of the contemporary cultural mainstream, align themselves with a particular historical lineage, and offer a cultural alternative in which legitimacy is grounded in reference to authenticity and historical fidelity" (1999, 66). However, those rockabillies who eventually became psychobillies were not actually diehard revivalists. They were generally not interested in rockabilly because of a nostalgic appreciation for the 1950s but rather because it was anti-fashionable and represented a rebellious, nonconformist ideology and attitude that they identified with. They also found these characteristics in a new style of music that emerged in London in the mid-1970s: punk.

Punk Revives a Rock 'n' Roll Approach (Mid- to Late 1970s)

When punk arrived in England in the mid-1970s,[6] some recognized it as the back-to-the-basics return to rock 'n' roll that it was (Morrison 1996, 225). Developed as a response to the perceived pretentiousness, extravagance, and commercialization of mainstream arena rock in the mid- to late 1970s, punk eschewed the complex style, form, and instrumentation of progressive rock and "art" rock in favor of a stripped-down, early rock 'n' roll approach. Just as rockabillies had, they played raw, amateur-friendly, three-chord songs as a basic combo (one or two guitars, bass, drums, and vocals) and were influenced by the nonconformist spirit and unbridled energy that motivated and characterized those rebellious early rock 'n' rollers. Punks appropriated not only the Teddy Boy designs that Malcolm McLaren sold in his store but also the music. As Kenneth Partridge points out: "Eisenhower-era hillbilly rebels like Elvis Presley, Gene Vincent, and Jerry Lee Lewis were the Johnny Rottens of their day. Recognizing the kinship, many of the first-generation U.K. punks nicked '50s fashions and hairstyles, and their simple three-chord bashing harked back to rock's early days" (2015). Ted Polhemus similarly describes the relationship between punk and rockabilly:

> To make the connection one must forget the soft drizzle of senti-mentality which in the end became all too typical of the rockabillies

(Elvis singing about Teddy Bears in Vegas) and go back to the angry, licentious snarf of their early days. From this perspective it is clear that the thumping beat, the in-your-face sexuality, the deliberate shunning of prissy sophistication and the greasy quiffs of the early Rockabillies were in tune with Punk's gutsy spirit of raw rebellion. . . . The common denominator is rock 'n' roll energy in its purest form. (1994, 102)

So even while punks clashed with Teds and rockers on the streets in the mid-1970s, some perceptive youth recognized the common underlying rebellious ethos; DIY musical sensibility; working-class identity; and nonmainstream, anti-elite impulse of their subcultures. For example, P. Paul Fenech of The Meteors identified as a rocker and spent his weekends fighting with punks (Decay 2004), yet he appreciated the similarities between rockabilly and punk, as he told *Sounds* magazine in 1981:

I've always really liked [rockabilly and rock 'n' roll]. It gets in the blood. That and punk are the only two forms of music I really care for. Rockabilly was like the punk of the Fifties; it didn't get played on the radio to begin with because they said it was the Devil's music. The musicians in the Fifties never had thousands of pounds or anything, and they couldn't afford nice clothes, and they all came from slums and places like that, just like a lot of the punk musicians. (quoted in Wall 1981, 14)

Others who would become psychobillies observed the commonalities as well. Kim Nekroman, singer and bassist of psychobilly band Nekromantix, remembers, "My mom was into Johnny Burnette and Elvis, and in the mid-'70s when punk came about, I automatically connected the two" (quoted in Downey 2004, 77). Similarly, lifelong psychobilly fan Craig Brackenridge remembers: "Early rock'n'roll and punk both appealed to me and plenty of kids my age. The first singles I bought were by Darts [popular 1970s rock 'n' roll revivalists], Stiff Little Fingers [a punk band], and then neo-rockabillies The Stray Cats" (quoted in Peacock 2015, 33). Steve Whitehouse loved rockabillies such as Elvis, Eddie Cochran, and Bill Haley, whom he described to me as "the punks of the Fifties," but he also listened to the punk and new wave bands that emerged in the mid- to late 1970s.

Thus, while those who only liked rock 'n' roll and rockabilly were perhaps committed to the music for its nostalgic associations and its attempted "authentic" reconstruction of the past, those who liked both rockabilly and punk were not. They were interested in drawing on any subcultural style—past or present—that represented their working-class identities, nonconformist attitudes, and rebellious ideologies. They also loved to transgress expectations and test boundaries, enjoying the reactions they received when they brought punk elements into the rockabilly scene because the two sub-cultures were largely understood to be rivals. Alan Wilson, for instance, delighted in how his interest in punk bothered rockabillies: "I remember going to rockabilly gigs and I'd dyed my hair pink at a time when no one did that in that scene. I was like sixteen, seventeen years old, it was around 1977 or 1978, and I only did it to piss everyone off, you know? And I did! People that used to speak to me suddenly didn't wanna now. They just thought: 'Well, he's a punk now.' I did it all just for a reaction, really." He described a gig his rockabilly band, The Dixie Rebels, played with punk band Vice Squad. The Teddy Boys had no interest at all in the punk band, further fuel-ing his desire to push back against their "narrow-minded" ways:

> It was being filmed for television and the audience were 50 percent punks for Vice Squad and then about 50 percent rock and rollers, Teds, who had come to see us. And the BBC were having a heart attack 'cause they thought there was gonna be a big fight. What it proved to me was the punks were so much cooler because the punks all went crazy for us, but the Teds walked out when Vice Squad came on. The Teds were so kinda narrow-minded about it, but the punks were going crazy. So I thought: "That's pretty cool." And I could see again that it kinda pissed off the Teds, so again, my nature is that makes it more attractive to me. I guess you could say I was a rebel.

This expressed desire to disrupt the limited vision of the revival movement came up repeatedly in my interviews with first-wavers, suggesting that they were more interested in embodying the rebellious ideology of rockabilly than in dogmatically preserving the music and style in a historically accurate way.

Breaking Away from Authentic Imitation: Neo-Rockabilly (Late 1970s and Early 1980s)

Those youth who most embodied the rebellious attitude that had initially driven both rock 'n' roll and punk quickly tired of the predictable note-for-note covers that had become the mainstay of the 1970s rockabilly scene. They experimented with their rockabilly style, bringing in elements from punk and new wave. These bands, who sounded different from the status quo on the revival circuit, came to be known for their new approach to rockabilly and were thus dubbed "neo-rockabilly." As Steve Whitehouse remembered:

> Steve: The reason that *neo*-rockabilly came to pass is because people were pissed off with the same—I was really pissed off—with the same fucking covers.
> Kim: Just imitation over and over?
> Steve: Over and over and over. You'd go to the shows, there'd be "Tear It Up" and "Be-Bop-a-Lula."
> Kim: Just done the same way? It wasn't altered?
> Steve: You had to sound just like Gene Vincent. You had to sound just like Bill Haley, Elvis Presley. It's been done so many times, and the reason that neo-rockabilly and psychobilly came to pass is because people wanted to smash that mold.

Clint Bradley tried to break that mold when he formed a band in 1978, at age fifteen, that combined his interest in both rockabilly and punk: "For me, it all went hand in hand, it was all about energy, working-class kids giving it some. . . . The two things together [punk and rockabilly] were explosive, at a time when that sort of thing was unheard of. Most of our songs were our own, we were just doing what felt good" (*DogEatRobot Fanzine* 2013a). Clint soon discovered, however, that the rock 'n' roll and rockabilly scene in London did not welcome his contemporary interpretation of 1950s music:

> After a while we started to get gigs on the rock 'n' roll circuit, and were very quickly told that what we were doing wasn't going to please the hard core of the scene in London. . . . I can still remember the first time we played in London. This agent called Lee Allen said, "Well I'll get you some gigs lads, but you need to do more covers and stop sounding so punk, stop wearing Doc Martin [*sic*] boots and get rid of the Gibson SG and replace it with a Gretsch semi acoustic." I was becoming really conscious of the fact that I wanted to write and play my own songs, about my own culture and the things going on around me. I mean I loved rockabilly music, but I couldn't relate to the lyrics of a lot of the songs, because they were about another youth culture from another country and time. It was people like Joe Strummer [of punk band The Clash] who were writing about things I understood and could see around me. And I wanted to call the band Spurdog but the agent said, "No, it's too new wave," and came up with this bloody ridiculous name of Tony and the Tennessee

Rebels. I mean what the hell had that got to do with four kids from an English dockland city?" (4).

His band collapsed under the challenges of performing a style of music that did not cater to the rockabilly revival community's demand for strict imitation of the classic genre. In 1980 he joined up with Carlo and Stefano Edwards, two rockabilly musicians from a Gene Vincent tribute band who shared Clint's frustration with the limitations of the scene; Carlo felt "locked in a creative prison and was busting to get out," and Stefano was "capable of creative drum patterns way beyond the confines he'd been given up until then" (2). By this time, Clint found that some fans were ready for the "neo-rockabilly" style that The Blue Cats represented:

> It was very different back then. We had to make our own scene because the purist rockabilly fans didn't like it when we played our own songs in our own style. . . . We got some grief from the music fascists but a lot of the kids were ready for what we were doing and just shouted louder than the moaners. . . . We very soon started to play our own gigs outside the old scene and so the neo-rockabilly scene was born. . . . We played in places like Dingwalls, Marquee Club, Rock Garden, Hope and Anchor, and others around London and that's how it all began . . . People that wanted to see us doing our own thing could come and see us in our own right without any grief. (2–3).

In clubs that catered to punk, oi, and new wave, The Blue Cats were freed from the limitations of the rockabilly scene and found fans who welcomed their unique approach.

Like The Blue Cats, bands including Restless, The Polecats, The Sharks, Levi and the Rockats, and Stray Cats mixed rockabilly with the sonic and sartorial aesthetics of punk and new wave, cultivating a fan base outside the traditional rockabilly circuit. Appearances by the Polecats and Stray Cats on *Top of the Pops* further exposed England's youth to the possibilities of mixing traditional elements of rockabilly with contemporary influences. Steve Whitehouse was excited by Stray Cats' "highly colorful, electric look, like the fifties on acid." He admired their commitment to the "authentic" upright bass and to a wild performance style he associated with the original rockabillies, but he also celebrated their exaggerated, nonauthentic interpretation of 1950s fashion and their eclectic integration of new wave and punk elements:

They were these sweaty, zitty kids with huge, over-accentuated quiffs and battered leather jackets and I thought they were just wonderful. Even though they were American, they were working the London circuit and you'd read reviews of them playing clubs like Dingwalls and see photos where they were just sweating their balls off. They were brilliant, really electric. They had a great double bassist in Lee Rocker, so it was proper rockabilly music as far as I was concerned. It was what I was looking for. (quoted in Peacock 2015, 33)

By refusing to play only reconstructionist covers of rock 'n' roll and rockabilly, neo-rockabilly bands paved the way for the development of psychobilly. As Alan Wilson put it: "The Blue Cats, and other bands that weren't exactly imitating the 1950s sound, were kind of a bridge between the rockabilly scene and the psychobilly scene. The difference, with hindsight, is very slight. It's a very short step from rockabilly, to what people have since called neo-rockabilly, to psychobilly." According to many, that next step was taken by The Meteors with their "psychotic," perverse, and macabre interpretation of rockabilly.

"The Cancer on Rock 'n' Roll": The "Mutant Rockabilly" of The Meteors

Psychobilly fans endlessly debate the origins of the genre. Many of my interlocutors argued that some of the theatrical "shock 'n' roll" performers of the 1950s and 1960s could be considered the first artists who cultivated a psychobilly sound and attitude. They described Screaming Jay Hawkins, whose theatrical stage shows featured him emerging from a coffin to sing his popular rock 'n' roll song "I Put a Spell On You," or Screaming Lord Sutch, who dressed up as the famous serial killer to perform his rock 'n' roll hit "Jack the Ripper." Because psychobilly is defined in part by its tongue-in-cheek engagement with the macabre, Hawkins's use of "voodoo stage props, such as his smoking skull on a stick—named Henry—and rubber snakes" (Komara 2006, 415) and Sutch's horror-themed productions represent psychobilly antecedents. Many fans also suggest that the uninhibited and rebellious rockabilly artists of the 1950s were the original psychobillies; as Steve Young of psychobilly band Surfin' Wombatz told me: "Johnny Burnette, to me, there's no difference to psychobilly. It's wild, mad, you know." Indeed, this is probably why The Cramps, a garage/trash band that had incorporated elements of rockabilly, punk, and 1950s horror B movies into their style years before the psychobilly subculture developed, used the word "psychobilly" on their concert posters in 1976 to describe their performances. As their guitarist, Poison Ivy Rorschach, explained: "To us, all the '50s rockabillies were psycho to begin with; it just came with the turf as a given, like a crazed, sped-up hillbilly boogie version of country" (Spitz and Mullen 2001, 34–35). But The Cramps refused to be "shoehorned into any stylistic box" (Partridge 2015), denying that they were a psychobilly band once the word came to be associated with the subculture that developed in the early 1980s (Downey 2004, 78).

The same year that The Cramps used "psychobilly" on their concert posters, Johnny Cash released a song that also featured the word. "One Piece at a Time," penned by Wayne Kemp, narrates the story of a Detroit factory worker who slowly but persistently steals Cadillac parts from his job. It takes him almost twenty-five years, from 1949 to 1973, to build his dream machine from these contraband treasures. At the end of the song, Cash identifies his mutant, mismatched creation as "the Psycho-billy Cadillac" and describes its oddball qualities, such as having three headlights and only one tailfin. When his wife sees it, she has her doubts, and the people in town laugh at it. But not only does it run, Cash is proud of it. He likes that his one-of-a-kind machine stands out, and he celebrates his creative resourcefulness, boasting that it did not cost him anything. Although songwriter Kemp never explained how he arrived at the word, the "psycho" prefix in his description of the Cadillac likely denoted the "crazy," mixed-up appearance of the car, its mutant combination of parts from different years. Most likely derived from "hillbilly," the "billy" suffix already had been borrowed to create the portmanteau "rockabilly" and signified rural, white, working-class southerners. The "Psychobilly Cadillac" was as an apt metaphor for the genre that developed in the early 1980s: rockabilly mutated with appropriated parts of popular culture from different years, born from a working-class desire to make do with what one can access, something that drives everyone wild, something with which psychobillies proudly identify even if—or, rather, *because*—it looks quite strange to others, something that is one of a kind.

But while The Cramps and Wayne Kemp used the word "psychobilly" in the 1970s, it was The Meteors who developed the specific musical style that came to be associated with the word in the early 1980s, and it was around them—and the bands they inspired—that the subculture grew.[7] Craig Brackenridge describes the undeniable role The Meteors played in the development of the psychobilly subculture:

> While the origins of psychobilly are as wild and varied as the genre itself, there can be no real doubt that The Meteors have always been at the eye of the psychobilly hurricane. . . . For most psychobilly fans

from the early 1980s and beyond, it was seeing or hearing The Meteors for the first time that brought psychobilly to their attention and even members of some other pioneering psychobilly bands, such as Pip Hancox of the Guana Batz, have openly admitted that it was The Meteors that drove them to form a group and create their own rockin' racket. (Brackenridge 2007, 18)

Most psychobillies who participated in the first wave can still recall the exact moment they first heard The Meteors' music, recognizing it as a completely unique style that brought together rockabilly and punk with a brand-new style of lyrics and performance. Indeed, even though more than thirty-five years had passed, all the first-wavers I interviewed were able to recount precisely where they were and how they felt when they heard The Meteors for the first time, saying things such as "it hit me right between the eyes," "it blew me away," and "it was just what I'd been waiting for." They remember that moment clearly because their discovery of The Meteors introduced them to a subculture that most of them still strongly identify with and are committed to today. As one first-waver told me, "Once I heard their music, I've never looked back." Accordingly, I delve into The Meteors' transition from rockabilly to psychobilly in some detail here in order to unpack how their unique characteristics served to bring together a sub-cultural community of rebels.

Before they formed The Meteors, P. Paul Fenech (vocals and electric guitar) and Nigel Lewis (electric and upright bass) played in rockabilly bands such as Raw Deal and Rock Therapy in the late 1970s. They wore Teddy Boy and rockabilly clothes, played for audiences of Teds and rockers, and covered the songs or closely imitated the style of 1950s artists such as Gene Vincent, Bill Haley, and Johnny Burnette. It was not long before Fenech and Lewis wanted to push the limits of the revival scene, and they began to experiment with a wilder and more eccentric approach to their music, lyrics, and live performances. Pat Panioty (rhythm guitarist/vocalist of Raw Deal) recalls a Raw Deal performance in Manchester that was quite unlike most rock 'n' roll gigs: "A Ted was standing there taking the piss for some time out of Paul, who was onstage in a long black coat. After absorbing the guy's 'mouth' for some time, Paul opened the coat up, underneath which he had a dildo strapped on. As he squeezed the balls, he covered the guy in milk!" (quoted in Fenech 1995, 5). Later, at The White Hart in Tottenham, Nigel seemed to lose control, smashing his double bass and proceeding to rip up the stage with the microphone stand while P. Paul rolled about on the floor (Fenech 1995, 5–6). Panioty remembers it as "the gig that changed Nigel from a quiet man into a monster" (quoted in Fenech 1995, 5). Marc Fenech (P. Paul Fenech's brother) recalls, "By the end of the song (which is only about one and half minutes!) the landlord had already set the dog on them! Raw Deal would never perform again. . . . What could follow that?" (6).

The rhythm guitarist and drummer left the band for fear of treading into uncharted territory that was too far outside the lines of the established rockabilly sound and scene. On the sleeve of one of their records, Fenech and Lewis describe this moment in their band's history: "Terry and Pat were not up to the trouble it caused" (The Meteors, *Teenagers from Outer Space* inner gatefold sleeve, 1986). The Meteors' manager, Nick Garrard, remembers the different perspectives of the band members: "Terry [the drummer] was content with the Ted circuit, Pat was happy looking cool and rockin' away (and he did both perfectly) while Nigel and Paul wanted to take rockabilly somewhere further and weirder" (quoted in Fenech 1995, 6). Committed to creating an original style of music and pushing beyond the conventions of the rockabilly scene, Fenech and Lewis formed The Meteors in early 1980 and recruited Mark Robertson, a drummer from a punk band who wouldn't shy away from playing loud, fast, and hard.

The Meteors demonstrated their commitment to rockabilly in several ways. For one thing, their band name conveyed their knowledge of obscure 1950s music: their earlier band, Raw Deal, had been named after a 1956 rockabilly song by Junior Thompson, and The Meteors were Thompson's backup band. Fenech and Lewis may have been extra keen to adopt that particular band's name because the members of the original Meteors had died in a plane crash, an odd bit of trivia that would have reflected their obsession with the twisted and morbid. Their musical style was firmly grounded in rockabilly: Lewis slapped away on the upright bass, and Fenech picked out rockabilly guitar licks and solos. They also proved their familiarity with 1950s repertoire, as they had in Raw Deal and Rock Therapy, cranking out covers of tunes by Roy Orbison, Sonny Burgess, Johnny Burnette, Rose Maddox, and others. However, they played these covers, as well as their own original songs, faster, heavier, wilder, and louder than typical rockabilly bands at the time, and they screamed, growled, and moaned more.

They owed some of this extra energy to their punk-ish interpretation of rockabilly, demonstrating their refusal to accurately imitate the music of the past. Fenech explains: "We just made a kind of mutation, the way we saw it, with a bit of punk in it, a lot of rockabilly influence, but our own sound really. We weren't trying to copy the records exactly like bands were trying to do. I mean it's better to play those records—you can't copy Gene Vincent, it's stupid, you might as well play the records, you know? We wanted to make our own sound, and we did" (quoted in Decay 2004). In 1982, Fenech described their sound as "mutant rockabilly": "That's what we call it because we've taken rockabilly and changed it. We've put a bit of punk in it and made it more lively" (quoted in *News Beat* 1982). As P. Paul told *No Class Fanzine* in 1981, he wanted to reintroduce the wild and raw sound that seemed to have been lost in both rockabilly and punk in the early 1980s: "Basically, the songs are just a cross between rockabilly and early punk. It's the feeling that the early punk stuff generated before it got commercial" (quoted in *No Class Fanzine* 1981). They also celebrated the working-class, anti-elite sensibilities that characterized both rockabilly and punk: "It's a bit like the early punk thing, the way we play rock and roll; lots of energy, no pretty clothes or anything like that" (quoted in Wall 1981, 15). The Meteors also fostered a DIY approach that had guided both rockabilly and punk, as their drummer Mark Robertson explained to me:

> Mark: The punk influence was more to do with the do-it-yourself
>   side. The fanzines, the print-your-own T-shirts.
> Kim: So, more the cultural side?
> Mark: Yeah, get a band together. Don't take fifteen years to learn.
> Kim: Yeah, be DIY.
> Mark: Just go play. I think that was the punk influence for us.

This influence from punk gave the band a "trashy" quality even while their technical rockabilly chops still stood out, as suggested by this *Sounds* magazine review of their seven-inch single "Radioactive Kid": "Imagine the worst punk band you ever heard gone fashionably rockabilly. Done so? That's this awful/great disc. The flip, 'Graveyard Stomp,' starts all fever-ish and soon degenerates into something much, much worse. Nice" (Robertson 1981). The Meteors were so pleased with this review that they included it on their 1986 *Teenagers from Outer Space* record gatefold sleeve, perhaps delighted that their experimental sound was interpreted as degenerative.

Fenech and Lewis refused to write typical rockabilly lyrics about bopping the night away, rocking the town, rockabilly clothes, going out with a girlfriend, or Cadillacs, noting that those themes did not reflect their daily lived experiences, hobbies, or interests (Wall 1981, 15). As Mark Robertson told me:

> Mark: We were in London in the late 1970s, early 1980s, and so we
>   didn't want pink Cadillacs, high school cuties, so we—
> Kim: Why didn't you want that?
> Mark: Because, that was just not what you did. I mean, we're talking
>   about the beginning of Margaret Thatcher.
> Kim: It didn't apply? It wasn't relevant?

Mark: Well, you know if you had a Cadillac, someone scratched it. And the weather wasn't such that you wanted one, right, and nobody really wanted one. It wasn't an aspirational thing.

Not being able to relate to the topics that rockabilly songs were generally about, they wrote instead about what they did know: horror movies and macabre subjects. Mark recalled: "We used to go out on Saturday and watch horror B movies. Like, *Teenagers from Outer Space* is a B movie. We used to watch *Plan 9 from Outer Space*, and the really Edward D. Wood shit, you know. *The Day the Earth Stood Still*. So, that's the sort of influences. It was all very, very tongue in cheek, but it was better than, you know, 'I've got a Pink Cadillac. I've got pink pants.'"

As noted by Nathan Katz, a revival of B movies in the early 1980s provided psychobillies with an escape from the problems of recession-riddled England: "Psychos gravitated towards these movies due to their lack of seriousness, mindless gore, and enjoyed the throwback to the original B-movies of the 1950s" (2012). The Meteors, and many other first-wavers I interviewed, loved going to these silly films to escape the real world, as is discussed further in Chapter 3. They were also inspired by early rock 'n' rollers who had already explored bizarre and macabre topics, as noted previously. For instance, Marc Fenech recalls that his brother was a fan of 1950s–1960s "shock 'n' roll" songs such as "I Put a Spell on You" (Screaming Jay Hawkins, 1956), "Dinner with Drac" (John Zacherle, 1958), "Haunted House" (Johnny Fuller, 1959), "Rockin' in the Graveyard" (Jackie Morningstar, 1959), and "She's Fallen in Love with a Monster Man" (Screaming Lord Sutch, 1964), and covered some of these songs during early Meteors sets (Fenech 1995, 7).[8] Fenech also told the press that "a lot of the inspiration for our songs comes from my interest in voodoo and [black] magic" (quoted in Wall 1981, 15). The Meteors drew on all these influences, writing songs that were very atypical for rockabilly: "My Daddy Is a Vampire," "Maniac Rockers from Hell," "Radioactive Kid," and "Graveyard Stomp." They identified as alien invaders who attacked humans in order to rule the entire cosmos in "Attack of the Zorchmen," and they sang about earwigs crawling into their brains through their ears and coming out their eyes in "Earwigs in My Brain" (both on *In Heaven*, 1981). Their celebration of these taboo topics underscored their difference from rockabilly—and even most neo-rockabilly—bands, expressed their "deviant" identity, and represented their desire to transgress society's dominant values and norms.

Their live performances were also atypical for rockabilly venues and crowds, influenced as they were by the theatricality of shock rockers such as Screaming Jay Hawkins and Screaming Lord Sutch; the unbridled energy of

Figure 1.1. P. Paul Fenech, covered in chicken blood, on the cover of *Sounds* magazine, April 18, 1981. Dubbing Fenech "The Psychobilly Kid," the corresponding article confirmed the name of the subculture and conveyed its nonconformist and rebellious characteristics. (Sounds *magazine, April 18, 1981.*)

original rockabillies such as Jerry Lee Lewis; and the crazed, unpredictable, defiant attitude of punks such as Johnny Rotten and Sid Vicious of the Sex Pistols. Most famously, Fenech often performed with chicken blood running down his chin, behavior he claimed to have borrowed from occult fertility rites that fascinated him (*No Class Fanzine* 1981). In 1981 *Sounds* magazine featured a cover photo of P. Paul Fenech with a crazed look in his eyes and blood dripping down his face, dubbing him "The Psychobilly Kid" and effectively giving the subculture a name to rally around (see Figure 1.1). The article describes the contrast between the wild intensity of The Meteors' shows and typically tame rockabilly performances at the time: "A gig murdered by fouled up equipment and yet brought back to life like some Frankenstein's monster by their almost insane will to play . . . injecting life, energy and meaning into what could so easily have been just another rockabilly yawn. Nigel Lewis roared ghoul-like over black, demonic riffs" (Wall 1981). They developed a reputation for acting bizarre and unhinged, as a *New Musical Express* review of a Meteors show at Dingwalls in 1981 conveys: "The double-bassist looks like one of those vulnerable, mid-west psychopaths you see in films about deathrow, a victim of his sorry circumstances. He looked like he might strangle his instrument, or random members of the audience, if he played a bum note" (Ruthren 1981). Fenech often appeared possessed, rolling his eyes about and shaking convulsively while he sang songs such as "The Crazed" (*In Heaven*, 1981), about beheading people in the park at night. He taunted rockabilly crowds, spitting "suck my cock" at them before launching into "I Don't Worry About It," a song that exemplified The Meteors' irreverent and unapologetic attitude as Fenech defiantly sang about doing whatever he wanted to do and that he would continue to rebel against the rules even after being punished for breaking them (Dipple 2015).

In short, "the combination of faster tempos, edgier subject matter, and scratchy, screechy vocals . . . gave tunes like 'Shout So Loud,' 'Maniac,' and 'Psycho for Your Love' enough attitude to signal the start of something new," as Kenneth Partridge (2015) observes. And audiences either hated The Meteors or loved them. Fenech remembers that his band's music provoked two very different reactions: "We caused a definite split between Teds and psychobillies. We made a definite change. People threw cans at us or threw underwear at us. It wasn't a part of the rock'n'roll scene. It was a separate entity. I kinda look upon it as being like a cancer on rock'n'roll" (quoted in Decay 2004).

Rock 'n' roll and rockabilly purists were offended by The Meteors' bastardization of the classic music they revered. For instance, a Teddy Boy by the name of "Sunglasses Ron" lamented that "punkabillies" had ruined the atmosphere at rock 'n' roll shows:

> In this country it's gone right down. Very few of the old clubs are left. What there are, they're getting over-run by these youngsters out there—punkabillies, or whatever they are, you know. A lot of people like myself who are still about just don't bother any more, it's just not worth the effort. You can go there and mix, but when you get up and you jive with your wife, and you get a dozen kids who are pogo dancing[9] around you, you think, what's going on?, you know. Are we listening to the same kind of music? . . . Let 'em have their own do and let them have their music there, but for Christ's sake let us have our music, you know? There's not enough of our lads left. (quoted in Décharné 2010, 293)

In *Sounds* magazine, P. Paul Fenech expressed his frustration at the narrow-mindedness of the rock 'n' roll revival circuit: "They didn't like us because we had a punk drummer, and had punk influences in the music. We don't play what they called 'authentic' rockabilly, and the old dinosaurs that go to those sorts of places didn't like it" (quoted in Wall 1981, 14). They were heckled during their first appearance at Rockabilly Night at the Sparrow Hawk in London, and at their second show, at The Cavern in Northwest London in

August 1980, the audience hated them so much that they were asked to leave the stage for their own safety (Brackenridge 2007, 20). In an interview with *No Class Fanzine*, The Meteors' drummer, Mark Robertson, recalls this performance: "They called us punks, 'coz I had funny colour hair. The manager brought this procession of Teds into the dressing room to say they didn't like the band" (*No Class Fanzine* 1981). P. Paul Fenech continues: "So, I said 'How comes you don't like us then?' He said 'Your drummer can't play cos he's got green hair.' Honest. So fucking pathetic. I whacked some guy with a baseball bat. It was grand" (quoted in *No Class Fanzine* 1981). Nigel Lewis told *Sounds* magazine that this actually revealed the "inauthenticity" of the rockabilly revival scene, which had forgotten the rebelliousness of the original rockabillies: "I mean, it's a joke. Sonny Burgess in 1957 had bright red hair and Wee Willy Harris had orange hair and that didn't stop them playing rockabilly. These people are so prejudiced it's sick" (quoted in Wall 1981, 15).

While The Meteors' music offended many Teds and rockers, it attracted those rebellious youth who wanted something a little bit different from the same old fare in the rock 'n' roll and rockabilly revival scenes. Alan Wilson was one of those nonconformist youth who loved The Meteors' unconventional approach to rockabilly, as an extended excerpt from my interview with him demonstrates:

> One day I was doing a gig with my band The Dixie Rebels in a huge venue with the Flying Saucers, supporting them. During the break between sets, the DJ played a record and the dance floor just emptied except for about three people. I thought these three people were fighting because of what they were doing on the dance floor. So I thought: "What's happening?" Then I realized they weren't fighting— this was actually part of their kind of dance thing they were doing. It wasn't called wrecking[10] or anything then. They were on the floor rolling about. I thought: "I really like this record." Because three people—only three people liked it and everyone else hated it—it made it more attractive to me. So I went to the DJ and asked, "What was that record you just played?" And he said, "Oh, it's this band called The Meteors and it's their first single." So I went out the next day and bought it. And then the first album [*In Heaven*, 1981] came out. And I remember, to this day I can still remember going into—in them days, you could listen to it first in the record shop, they would actually play you a track and then you'd go, "Yeah, I want it or I don't." The Meteors album came out and it was in the rockabilly section 'cause there was no psychobilly section then, so I said, "Can you play it for me?" And he put it on and you get that little chant

thing at the beginning, then he goes, [vocalization of the bass line], I said, "I'll have it." Literally, two bars in and I'm like, "Yeah, I'm getting the money out." That first Meteors album, for me, that just opened up a whole new world. It wasn't just me. Everyone that I knew just suddenly went, "Wow. This is great." Everybody that I knew back then, that first Meteors album switched them and a lot of rockabillies became what later became known as psychobillies. At the same time, some rockabillies kind of went more retro and said, "Oh, we don't like this new stuff," but a lot of them went, "We do like this." And I think—I don't know, I'm not the authority on this—but for me, that was the start of the psychobilly scene, the first Meteors album. For me, it just turned me on like nothing else. And I think if you interview lots of people, they'll probably say the same.

Indeed, all of my first-wave interlocutors latched onto The Meteors as soon as they heard their unique interpretation of rockabilly. Norm Elliott, for instance, recalled:

I was a young teen on the U.K. rockin' scene, [listening to] rock 'n' roll, rockabilly, etc. We heard about this crazy new band from London who played wild, wild rockabilly, but instead of bopping [the way that traditional rockabillies danced], the young crowd pushed and punched each other. When their first EP came out, we were hooked. It was ours, something of our very own instead of borrowing from our fathers' generation! All of a sudden when the *In Heaven* album came out, my parents were telling me to "turn that rubbish off"! That's how it should be! Every generation needs something of its own that the previous generations don't understand. Oh, and we soon found out Meteors' live shows were just as wild as we were told! Great times.

Together, these fans of The Meteors' new approach made their departure from the rockabilly revival circuit to clubs where they could find other open-minded youth who appreciated the experimental combination of rockabilly, punk, and horror subjects.

Forced off the Rock 'n' Roll and Rockabilly Revival Circuit, Psychobilly Brings Punks and Rockabillies Together

The reaction of the Teds and rockabillies to The Meteors' unconventional brand of music soon made it difficult for the band to play the venues in which they had started their career. Banned from the rockabilly circuit, The Meteors looked elsewhere for youth who might actually enjoy their psychotic rockabilly-punk-horror hybrid. Nick Garrard booked them with punk bands including The Clash, The Damned, and the UK Subs, and they played Dingwalls, The 100 Club,[11] The Marquee Club, and The Hope & Anchor, venues that tended to showcase punk or new wave music rather than rock 'n' roll and rockabilly (Peacock 2015, 33). Garrard came up with a creative way of introducing The Meteors to youth who might not frequent these clubs, featuring them in a short movie that aired in the theaters before *Dance Craze*, a film about the ska revival. Craig Brackenridge describes the offbeat *Meteor Madness* short:

> This seventeen-minute short featured performances from The Meteors squeezed into a whacko B-movie plot about the Devil (played by Brit actor Keith Allen) and his fiendish plot to destroy the world through a dastardly keep-fit regime (!?). After what seems like endless bouts of Allen's goofing, The Meteors appear (literally) in a puff of smoke, run around the streets of London for a bit then burst into a live performance in a tiny club. (2007, 20)

The four Meteors songs that appeared in the film were released on the band's first EP, *Meteor Madness* (1981): "Voodoo Rhythm," "Maniac Rockers from Hell," "My Daddy Is a Vampire," and "You Can't Keep a Good Man Down." On the sleeve of the record, the director of the film describes the plot almost as an allegory for the birth of psychobilly itself:

> Boredom, Rockabilly, Keep Fit, and Demonic Behavior combine any way you like to create Psychobilly—and Meteor Madness. The Devil only wants to save the World. He believes Athletics is the way, but the World says no: All we want is fun, something to shake off those cobwebs, and through the good fortune of yet another of the Devil's bogged-up experiments, they get it. Once again Satan gets it wrong and instead of the perfect athletes he so desires, The Meteors, Maniac Rockers From Hell, are born. They escape his world of linament and press-ups to play their mutant music and blast the World's boredom clean away.

The film's narrative symbolically reflects how The Meteors saved bored rockabillies from the conventionalization and commercialization of their scene and won over fans who were eager for something really wild, rebellious, eccentric, and twisted. It also represents The Meteors and their psychobilly music as the product of hell, symbolizing the profane, transgressive, and subversive nature of the new subculture.

For punks and rockabillies who discovered The Meteors through such nontraditional circuits, the band represented common ground for two subcultures that, even though they shared certain qualities, had been at odds with each other. Craig Brackenridge paints a picture of this early 1980s context:

> A school in the East Midlands, new term 1981–82. A new boy enters the class and is introduced by the teacher. He has spiky hair and wears a T-shirt, Doc Martens and tight denims with tiny turn-ups. He is instructed to sit [in] the nearest empty seat. The boy beside him has a flat-top and wears a tartan[12] shirt, crepe shoes and loose denims with big turn-ups. As the latest addition to the class takes his seat he mutters to his new neighbour "Rockabilly bastard!" "Fucking Punk" replies his schoolmate, and they glare at each other menacingly. One year later they are wrecking wildly together at a Meteors gig—best of mates. (2007, 11)

As previously explored, The Meteors' rockabilly-punk hybrid attracted those who recognized the common musical and ideological characteristics that defined both styles of music. But the band especially attracted those who were frustrated by the mainstreaming and dilution of both the punk and rockabilly subcultures. Craig Brackenridge, for instance, remembers feeling that rockabilly had already "drifted dangerously close to the mainstream and the fancifying effect of major record label neutering" (2007, 13). Some punks were frustrated that their scene, too, had lost some of its initial creativity and licentiousness. Mark Robertson told me that he was compelled to team up with Fenech and Lewis in part because "punk had actually started to get really boring by then. I mean, I was in Manchester in 1976. So, I saw The Clash in '76. I saw the Banshees, '76. It was very primitive, raw. But by '78, '80, it was becoming very formulaic. I started to get bored with punk." Nick Garrard describes the band's early fans as "rockabillies bored with the scene and a new generation of punks with G.I. haircuts and quiffs, inspired by The Stray Cats, but looking for something less 'pop star' to latch on to" (The Meteors, *Teenagers from Outer Space* inner gatefold sleeve, 1986). Thus youth from both punk and rockabilly backgrounds (and particularly those who already liked both), disillusioned with the stagnation and corporatization of their scenes and eager to find something that would revive the wild impetus of both genres, were attracted to how The Meteors' music, attitudes, and unpredictable performances willfully defied authority, convention, mainstreaming, and sophisticated styling.

The Meteors also attracted those who enjoyed the band's rejection of rockabilly and punk clichés. Punks who wanted something other than songs about politics appreciated that The Meteors insisted on a "politics and religion free zone." They liked the loud, fast, aggressive punk sound of The Meteors while enjoying a respite from social and political critique. Some rockabillies were also excited to find a band that rejected the clichés that plagued the genre's lyrics. Norm Elliott found psychobilly's topics a relief from the lyrics of traditional rockabilly: "For a rebellious rock 'n' roll teen, it was refreshing to hear those themes instead of bloody songs about love or pink peg trousers." Alan Wilson remembered the similar impact The Meteors had on him as a young rockabilly musician:

> That first Meteors album, for me, that just opened up a whole new world. It was because they weren't singing about Saturday night and petticoats and poodles and drive-ins; they were singing about kinda science fiction things. And I think Nigel's stuff was a little bit more tongue-in-cheek, like "Earwigs in My Brain" and stuff like that. Obviously that's not real, and it's all kinda science fiction and a bit sort of pretend, and it was just so exciting for me, you know? I suddenly realized when the Meteors stuff started coming out, I thought: "Do you know what? You don't have to sing about things you don't really know about. You can just sing about anything. This is great!"

Likewise, O'Prez loved the rebellious attitudes and wild energy of 1950s rockabilly, but "first got an inkling that I liked something different" when he heard a band called Those Handsome Devils, and then the Guana Batz, who played rockabilly at a faster tempo and "weren't sticking to a set of rules." He told me that most rockabilly at the time was "the same shit, 'a rockin on a Saturday night, rockin' with my chick.' I just turn it off. I've no interest. It meant fuck all to me." When I asked him why he did not relate to the lyrics, he pointed out that the postwar context was different in Ireland and England: "I suppose over there [in the United States] in the 1950s it was about cars, and bopping on a Saturday night. Over here it wasn't. So we don't give a shit." Instead, he was excited that psychobilly bands were singing about "something more original." For him psychobilly was the perfect mix of rockabilly, punk, and horror movie themes: "It had aggression. It was faster. And it was about horror movies, which was all I watched—and still do."

Some fans of The Meteors were inspired to develop their own versions of "psycho rockabilly." Alan Wilson, Steve Whitehouse, and Paul "Hodge" Leigh had been playing the rockabilly circuit as The Sharks but were excited about the changes that were happening around The Meteors. Alan remembered: "There was this other thing going on within the scene where when you would go to gigs, the look of some, just a small element of the crowd, the look was different. And I could sense that there was something changing. Some of these rockabilly people didn't like this other element coming in, so that made it more attractive to me straightaway because I always go against the grain a little bit." For "Hodge," who listened to punk and ska before joining The Sharks, psychobilly had something that was missing from the classic rockabilly that his classmate Steve Whitehouse played for him: "As soon as I heard The Meteors it was, like, yeah, I'm definitely into this. I liked Mark Robertson's punk aspect combined with Nigel's and Paul's rockabilly background. It was just different than that rockabilly thing. It was more than singing about pink pegs [trousers] and Cadillacs. I liked the aggression of it, and I thought: 'Well this, I can get into this,' and that was pretty much what did it."

The Sharks started to write original songs that were about offbeat topics such as serial murderers, and they played a faster and louder version of rockabilly than they had before. But like The Meteors, they had a difficult time finding fans who appreciated their new style of music. Alan recalled:

> We were in a no man's land because rockabillies didn't like this new thing that was happening—we were too fast or too loud, and we didn't play the covers they wanted to hear. So you couldn't play at a rockabilly gig. And the rock 'n' roll gigs, like the Teddy Boys and that, they hated anything to do with it, and so you'd just get gigs and hope someone would come. My memory of the early Sharks gigs was that no one liked us. We didn't have an audience, to be honest. Everyone hated us because there was no psychobilly scene really yet, and the rockabillies didn't like us. We were just desperate for gigs, so we'd do a gig at a rockabilly club and we'd get booed off. At one gig at a rock 'n' roll club, they hated us so much, they actually switched the power off halfway through our set. The sound guy was telling us, "Stop! Stop playing," and we didn't. So they pulled the plug on us. And there were probably 200 people in that club, and 195 in the rock 'n' roll or Teddy Boy types, and there were about 5 what we would now call psychobillies. And when they pulled the plug, there was a massive riot, and these five kids smashed the place to pieces. They went into the toilets and pulled the sinks off the walls, so there was water squirting everywhere. Then they came out into the dance floor with the sinks and threw them at the Teds. They went mad, 'cause they really didn't like each other those days. And we just stood on stage thinking: "Oh

fuck, what do we do?" And it was just crazy, so we had to leave there pretty quick.

The Sharks, King Kurt, Guana Batz, Demented Are Go, and many other bands from the United Kingdom joined The Meteors in rejecting the conventions that had characterized rock 'n' roll and rockabilly in the late 1970s and early 1980s. They hybridized rockabilly with other styles, such as punk, new wave, heavy metal, and ska, and each band had a slightly different style. They rejected the clichés that characterized rockabilly music, composing lyrics about any topics they wanted, whether they were silly or macabre, fantastical or based on everyday life. By 1982 these bands had won over enough fans to fill the downstairs assembly room of the Clarendon Hotel to capacity, leading the venue's promoter to host psychobilly events on Saturday nights in the upstairs ballroom. Dubbed "The Klub Foot," this venue became the "undisputed epicenter of the rapidly-expanding psychobilly scene; attracting quaffed-up and flat-topped disciples from all over the UK and beyond" (Peacock 2015, 35). The next chapter explores what those events were like and how they established the over-the-top, profane, and transgressive quality of the behaviors, performances, and style that came to characterize the subculture.

Concluding Thoughts: The Relevance of the Past in the Present

Kenneth Partridge describes psychobilly this way: "When punk and rockabilly had a baby, the little bugger wasn't pretty. Called psychobilly, the greasy mutant lovechild and its birth were both figuratively incestuous and totally inevitable" (2015). He alludes to punk's development from rock 'n' roll and the rebellious attitudes that characterized both. The continued impact of rock 'n' roll is also reflected in the lyrics that open this chapter. The Sharks sing about hearing a "strange sound," a "crazy phantom rocker sound," underscoring how the specter of wild 1950s rockabilly haunted the sonic landscape of the 1970s and 1980s and still does so today, as the rockabilly revival, neo-rockabilly, and psychobilly subcultures still engage with it. As The Sharks suggest, psychobilly was both new and old, driven by a phantom sound from the past that was relevant and exciting in the present. The interest in rockabilly, vis-à-vis the revival movement and then the development of neo-rockabilly and psychobilly, demonstrates how the rebellious ethos, wild energy, and working-class determination to find self-expression against all odds still resonated long after the 1950s. As Walter Benjamin suggests, "Every image of the past that is not recognized by the present as one of its own concerns threatens to disappear irretrievably"

(1968, 257). Rockabilly has clearly not disappeared, for subculturalists continue to relate to how it reflected a nonconformist outlook and spirited defiance of traditional norms and cultural expectations.

But this chapter also draws attention to the different degrees to which revivalists may be "haunted" by the past. As suggested previously, the rockabilly revival was characterized by what Tamara Livingston calls "the pursuit of authenticity" (1999). But neo-rockabillies and psychobillies were not content to replicate 1950s music, and they broke away (and were pushed away) from the revival circuits. They were not interested in living in a time bubble, as Mark Robertson told *Sounds* magazine: "If you've been through the Fifties, been through the Sixties, the Seventies, and gained a bit from each era, you can't help but make your own sound, whether it be rockabilly or whatever, be a bit more modern. If you've listened to the Sex Pistols you can't go on stage after that and play as if they'd never existed" (quoted in Wall 1981, 15). This historical understanding of the shift from rockabilly to the development of new subcultural styles corresponds with Livingston's understanding of the life span of music revivals:

> I would suggest that when there is no longer an overriding concern for "authenticity" (i.e. style markers that are consciously employed for historical reference) and the "tradition" is felt to be too constricting of a reference point by the majority of revivalists, that revivals break down into different styles. In such cases revivals may stimulate new innovative styles and thus cease to exist primarily as a revivalist genre. On the other hand, revivalist strains of a genre, distinguished by the term "traditional," may exist alongside new styles generated by, or merging with, revivalist genres. (Livingston 1999, 80–81)

Supporting Livingston's suggestion, this chapter's analysis of psychobilly's origins reveals how some youth rebelled against the constraints of the nostalgic Teddy Boy and rockabilly scenes and generated the more experimental and diverse neo-rockabilly and psychobilly styles alongside the more traditional revival.

Some scholars have criticized how the past has continued to haunt us. As fashion scholar Heike Jenss notes in *Fashioning Memory*, postmodern discourse suggests that "the ongoing aesthetic immersion into the past among younger people may read as a sign of cultural regress or as indicating a lack of, or even inability for, cultural inventiveness" (2015, 2). Simon Reynolds, for instance, has reflected on "pop culture's addiction to its own past," whereby "the scope for imaginative reworking of the past—the misrecognitions and mutations that characterised earlier cults of antiquity like the

19th-century gothic revival—is reduced" (2011b). In *Retromania*, Reynolds worries that "the sensation of movement, of going somewhere, could be satisfied as easily (in fact, *more* easily) by going backwards within that vast past than by going forwards" (2011a, xx). He also "registers alarm about the disappearance of a certain quality in music: the 'never heard this before' sensation of ecstatic disorientation caused by music that seems to come out of nowhere and point to a bright, or at least strange, future" (2011b). Similarly, Fredric Jameson suggests that we are disengaged from the present, relying on our "pastiche of the stereotypical past" while becoming "increasingly incapable of fashioning representations of our own current experience" (1991, 21). These postmodern critics imply that our "unhealthy fixation on the bygone" (Reynolds 2011b) prevents us from being "present" and from having a contemporary identity. As suggested in the Introduction to this book, this postmodern perspective has equated the fragmentation of youth's identities with the death of subcultures. This led *Spin* magazine to publish the following in 1991:

> Magazines and newspapers such as *Time* and the *New York Times* are . . . comparing you unfairly to the dynamic and euphoric baby boomers—the authentic prototype of youth culture, at least as they would have it. They're saying you, the members of the twentysomething generation, have no distinctive identity, no culture to call your own, only recycled bits of the past. Ask yourself this question: Do you recognize yourself in this portrait? No? We didn't think so. (Owen 1991, 68).

Jenss (2015) counters such postmodern arguments by exploring how "1960s stylers" creatively reimagine and transform vintage fashion. She argues, "Something of the past must resonate in the present—it must be recognized" in order to be revived; it must be meaningful and significant to those who actively look to the past to fashion their contemporary identity (6). Drawing on the work of Judith Butler, Jenss considers the act of "doing memory," made visible through the ways that vintage enthusiasts actively make the past present in a performative, rather than reproductive, way. Similarly, Angela McRobbie finds secondhand clothing "neither nostalgic in essence nor without depth," as "nostalgia indicates a desire to recreate the past faithfully, and to wallow in such mythical representations" (1988, 41). Secondhand style, on the other hand, reflects a conscious criticism of mainstream culture and a "willfull anarchy" that subverts contemporary conventions (42). Pat Gill also challenges postmodern views, analyzing how contemporary television shows and films set in the past reflect "a very real apprehension of the disturbed present and the potentially apocalyptic future" and are "a vivid representation of present concerns and circumstances" (1997, 163). In other words, these scholars suggest that our interest in the past is not representative of "yet another cultural re-run" (McRobbie 1988, 48) or a desire to return faithfully to the past due to a loss of faith in the future, but rather is indicative of a strategic and playful rediscovery of the past that allows us to creatively reimagine and comment on the present.

I also do not interpret psychobillies' use of 1950s rockabilly as evidence of cultural regression, an inability to creatively develop new art, or a tendency to live falsely in a distorted past instead of engaging in the present and looking forward. This chapter demonstrates not only how the rebellious ethos of 1950s rockabilly continued to be relevant to British teens in the 1970s and 1980s but also how they actively transformed the sounds of the past into something different and new, something that resonated with them in the present and mediated their contemporary experience. As Norm Elliott remembered, psychobilly felt like something he could call his own: "When psychobilly came along it just spoke to me and moved me like nothing had before. As I said before, it was OURS!!!" These fans recognized and related to the rebellious ideology and working-class sensibilities that motivated rockabilly in its own time, but their identification with it was filtered through the lens of their contemporary experience, and they updated their style and lyrics accordingly. They embodied the rebelliousness of the original rockabillies so much that they refused to be straitjacketed by anything, including rockabilly. As Nigel Lewis of The Meteors says, "I wanted to be like the original rockabillies and try new things. After all, rockabilly would not have begun if musicians didn't try out new sounds" (Lewis 2010). As illustrated by my interviews with first-wavers, psychobilly offered the "never heard this before" excitement that Reynolds suggests has been lost in retro revivals. The inventiveness of The Meteors inspired other musicians to continue to experiment, as the following quote from a member of the psychobilly band Batmobile suggests: "Just listen to a lot of music, be inspired by a lot of people, but do your own thing with it" (Psychomania TV 2016). Thus, I understand early psychobillies' creative synthesis of rockabilly, punk, and horror (among other things) as an act of agency that helped them look to the future rather than retreat into the past. As one musician stated on a Facebook group for psychobilly fans: "Psychobilly is about the now and the future, NOT the past. Nostalgia is for rockabillies."

The desire to "do your own thing" aptly sums up the development of psychobilly as documented in this chapter. I have relied heavily on the recollections of first-wave psychobillies in order to highlight their understanding of how their rebellious identities compelled them to repeatedly refuse the status quo. They rejected mainstream trends in their preteen and teenage years, preferring the anti-fashion of rock 'n' roll to corporate disco, progressive rock, or pop. Once rock 'n' roll became popular, normalized, and commercialized during its mainstream revival in the 1970s, and its rebelliousness was diluted, those nonconformist youth moved on to more obscure rockabilly tracks and soaked up the countercultural punk and new wave movements. Frustrated by the restrictive clichés and mainstreaming of both rockabilly and punk, they then moved in a "neo" direction. The Meteors upped the ante further, transgressing norms of performance and breaking all expectations about lyrics. This history of psychobilly's early development thus underscores how the genre attracted nonconformists, who distanced themselves from mainstream trends and normative expectations. They liked being outcasts even among outcasts, gleefully flaunting green or pink hair in a crowd of greased-up Teddy Boys and rockabillies. They were glad that their "punkified" music offended rock 'n' roll and rockabilly "purists." Psychobilly became a home for those subcultural young adults who refused all expectations—even subcultural ones.

This chapter also draws attention to the consequences of psychobilly's defiance of subcultural norms: its exclusion from the revival circuit. Psychobillies needed to create an alternative space where they could be free to move, behave, and perform as they wished. This desire to freely express themselves underscores this book, and thus it is important to establish from the outset that they were not able to do so within the confines of traditional and nostalgic rock 'n' roll and rockabilly outlets. Psychobillies found their own ways to develop outside of the rules and regulations that characterized other subcultures at the time. The next chapter explores how they cultivated for themselves a space to improve their lived experience: to have fun, perform what they wanted to, shock the squares, cultivate an interest in nonmainstream tastes, and transgress hegemonic norms.

CARNIVALESQUE EVENTS AND
TRANSGRESSIVE PERFORMANCE

Celebrating a Counterhegemonic Ideology

Here we go again, we're still being called a '50s band
What's it gonna take to make you people understand
We're playin' psychobilly 'cause that's what we must do
What's it gonna take for us to get through to you
We had to leave America 'cause people there are square
They laughed and called us names and they laughed at our big hair
We tried to make it there but people don't wanna know
The only thing for us to do is pack our bags and go

—THE QUAKES, "Pack Our Bags and Go," *The Quakes*, 1988

Rejected by the Teddy Boy and rockabilly purists, neo-rockabilly and psychobilly bands found alternative venues that accepted their unique brand of music and performance, as well as their fans' already infamous behavior. London venues including the Klub Foot, Dingwalls, The 100 Club, The Marquee Club, The Hope & Anchor, and Feltham Football Club became regular haunts for bands who pushed beyond the traditional conventions of rockabilly, such as The Meteors, King Kurt, The Sharks, Guana Batz, The Krewmen, Demented Are Go, Frenzy, The Quakes, and Batmobile.[1] Some musicians outside of the United Kingdom who had caught wind of the developing subculture uprooted their lives to follow their passion for this new brand of nontraditional rockabilly. For instance, Paul Roman of The Quakes was from Buffalo, New York, but recalled that "there was no scene there [in the 1980s]. Zero. No one that came to see us looked like us or knew what we were doing." As described in the song that opens this chapter, the "squares" in the United States did not appreciate the band's strange sound and big quiffs. Paul packed up and headed to London, where a community of neo-rockabilly and psychobilly fans enjoyed something other than "authentic" rockabilly. Of the places The Quakes performed, no club defines the subculture more than the Klub Foot, the upstairs ballroom of the crumbling Clarendon hotel-pub in London's Hammersmith Broadway.

Built in the 1930s, the art deco hotel-turned-pub became known for its lively punk, trash, and psychobilly shows by the early 1980s. When owner John Curd noticed that the downstairs function room regularly exceeded its capacity, he started promoting Klub Foot shows on Saturday nights in the creaky upstairs ballroom. Here, from 1982 to 1988, neo-rockabilly and psychobilly bands found an audience that embraced their nonconformist lyrics, sound, and performance style. The *Stomping at the Klub Foot* series,[2] which featured recordings and photos of live performances, furthered the legendary status of the venue and "spread the sickness" (a phrase often invoked by psychobillies) to those who lived far away from London or were too young to experience the madness firsthand[3] (see Figure 2.1). Not only could they hear the bands who were inventing this new style of music; they could also see how psychobillies in London dressed and styled their hair, gaining valuable subcultural capital.[4] Lois Pryce remembers studying the albums as a "loud, lairy, silly 14-year-old" in Bristol:

> I could quote every lyric and liner note from all of them. I studied the covers of the LPs with a mixture of awe and envy, taking in each detail of the group shots of the audience, clearly drunk out of their skulls, playing up to the camera, covered in sweat and tattoos with their insane haircuts and ripped-up jeans, pints of snakebite sloshing wildly as they gurned [made a grotesque face] for the photo outside the legendary venue. Oh, to visit The Klub Foot, to pass through its hallowed doors and feel its sticky carpet beneath my Dr Martens [*sic*]. Oh, to be on the cover of one of those albums, I would fantasize from my bedroom 120 miles away as I patiently painted a logo of The Meteors on to my school-bag. (Pryce 2015)

She was finally able to make the pilgrimage to the Klub Foot just before the hotel was demolished in 1988. Psychobillies like Lois came to the Klub Foot to affirm their membership in this alternative subculture, to "find their tribe,"[5] as some of my interlocutors put it, and to feel part of a community of

Figure 2.1. The cover of Stomping at the Klub Foot, volume 5. In the 1980s many young people learned about psychobilly music and fashion via this series of live recordings from the Klub Foot. Note the range of psychobilly wedge hairstyles worn by both men and women. (*Used with permission from Cherry Red Records.*)

other "Others" who looked and behaved like them. They came to escape the regulations and norms of hegemonic culture and to perform their nonconformist identities and values. They came to have fun, to "get out of their heads" as they drank, wrecked, bled, sweated, and enjoyed spectacularly wild performances, forgetting about the socioeconomic marginalization that characterized their lives as teens and young adults in Thatcher's England.

This chapter explores the theatrical performances, typical behaviors, and unique style that defined the subculture at the Klub Foot and continue to characterize psychobilly events today. I consider how psychobillies resist society's regulations, break taboos, liberate their bodies from social and self-control, and contest norms at these events. I compare these transgressive performances to carnival celebrations, which also represent a liminal utopia: a time out from the everyday world that allows participants to both escape hegemonic culture and critically express their frustration with it. This provides psychobillies with a sort of "rock 'n' roll therapy": they forget about their problems while expressing themselves as they want. While psychobillies do not frame their transgressive practices as "political," I suggest that these carnivalesque acts express a subcultural resistance to hegemonic systems of power (S. Greene 2012; Haenfler 2016) and represent a "politics of survival" that allows subculturalists to exercise sovereignty over and thus improve their lived experience (Maffesoli 1996; Riley, Griffin, and Morey 2010; Dimou & Ilan 2018). Although I focus on the significance of the Klub Foot as the space where the subculture's carnivalesque performances, behaviors, and style were most famously cultivated during the first wave, I supplement archival descriptions and recollections of past events with more recent ethnographic observations to demonstrate how these transgressive qualities still inform psychobilly events some thirty years after the subculture's birth.

Carnivalesque Events: Sites of Resistance
or Escapist Fun—Or Can They Be Both?

Surrounded by low-income public housing, the Clarendon Hotel that housed Klub Foot events in its basement was never described as "well-maintained." Steve Young from Surfin' Wombatz smiled as he described what the venue was like in the 1980s: "It was a horrible, run-down, nasty old hotel, falling to bits, probably ridden with asbestos. Definitely damp and black mold. Stinking of piss. And one flight up was the toilets until it overflowed and rained down the stairs." And yet he absolutely loved it: "It was basically our life in the early '80s for anyone that was into that sort of music." He mentioned that there were abandoned hotel rooms upstairs, but he could not recall anyone ever exploring them. I asked him why not, since it seems abandoned hotel rooms at the legendary venue would have been perfect places for psychobillies to indulge in a variety of forbidden and clandestine acts. Steve responded that he could only speak for himself, but he was always more interested in the show and the bar. I then asked Roy Williams, founder of neo-rockabilly and psychobilly label Nervous Records, if he recalled anyone ever exploring the rooms at the Klub Foot. He thought it would have been too dangerous to do so:

> The building was falling down. I knew a manager there and he told me the only thing holding that building together was—in the main hallway there were a pair of sliding doors. These sliding doors had a massive metal frame. Without that, the club would have come falling down. It was unsafe. You could sit down in the middle place, in the bar there, and have a drink. You'd know when a band was coming on because you would see the light start to swing a bit. It was scary, but it was a fun place.

Due to the venue's deteriorating condition, Klub Foot attendees were free to do whatever they wanted, so they wrecked, drank, and participated in wildly theatrical performances. As this chapter describes, the artifacts of their revelry—lost watches, smashed eyeglasses, blood, beer, vomit, urine, flour, baked beans, and even fishheads and mutilated rabbits—littered the floor after gigs.

The decay of the Clarendon was evidence of the effects of economic recessions that destabilized England in the mid-1970s and then again in the early 1980s. Music journalist Jon Savage describes the "apocalyptic" conditions that characterized England in 1976 and contributed to the growth of punk:

England's crisis had become what Stuart Hall calls 'the articulation of a fully fledged capitalist recession, with extremely high rates of inflation, a toppling currency, a savaging of living standards, and a sacrificing of the working class to capital.'[6] . . . The consensus that had governed postwar politics and social life was cracking up. This consensus, partly inspired by the century-long democratic ideal of American consumerism, was not only inadequate against the recession of the mid-1970s but also patently untrue: one had only to look at the decaying inner cities to realize that poverty and inequality, far from being eradicated, were visible as never before. (2002, 229)

When Prime Minister Thatcher and the Conservative Party came to power in 1979, they attempted to tame high inflation rates by shifting from state-run institutions to privatized corporations, dramatically cutting benefits and public services, increasing interest rates, and prioritizing the service industry over manufacturing (Dean 2013). As companies reorganized themselves, unemployment rose rapidly, from about 3 percent of the population in 1979 to about 12 percent in 1984 (Office for National Statistics n.d.). Among those hardest hit during the recession of the early 1980s were members of the working class; for instance, twenty coal pits were forced to close down in 1984 alone, putting thousands out of work (BBC 2013).

Jane Dipple situates the development of psychobilly in the early 1980s within this context of Thatcherism and Conservative Party policies, which severely impacted the poor and working class. She observes that the subculture emerged just after the 1980 Housing Act further stigmatized and subordinated those who were not able to achieve the socioeconomic mobility that the government encouraged:

Working class people were forced to become aspirational—to desire wealth and ownership or lose out, subsequently the poorer working class and unemployed became even further marginalized and criminalized by the right. In London, whilst some areas were capitalizing on a new-found affluence boosted by the buying and selling of council houses in prime locations, people from the most rundown areas, unable to shift, were subsequently trapped by the circumstances of location. (Dipple 2015, 93–94)

She suggests that "it was out of these locations the psychobillies emerged . . . from small pockets of deprivation, mainly in South East England" (94). The neighborhoods where psychobilly venues were located, like the members of the subculture themselves, were "deeply affected by Thatcher's regime, impoverished and marginalized by government policy and routinely over-looked by those who had benefitted most from Thatcherism" (100).

The decrepit venues that hosted events during the first wave of psycho-billy's development, such as the Clarendon Hotel and Feltham Football Club, were perfect spaces for the carnivalesque performances that came to define the subculture. In these dingy buildings that no one cared about and that were already falling apart, psychobillies were able to indulge in wildly trans-gressive behavior. What more damage could be done to these venues? In other words, those whom Thatcher had abandoned appropriated the places that Thatcher had abandoned, using them for their own purposes and plea-sure to relieve the anxieties that Thatcher had created. There, they could let off steam and find a way to enjoy life for a few hours. There, away from soci-ety's restrictions and regulations, they did as they pleased and expressed themselves as they wanted. I suggest that these subcultural events offered the opportunity to negotiate experiences of socioeconomic marginality; psycho-billies let loose and had fun while expressing their resistance to hegemonic authority, performing rebellious values, behaviors, and identities.

This perspective is, on the one hand, indebted to the work of scholars from the Chicago School (A. Cohen 1955) and Birmingham's Centre for Contemporary Cultural Studies (Hall and Jefferson 1976; Hebdige 1979; Hall 1981), who understood subcultures as a response to social and eco-nomic marginalization caused by postwar structural changes. I remind readers that many subcultural theorists, especially those associated with the CCCS, have been criticized for overtheorizing subculture as an arena in and through which a counterhegemonic struggle against the powerful is engaged, wherein heroic resistance is expressed by the working class. Post-subcultural scholars suggested that youth are motivated by a classless, hedo-nistic pursuit of pleasure rather than a desire to express resistance to the dominant culture; they argued that people come together primarily to have a good time with others who share their interests (see, e.g., Melechi 1993; Rietveld 1993; Thornton 1996; Redhead, Wynne, and O'Connor 1997; Ben-nett 1999; Miles 2000; Muggleton 2000; Chaney 2004). Were venues like the Klub Foot sites of counterhegemonic resistance or of escapist fun, where fans could collectively enjoy a new type of music? I argue that they were both: those who suffered under the recession attended psychobilly events to have fun and share eclectic interests with other like-minded individuals, but they did so by transgressing hegemonic cultural expectations, resisting and rejecting the system that oppressed and suppressed them.

As post-subcultural scholars have suggested and my interlocutors con-firmed, psychobilly events are first and foremost a time and place for fun.

Participants are not motivated by an explicit political agenda of resistance against the institutions that manufacture their socioeconomic marginalization. After I asked O'Prez several questions about why he has liked psychobilly for over thirty years, he distilled his interest in the subculture down to the following response: "It's a bit of fun, isn't it? There's no political bullshit or any of that stuff like there is in punk. It's all a laugh really." Like many others I interviewed, he said that when he discovered psychobilly in the early 1980s, he liked that it was a faster and more aggressive type of rockabilly, dealing with topics that reminded him of the horror movies he loved. He liked the speed and attitude of punk but was not interested in political discourse. While punks used music to express their frustration with Thatcher's policies, first-wave psychobillies told me that they used music to escape their experiences of poverty and their disillusionment with the future. Steve Young, for instance, suggested that part of the reason he appreciated the subculture in the early 1980s was that it allowed him to forget about the problems that affected working-class youth like himself: "Back in the '80s, England was so shit for working-class kids that Saturday at the Klub Foot was what you lived for." When I asked him to explain why life was "so shit" in the early 1980s, he explained:

> Steve: Industry was changing, becoming more automated, and basically you were fuckin' out of work. There were like three million unemployed. And also the Cold War was at its height. I don't know if you had it—you had the "duck and cover" thing in the '50s, right?
>
> Kim: Yeah, my parents had those in school.
>
> Steve: Yeah, well over here that was in the '70s. And you'd get public information films on TV. . . . It was like a five-minute TV film, "you can die tomorrow." Soon there was a slight thawing of the Cold War and glasnost had started, but there was still that sense that—but it was still going on, you know? You've grown up thinking: "Oh, I might get incinerated any minute." Then you've decided, like: "Right, well fuck this, I'm going to get into this alternative lifestyle of music." You got to get into that, and girls. But '82, what comes along? Fuckin' AIDS: "You're all gonna die of AIDS if you look at somebody." You know? It was fuckin' nihilism as far as I'm concerned. Back in the '80s, the early '80s, it was a bit of nihilism, it really was, because we did all think: "Fuck this, the end." Rock 'n' roll, it's escapism, and it's about having fun.

Steve described himself, and many of his psychobilly mates, as "extremely left-wing," and he was critically aware of the conditions that affected his everyday experience, as demonstrated by his detailed description of the political, economic, and cultural context of the late 1970s and early 1980s. Yet his reaction to these structural and cultural conditions had been to go out and have as much fun as possible rather than engage in political activism. The future seemed too hopeless, bleak, and depressing, and the best recourse was to enjoy every night as if it might be his last.

Aileen, a musician who performs in both psychobilly and punk bands, felt that these escapist tendencies continue to differentiate the two subcultures today:

> Aileen: I quite like the idea that "Psicholand" [a reference to part of a Nekromantix song, "Alice in Psycholand"] is this kind of escapism place—
>
> Kim: This kind of alternative reality?
>
> Aileen: Yeah, see, 'coz looking at a lot of these people at Bedlam [a psychobilly festival]. . . . It's just like they probably have a shit job or they're unemployed and most of their time is probably spent either doing a job that's a lot of fuckin' work or pissing around on Facebook 'coz they're unemployed. So like Bedlam and gigs is a place where they can go and see their mates and just enjoy time spent not having to deal with the fact that they're working a shit job or they're unemployed.
>
> Kim: How does it compare to your experience in punk?
>
> Aileen: A lot of the DIY punk and the ska and stuff that I listen to, especially the DIY punk now is like, you know, the music can be fun and interesting, and like fun to dance to, fun to listen to, fun to go out to. But at the end of the day, the lyrical content is still like talking about Tories, anxiety, and stuff. It's discussing socio-economic and like social-political and like social-emotional problems like as a lyrical content in a way that's dancey and upbeat. Whereas what psychobilly's doing is like: "Fuck all that for a night." It's like: "We know it's shit, we're focused on the fact that it's shit constantly, so we're just gonna avoid the fact that it's shit for a night."

Aileen's analysis corresponds with what many of my interlocutors told me: they are frustrated with various aspects of their daily lives, but they want to use their leisure time *not* thinking about those problems. For instance, Pammy told me: "The very best thing about psychobilly is that it's typically politics-free. I love being able to turn on some music and turn my brain off for a while. I want to enjoy my music, not think about it. One of the main reasons I never liked punk is because it was too political for my liking." Similarly, Randy told me he liked psychobilly shows because "they don't feature politics and religion. It's all about horror, having a good time, and chilling with friends."

Indeed, one of the defining characteristics of psychobilly is its apolitical-ness. The phrase "Fuck politics, fuck religion, dance with a chainsaw," taken from the full title of The Meteors' song "Chainsaw Boogie" (from *Hell Ain't Hot Enough for Me*, 1994), has become the motto of the subculture, one that is strongly enforced. When a member of the Psychobilly Worldwide (n.d.) Facebook group posted a meme having to do with the 2016 U.S. election, the moderator reminded users: "I'm only going to say this once, because every-one should know. Psychobilly is a politics free and religion free zone. That has been a big part of the psychobilly community long before facebook or the internet. If you don't understand that, fuck right off."[7]

In an interview with *Alternative Press*, Kim Nekroman of Nekromantix describes the lack of attention to politics that defined the subculture: "We are all different people and have different political beliefs. Psychobilly is all about having fun. Politics is not fun and therefore has nothing to do with psychobilly" (quoted in Downey 2004, 78). Like those Nekroman describes, my interlocutors had a range of personal beliefs: some had a very clear sense of their liberal or conservative values and participated in elections, while others were staunchly uninterested in contemporary political matters. Regardless of their individual leanings, they all thought of psychobilly as a place where one did not talk about politics. This was aptly demonstrated by a cartoon that went viral in 2016 on online psychobilly forums. The cartoon exaggerated stereotypes about various subcultures, pointing out the thing that each subculture is understood to hate the most. It suggested that straightedge punks (who are often vegetarians) want to kill carnivores, goths want to kill themselves, punks want to kill Nazis, Nazis want to kill everyone except Hitler, and black metalheads want to kill Christians. The ideology of psychobilly, however, is summed up thus: "Let's get some booze and party hard!" Below the cartoon, a caption reads: "Psychobillies: For almost 30 years just enjoying life and rock'n'roll." True to the subculture's philosophy, psychobillies are represented as not having a political motive; they just want to have fun. The viral image captured the subculture's sense of its own difference from other ideologies, evoking the way psychobillies distance themselves from a clear political motive and consider members of other subcultures to be motivated by politicized agendas.

This insistence on having fun and escaping the realities of their socioeconomic marginalization through apolitical entertainment, drinking, and partying might appear to be evidence that psychobillies implicitly consent to the hegemonic and systemic structures of power that subordinate them, or at least fail to resist them. It could seem problematic that psychobillies are not interested in addressing political concerns or drawing attention to the social and economic inequalities that affect their lived experience. This criticism is often levied against heavy metal by progressives, as Deena Weinstein observes: "The progressives repudiate heavy metal because it substitutes hedonistic ecstasy for the political commitment and social concern that they would like to see in popular music" (2000, 237–238). This is what Max Horkheimer and Theodor Adorno of the Frankfurt School were concerned about in the 1940s when they suggested that popular entertainment prevented the masses from critiquing or "refusing" (in Marcuse's words, 1964) the hegemonic social order (Adorno [1941] 1990; Adorno and Horkheimer [1947] 2002). They argued that mass culture represented a "flight" from "the last remaining thought of resistance" (Adorno and Horkheimer [1947] 2002, 144) and precluded the working class from actively shaping their own future: "Instead of utopia becoming reality it disappears from the picture" (Adorno [1967] 1981, 132). The legacy of the Frankfurt School's argument continues to influence scholars who "dismiss popular culture as little more than escapist, formulaic, mindless trivia imposed on an uncritical mass in order to shape consumer consciousness and diffuse opposition" (Kelley 1992, 1400). For instance, some post-subcultural theorists who analyze electronic dance music culture imply that clubbers are concerned with the pursuit of ecstasy, rather than a politics of identity. As Shane Blackman notes, the post-subcultural theory of Antonio Melechi (1993) and Hillegonda Rietveld (1998) "puts pleasures first, arguing that individual sensation is found in empty kitsch, intoxication and hedonism as new forms of self-expression where drugs and different types of dance music allow young people to implode with the pure joy of individualistic consumerism" (Blackman 2005, 10).

However, an understanding of how psychobillies "have fun" at events, as this chapter describes, reveals that the pursuit of pleasure is not simply an "escape" resulting in the loss of a subcultural identity, nullifying any possibility of collective counterhegemonic resistance. Psychobillies do frame their subcultural activities as an apolitical "escape," but what they want to escape is the hegemonic culture that has socially and economically marginalized them, and they do so by *escaping to* a utopia where they reject hegemonic ideologies, performing and celebrating nonconformist, alternative values, behaviors, and identities. At subcultural events, they contest norms, break taboos, engage in behaviors that are deemed inappropriate in other contexts, and resist social and bodily control by doing what they want with—and to—their bodies. They engage in multiple transgressions, or what Barbara Babcock calls "symbolic inversion": "'Symbolic inversion' may be broadly defined as any act of expressive behaviour which inverts, contradicts, abrogates, or in some fashion presents an alternative to commonly held cultural codes, values and norms be they linguistic, literary or artistic, religious, social and political" (1978, 14). Criminologist Jock Young points to the importance of having a "subterranean" space in which to engage in "deviant" practices, such as alcohol and drug use, that take one away from the alienating effects of capitalism: "They allow us to step out into a world free of the norms of workaday life. . . . It is fallacious to think of these episodes as escapes from reality; rather we must view them as escapes into *alternative* forms of reality" ([1971] 2005, 155).

By indulging in their subcultural interests and leisure activities, psychobillies have fun and enjoy release from the experiences of social and economic marginalization that characterize their lives. But they also actively construct an *alternative* reality, making visible their frustration with contemporary life. For Dick Hebdige, this transgression of normal codes of behavior has "considerable power to provoke and disturb" (1979, 92). Even though psychobillies attend events because they want to have fun and forget about their troubles, how they challenge the status quo and enact counterhegemonic values demonstrates their refusal to concede to systemic forms of power. They are "under-fucking the system," as Shane Greene puts it (2012), by working around capitalist society, living their lives as they want to, in their own countercultural ways. Transgression can be political in this sense, but it should not be forgotten that it is also fun, as Keith Kahn-Harris suggests in his exploration of the controversial characteristics of the extreme metal scene: "Transgression allows members to voice their frustration at the alienation and disempowerment produced by modernity. It produces excitement, unpredictability and joyous experiences of the body" (2007, 159).

In this chapter I compare the subcultural celebration and performance of nonconformity to carnival, that time and space wherein people behave in "unacceptable" ways and defy conventional expectations. Evolving from the Greek Dionysian Mysteries (Ustinova 2017), and later Roman Bacchus celebrations and Saturnalia festivities, "carnival celebrates temporary liberation from the prevailing truth and from the established order, it marks the suspension of all hierarchical rank, privileges, norms, and prohibitions," as suggested by Mikhail Bakhtin, the prominent scholar of medieval carnival ([1936] 1984, 10). "During carnival time," he writes, "life is subject only to its laws, that is, the laws of its own freedom" (7). Keith Nurse describes carnival as a "period of celebration of the body, of physical abandon, where licentiousness, hedonism and sexual excess are expressed in music, dancing, masquerading and feasting" (1999, 664). This transgressive behavior is a temporary escape from the prescriptive expectations normally associated with one's social status, a "breaking free" from both the restrictions placed on the lower class and the responsibilities and proper behavior typically required of the elite. Thus, Bakhtin argues, carnival allows people to momentarily escape their strictly defined roles and even provides an opportunity to *invert* the normal social order, resulting in a "world turned upside down," wherein the lower classes not only imitate but also parody the elite, and get away with it ([1936] 1984). As Mary Russo explains, "the masks and voices of carnival resist, exaggerate, and destabilize the distinctions and boundaries that mark and maintain high culture and organized society" (1994, 62).

Bakhtin and Victor Turner suggest that carnival's "rituals of rebellion and inversion" (Turner 1969) occupy a liminal space; they are allowed only during "a ritually organized time-out from the rules and regulations governing everyday life" (Halnon 2006a, 36). After the festivities are over, the world is turned "right-side up" again, and order is restored and revalidated (Handelman 1990, 51). Carnival has thus been understood by some to be a sort of "release valve" that permits citizens to occasionally "blow off steam" so that they will continue to accept hegemonic rule. As Terry Eagleton argues: "Carnival, after all, is a *licensed* affair in every sense, a permissible rupture of hegemony, a contained popular blow-off as disturbing and relatively ineffectual as a revolutionary work of art. As Shakespeare's Olivia remarks, there is no slander in an allowed fool" (1981, 148; emphasis in original). Peter Stallybrass and Allon White note that "politically thoughtful commentators wonder, like Eagleton, whether the 'licensed release' of carnival is not simply a form of social control of the low by the high and therefore serves the interests of that very official culture which it apparently opposes" (1997, 296). Alternatively, scholars have underscored how the critiques expressed during carnival festivities allow for an "experiment in alternate visions of the world" and can bring about social change and improve lived experiences in lasting ways (Pershing 1996, 234; see also Zemon Davis 1975; Schröter 2004; Halnon 2004; Vitos 2010; Santino 2011).

I suggest that subcultural events, such as carnival festivities, are important for improving the lived experience of participants: they provide an opportunity for psychobillies to escape their subjugated "everyday" lives; experience the release of physical abandon; critique hegemonic culture; and become masters of their own domain as they perform the ideologies, behaviors, and identities that they value for themselves. And just as carnival can have lasting effects for participants, so too can these subcultural events. I draw on the work of scholars who understand subcultural performance, like carnival, as a "politics of survival," a strategic attempt among subcultural-ists to improve their lived experience by enacting sovereignty over their own lives as they construct an alternative world of their own making (see, e.g., Maffesoli 1996; Greener and Hollands 2006; Halnon 2004, 2006a; Riley, Griffin, and Morey 2010; Dimou and Ilan 2018). As Kai Fikentscher suggests, events cultivated "outside the view of the general public eye" allow an alternative society to "be pursued, tested, revised, experimented with" (2000, 6–7). Subculture thus "provides the scripts necessary for individuals to pursue freedom from various forms of perceived oppression in everyday life" (Williams and Hannerz 2014; see also G. St. John 2009). Within their subcultural space, where the world is turned upside down, individuals can experience "the pleasure of producing one's own meanings of social experi-ence and the pleasure of avoiding the social discipline of the power-bloc" (Fiske 1989, 47). The carnivalesque performances that I consider here are a way for psychobillies to survive by constructing and enjoying their own ways of being. And even though they do so without the agenda of making a political statement, their nonconformist and transgressive behaviors and values make visible their disenchantment with dominant culture and chal-lenge the totalizing attempts of hegemonic systems of power.

Transgressive Performances: Breaking Taboos by Celebrating the "Grotesque Body"

> The Surfin' Wombatz hit the stage for the first part of a double bill of dementia along with Thee Waltons. Both bands deliver laugh-out-loud performances with so much going on onstage that you just can't turn away. The Wombatz certainly dress for the occasion but behind the wacky gear they have a solid rockabilly beat and are always worth watching. Glad to see their electric washboard was still an essential part of their sound but I don't remember seeing the bucket of "anal seepage" that they used at other gigs. Things are getting a little hazy and my eyesight was blurring with the booze by the time Thee Waltons appeared but their show was the usual mix of madness to a demented hillbilly beat. Pretty sure I saw some rubber chickens, dancing girls with guns and a roadie having his head (or back) shaved!!?? (Brackenridge 2014b, 15)

As evidenced by Brackenridge's review of a Pompey Rumble weekender in 2014, the enjoyment of spectacular and theatrical performances that include a variety of bizarre and unconventional elements is central to the psychobilly experience. This section considers the carnivalesque dimensions of psychobilly performances, which since the days of the Klub Foot have welcomed and celebrated traditionally "offensive" and "unacceptable" values and behaviors. Like carnivalian celebrations, typical psychobilly performances embrace what Mikhail Bakhtin calls the "grotesque" ([1936] 1984], drawing attention to those features and processes of the body that are usually considered taboo, repulsive, shameful, and degrading. This "highly transgressive, playful retreat from, and reversal, inversion, and debasement of the totality of officialdom" (Halnon 2004, 747) allows subculturalists to express their rejection of hegemonic norms and manifest an alternative world in which counterhegemonic values and behaviors are gleefully enacted.

In *Rabelais and His World*, Bakhtin analyzes the "grotesque realism" that characterizes carnival. During the "world turned upside down" context of carnival, norms about the body are subverted and inverted. That which conventional society normally represses and considers to be "grotesque" is celebrated and exposed, as the body's natural functions and processes are highlighted (Bakhtin [1936] 1984, 317–322).[8] Attention is paid particularly to orifices—the mouth, nose, anus, and sexual organs—where natural materials enter and exit the body, connecting the inside of the body to the outside world. Mike Presdee explains: "Bakhtin's writing places much emphasis on the body, most particularly on the grotesque body. In this sense he sees carnival as a celebration of the connectedness of the body to the world: through ingestion and excretion, birth and death, the grotesque constantly reminds us that we are not separated from Nature's cycle; we are not closed off and 'above' our natural context but are inherently part of it" (2000, 39).

In other words, grotesque realism highlights the natural processes through which the outer world and inner body are connected throughout the life cycle: we feed the body with food and drink and then eliminate them through defecation, urination, burping, and vomiting; we produce life within the body and then birth a child into the world; we feed a newborn with fluids that originate within the body; we are born into the world and then return to it through the inevitability of death. Bakhtin shows that through discourse, performance, and imagery, carnival reveals the processes— "eating, drinking, defecation, and other elimination (sweating, blowing of the nose, sneezing)" as well as copulation, birth, and death—through which the inner and the outer world become one ([1936] 1984, 317).

By focusing on these types of natural processes during carnival, we pay more attention to the body (especially its lower strata) than to the mind, inverting the body, like the social order:

> Thus carnival celebrates orifices and sex organs, extreme youth and age, sex, stomachs, birth and death. . . . Carnival, in its language and imagery, is not afraid of the "arse hole," the "prick" or the "cunt." Indeed, as carnival inverts the social structure, so too does it invert the body, for in the carnival universe the head (the location of reason) is uncrowned by the stomach, the genitals and the arse. Faeces and the fart, the burp and the belly laugh all become an integral part of the logic and language of carnival. (Presdee 2000, 39)

As Presdee notes, carnival's celebration of the body's earthly connection to nature "is wholly opposed to the sobriety of the classical body, separated from the process of life" (39). These are the natural processes of our bodies, which society hides and represses, making them private rather than public and censoring the public demonstration of them through embarrassment, disapproval, or even criminalization (Jervis 1999). In short, carnival allows the "taboo" to be staged and dramatized, rejecting civility and modesty through engagement with the grotesque body.

Psychobilly events exhibit extreme amounts of this carnivalesque fascination with the grotesque body, drawing attention to the natural processes, elements, needs, and actions of our living and dying bodies. Klub Foot performances were a messy celebration of food and drink, a reminder of the requirements of all our bodies. One of my interlocutors remembered a show in which the lead singer of the Deltas talked about the beans he had eaten for breakfast. He then poured a can of beans on the snare drum, added lighter fuel, and set them alight: "He started going berserk while playing this manic song and sending burning beans flying into the audience. I thought: 'This is a lot of fun.'" Berni Lumb, of first-wave psychobilly band Sgt. Bilko's Krazy Combo, remembers his own band's playful performances at the club with fond nostalgia: "Towards the end of the Klub Foot days we went through a phase of throwing buckets of wet fish and dried pasta into the crowd. You'd see immaculate quiffs full of wet smelly fish and during the quiet moments of a song you could hear the stomp of boots on dried pasta. . . . Heaven!" (Lumb 2007).

One regular Klub Foot band, King Kurt, helped set the precedent for the carnivalesque performances that came to define the subculture. Early fans knew King Kurt by another name—Rocking Kurt and the Sour Krauts—because the band distributed packets of sauerkraut to the audience during a show early in their career. To the glee of the band and the fans, a food fight erupted, and such stunts became an essential element of their performances from then on. Craig Brackenridge remembers the wild debauchery of

King Kurt's shows at the Klub Foot, particularly those moments when ingested food or drink spewed forth from the body:

> King Kurt gigs resulted in widespread attacks of flour bombs, eggs, shaving foam, fire extinguishers and anything else which came to hand—along with a few unmentionables. Drinking games were also part of the gig experience including a live favorite which would follow later in the band's career, the infamous "Wheel of Misfortune," a huge wheel [. . .] which punters were strapped to and spun [on] after being fed a bucket of booze through a hose. This often resulted in the victim being left in an unconscious stupor or forced them to let go a multi-colored fountain of puke. Snakebite was the supposed content of the bucket but many would shudder to think what foul potions were also added to the receptacle. (2007, 24)

Roy Maat adds: "I can still hear the dulcet tones of Smeg [lead singer of King Kurt] shouting 'Pipe in the bucket, 5–4–3–2–1 SUCK!!!!' Of course, those that failed got a bucket of the colored gunk chucked over their head. This, added to all the flour, eggs and baked beans that were already being chucked around the venue, made for a very messy evening" (2003). As psychobillies left the club covered in food, drink, and vomit, they defied codes of propriety about cleanliness and indulged in a carnivalesque celebration of what goes in and comes out of the body's orifices.

King Kurt's performances sometimes made the news, earning psychobillies a reputation for being "folk devils" known for their "deviant" behavior (Stanley Cohen 1972): "The band's outrageous live performances rapidly gained them notoriety and some music press. Lurid headlines in daily newspapers even warned of alcohol poisoning, dead animals launched into (and out of) the crowd and a variety of sex acts performed in the audience," all of which, Brackenridge suggests, were true (2007, 24). Given carnival's obsession with the cycle of life, it is not surprising that psychobilly performances engage transgressively, but comically, with sexual reproduction, as King Kurt did. I have seen performers and audience members expose their genitals, grab each other's breasts or crotches, wear exaggerated replicas of sex organs, and engage in real or simulated sexual acts. Brackenridge describes a performance at a festival in 2014: "The doors were barely open before opening act Dick Venom & the Terrortones hit the stage and within minutes their lead vocalist was standing on the bar waving his balls at the audience" (2014b, 14). Perhaps the most famous of all when it comes to sexual "deviancy" on stage is the band Demented Are Go. Steve Young laughed as he remembered Demented Are Go's performances at the Klub Foot: "They brought sex. They developed the sex gear—it was the rubber trousers and dildos hanging off his belt and all that." Stories of Sparky (the lead singer) simulating sex with a vacuum cleaner on stage have been passed down like legends. Repeated citations for public indecency and various other crimes eventually led to the band being banned from many stages (and even some countries).

Psychobillies are particularly preoccupied with the belly, that part of the grotesque body that most represents the processes through which the inner and outer worlds collide, by way of ingestion, digestion, and then elimination, and through insemination, pregnancy, and then birth. I have seen men in the wrecking pit lift their shirts to their nipples and then belly bump one another, and male performers rub their extended bellies with their hands in a ludicrously sexual way while leering at the audience with a gleam in their eyes. They smile as they exaggerate natural eruptions of the body—through which the inner becomes outer—calling attention to their burps, farts, and belly laughs.

Carnival highlights not only the beginning of the life cycle but also the end. Psychobilly performances, too, regularly play with death. As previously noted, tales about dead animals being used during King Kurt's performances made headlines. Nigel Lewis of The Meteors remembers one show in which their drummer, Mark Robertson, determined not to be outdone by King Kurt, started kissing and biting rabbit heads that were thrown onto the stage by the audience (Decay 2004). As is discussed in the next chapter, psychobillies regularly play with zombie imagery, symbolizing at once both death and life (or, rather, undeath). In one zombie performance that was replete with carnivalesque fascination with sex, death, and bodily fluids, at a Cold Blue Rebels show, the singer took a dancer dressed as a zombie into a coffin, simulated the act of oral sex, and then raised his head up, spitting fake blood at the audience.

Both fake and real blood frequently litter the floors of psychobilly performances, just as "the grotesque image displays not only the outward but also the inner features of the body: blood, bowels, heart and other organs" (Bakhtin [1936] 1984, 318). As noted in Chapter 1, P. Paul Fenech of The Meteors quickly became known for his tendency to spit chicken blood at the audience (Wall 1981). During my ethnographic fieldwork, I met several musicians known for their bloody performances. Vic Victor of Koffin Kats, for instance, routinely bangs his forehead against the fingerboard of his bass until blood runs down his face. When I asked him about it, he pointed out: "I used to do it every show, but my head took such a beating. It's real, and it does hurt after awhile. I don't do it for every show now, and there are some venues you play that just won't allow it. So now that we've been through the country a few times with that little trick, some clubs are hip to it, and they're like, 'no body fluids, no spitting.'" The guitarist, Tommy Koffin, added: "When we didn't have our own mics, we'd get charged for the mics, for bleeding out on them." Likewise, a musician from the now-defunct Texas psychobilly band Pickled Punks told me that they were banned from many venues for their transgressive performances. I saw the lead singer swing from the rafters of a venue and fall into the crowd, act in sexually transgressive ways, and bleed on stages. "We're like a freak show," the drummer, Destin, told me. "We're actually like Pickled Punks in a jar. People will stare at it and they're not really sure if they want to see it again. Maybe the crowd would like to see it again, but the people that have the venue don't really want that kind of stuff, don't really want to be associated with it. We're kinda like GG Allin.[9] They're not quite ready for it."

Carnival thus provides an opportunity to reject conventional norms of propriety about the body, as Karen Halnon suggests in her interpretation of Bakhtin's work: "The grotesque body not only exposes what is veiled (its genitalia, its smells, its eruptions) and what is hidden inside (its fluids, its "wastes," or its organs), but it also can be detected by movements such as spasms, tensions, popping eyes, convulsions of arms and legs, or hanging tongues" (2006b, 38). Psychobillies perform the grotesque body by moving in ways that reject notions of self-control: they hang out their tongues, lick the microphone, roll their eyes back into their heads, convulse, and spasm. They pick their noses (or sometimes each other's noses); expose their buttocks, genitalia, and bellies; simulate or perform sexual acts; bleed on stage or in the wrecking pits; play with dead animals; vomit, burp, and fart; cover themselves in food; and generally disobey just about every law governing "civil" and "proper" behavior.[10]

They embrace the grotesque body and "playfully dramatize and expose what is hidden yet common to all human beings" (Halnon 2006b, 38). This performance of the body's natural tendencies, which all people have in common, can foster intrascene unity. Carnival calls attention to the fact that all people, regardless of socioeconomic status, have the same natural bodies: all of us are tied to nature by the necessity of eating and eliminating, and we all will die. Carnivalesque performances, then, erase differences between people, reminding all members of society of their sameness. I argue that carnivalesque performances in psychobilly serve this same function. They create a sense of community among participants as they revel in the grotesque body together: all covered in baked beans, flour, and fishheads; all with the potential to vomit on the Wheel of Misfortune; all sharing the same body parts and blood that are exposed on stage and throughout the audience; all sharing the same bodily functions—burping, farting—which are exaggerated for comic (and physical) relief.

As Bakhtin ([1936] 1984) and Turner (1969) observe, societies have traditionally reserved the exploration of these taboo topics for carnival, a liminal time and space that is understood *not* to be everyday life. Once the world is turned right side up again, these same topics are off limits once more. Accordingly, the "imagery of grotesque bodies" that Karen Halnon finds in her study of "heavy metal carnival" bands (e.g., Alice Cooper, Ozzy Osbourne, Marilyn Manson, Slipknot, GWAR, Insane Clown Posse, and Cradle of Filth) "would be judged seriously vile, obscene, or disgusting . . . in ordinary life" (Halnon 2006b, 38). Subcultural performances, she suggests, thus represent "a creative medium for and by the people for imagining and living (at least for a few utopian hours) a radical difference from the everyday, oppressive status quo" (46). I also frame psychobilly performances as "carnivalesque" because they embrace and reveal the grotesque, "rebelling against potentially everything that is moral, sacred, decent, or civilized" (35). Psychobillies use their bodies as they want to, rejecting society's standards about propriety and decency. As Presdee argues, "the performance of carnival uses the body as the stage, claiming it back from those who wish to control it, who wish to appropriate that which it produces, to civilize it, or even to imprison it" (2000, 39–40). Accordingly, I understand psychobillies' carnivalesque performance of the grotesque as a way of claiming back their bodies: they refuse to veil or hide from view the natural processes that all bodies share. Their determination to violate accepted codes of behavior through their taboo engagement with their own bodies is testament to psychobillies' expressed defiance of regulatory restrictions.

It is also important to remember that liberating one's body from the norms of social and self-control is fun. Simon Frith emphasizes the ecstasy of jouissance that can be experienced when we free ourselves from the constraints of culture and enjoy pleasures of the body: "*Jouissance*, like sexual pleasure, involves self-abandonment, as the terms we usually use to construct and hold ourselves together seem to float free" (Frith 1981, 164–165). Indeed, we continue to participate in carnival celebrations in part because it is fun to free our bodies from the constraints and expectations that are normally imposed on them. Similarly, the carnivalesque performances that characterize this subculture allow psychobillies to enjoy using their bodies in undisciplined ways. We particularly enjoy doing that which we "know" we are not supposed to enjoy (or rather, if we consider Foucault's [1978] theories about the power of discourse to structure our understanding of the world, we enjoy doing that which we *have been conditioned to think* we are not supposed to enjoy). Film and media studies scholar William Paul argues that this is why many people enjoy horror movies that indulge in the grotesque: "There is a kind of defiant pleasure in regression, in wallowing in dirt as a way of rejecting social constraints. We take fierce pride in our body's ability to produce disgusting emissions, finding pleasure in them precisely because they are disgusting" (1994, 314). Through these carnivalesque performances, psychobillies have embraced the opportunity to freely inhabit their bodies in typically "unacceptable" ways, indulging in the pleasure of transgression and gleefully signifying their resistance to society's repressive norms.

Transgressive Behaviors: The Ecstasy of Wrecking and Intoxication

> Under the stage, a wrecking pit from hell. Violence, beer and alcohol spilled on anyone. This is psychobilly and everything is perfect for one and a half hours. About 3 am when their concert ends we begin to dance, stagger, or faint from alcohol abuse or who knows what else in any possible direction. We're drunk but happy, tired but excited, as we head into the darkness of Potsdam towards the hotel, ready for the usual early wake-up after 3 hours of "sleep" for the return trip. (*DogEatRobot Fanzine* 2013d, 26)

In this passage, the reviewer describes the pleasure of a psychobilly concert during which, for a short time, "everything is perfect." The show on stage is only one part of the utopic experience; the right combination of alcohol, wrecking, and a great performance can leave one feeling exhilarated. Deena Weinstein describes how heavy metal fans seek to attain an ecstatic experience that "eliminates calculative rationality and circumspective concern" (2000, 213). She suggests that the experience of ecstasy at a good show "removes the everyday-life world, with its remembrance of things past and the anticipation of things to come. It is the experience of falling into the moment" (213–214). An ecstatic experience allows participants to focus on feeling good in the present moment, unconcerned about the oppressive, alienating, or frustrating experiences that characterize their day-to-day lives. To achieve this feeling of ecstasy, concertgoers should have a "multisensory experience" that eventually "produces the final consummatory emotion, the experience of being totally relaxed and done in, 'wasted'" (214), as the reviewer feels at the end of the Psychomania Rumble. Norm Elliott similarly described to me the ecstasy he felt at shows, which gave him something to "live for": "We lived and breathed it. It was life! We'd get right in the pit just before show started, take our T-shirts off, and stuff them down the front of our bleached jeans. Then the band would start and we'd go mental. Everyone really, really went for it. We didn't need drugs. That music just sent us to another place, and we just went to another planet."

In this section I consider how psychobillies achieve this ecstatic sense of release through two typical physical experiences of bodily and mental abandon: wrecking and intoxication. Both of these behaviors are carnivalesque: through them, psychobillies break free from normative expectations about self-restraint and bodily control. Just as performances indulge in the natural processes of the body, wrecking and drinking disobey rationality and focus instead on the sensations of the body. As they do, the grotesque body is further revealed: as wrecking releases blood and sweat, and intoxication leads to vomiting, the barriers between the inside of the body and the outside world blur.

Also referred to as "going mental" or "stomping," "wrecking" describes the frenetic movement within a psychobilly crowd that "to the untrained eye, resembles a Wild West saloon brawl," as longtime fan Craig Brackenridge notes (2007, 19). Like the slam and mosh pits described by William Tsitsos (1999, 405–406), the wrecking "pit" is not a designated, marked-off area; pits form naturally when those who want to wreck begin to move around and engage physically with others around them. Not every song at a concert will generate a pit; the tempo of the song, the number of people in the audience, the popularity of the band, encouragement from the band to start a wrecking pit, and the general degree of excitement "in the air" can all determine whether a pit will develop. When pits form, audience members who are watching the band and do not want to get swept up in the movement of the pit move away from the area. People on the perimeter of the pit turn their attention away from the band to watch the action; brace themselves for the inevitable impacts from wreckers who are pushed into them; and keep an eye out for anyone who might need help, for instance if someone falls or takes a punch to the gut or a kick to the head that stuns that person and leaves them momentarily incapacitated[11] (see Figure 2.2). As in other subcultures, a lively pit is a usually an indication of the crowd's approval of the band and their performance on stage, as well as the popularity of the particular song (Tsitsos 1999, 405). Wrecking is considered by most psychobillies to be an essential part of the concert experience; fans find enjoyment not only in participating in the pit themselves but also in watching others wreck.

Less uniform in style than the pogo dance associated with classic punk, the moshing of heavy metal, or the circle pits of the hardcore scene, psychobilly wrecking pits exhibit a diverse range of movements. Participants move in unpredictable directions: some slam their bodies into each other while

Figure 2.2. A lively wrecking pit, whose energy, size, and speed—commonly considered essential elements of the ecstatic concert experience—can indicate the crowd's approval of the performance. (*Photo by the author.*)

punching their fists in front of them, others stand still and convulse on their own as if overcome by the music, and still others invent new moves on the spot. During a few years of my research, a trend developed wherein girls braced themselves in the middle of the wrecking pit and used both arms to quickly jab each other, as if rapidly hitting a punching bag, while others slammed into them from every direction. Some participants "clown around" in the pit, shuffling along like zombies with their arms raised in front of them, while others are determined to collide into everyone else with as much force as possible. The speed at which people move varies tremendously: the pit may move slowly as people casually walk around at a moderate pace; at other times bodies blur as they whiz by; and sometimes people move at different speeds within the same pit. The diverse ways people participate in the chaos of the pit demonstrate how fully psychobillies rebel against any disciplining of their bodies; they even refuse to rebel together in a consistent way!

When I asked my interlocutors why they enjoyed wrecking, they articulated that it helped them release tension and aggression, that the music *compelled* them to move in frenzied and spastic ways, and that they enjoyed the "feeling of community" that came from engaging together in a common subcultural activity with others they identified with. For instance, Aileen thought that wrecking evolved in the early 1980s as a way for "young men in the broken Britain" to release their anger: "The aggression is there. They're angry because they're being shafted [by the recession] and so like it comes out in different ways. It's a release. They just want to let go." She suggested that the thumping beat from the bass further created in them a desire to "go mental" and lose control. Steve Young agreed: "It *is* something in the beat, because I'm forty-eight now and the other night we went to see a concert. And I've got a bad back and I'm old but I couldn't help myself. I'm suffering for it now, yeah, oh yeah, just a bit. But I can't hold back, even at my advanced age." Similarly, O'Prez told me: "I get the fuckin' baloobas[12] when I listen to psychobilly." I asked him if he still "goes mental" when he hears it and he replied, "I still do here at nighttime. I go berserk. When you hear a bit, you just can't help it. Fuckin' hell. It just drives me berserk. I suppose the whole rhythm and beat of the music, it just makes you move." While some of my interlocutors enjoyed wrecking because of its social dimensions, O'Prez's suggestion that the music made him "go wild" even if he was listening to it alone underscored how the music itself, rather than the feeling of being in a crowd, compelled him to move.

William Tsitsos's analysis of slam dancing in the punk scene provides a useful model for understanding both the individual and communal aspects of wrecking. He argues that the chaotic nature of slam dancing reflects "the balancing of individuality and unity which punks undertake in formulating their ideologies of rebellion" (1999, 407). As an individual expression, "scene members . . . give the impression that slamdancing is just an adrenalised dance with no rules at all, in which impulsive urges drive dancers to act out spontaneously in any way they desire. This idea of the lawless individual in the pit reflects the vision of rule-breaking individuality which is such a large part of being a punk" (408). At the same time, "their actions while slamdancing are structured by 'rules' of the pit," such as moving together in the same direction, picking up those who fall, and using the same general body movements, all of which serve to generate a feeling of intrascene unity (408).

As in slam dancing, psychobillies' individual and unpredictable movements symbolize their desire to break rules and to rebel against the disciplining of their bodies by others. They enact control over their own bodies, using them as they want to and creating chaos with them. At the same time, as Tsitsos suggests, there is a general sense of "looking out" for the safety of others, reflecting a sense of intrascene unity that indicates participants' identification with one another as outcasts who share a common desire to rebel against mainstream and normative culture. Moreover, psychobillies must submit their bodies to the communal nature of the pit: even though they express their own individuality by attempting to move in their own ways, they ultimately cannot control how their bodies are impacted by all the other bodies. Wreckers may go into the pit as individual rebels, but they come out having been subjected to the forces of all the other rebel bodies. I argue that this is yet another way intrascene unity is directly embodied and fostered: psychobillies surrender their bodies to those around them, who literally "have their backs,"[13] not unlike "the trust falls" that are used for team-building exercises. Thus, wrecking represents both individual agency and unity with others, both self-control and the surrendering of control. Keith Kahn-Harris describes the similar contradictions found in extreme metal, wherein participants give themselves over to the collective while enjoying a sense of personal control and individual agency: "Extreme metal practices . . . are excessive, testing and breaking boundaries, invoking the joys and terrors of formless oblivion within the collective, while simultaneously bolstering feelings of individual control and potency" (2007, 30).

Giving up control of one's body is central to psychobillies' pursuit of an ecstatic experience. For example, a reviewer of the Psychomania Rumble describes the joy of surrendering to the pit: "Their show was devastating like always! Fuck, 45 minutes of pure violence, on the stage but especially under the stage in the middle of the wreck—bumps and punches have flown so fast to hit your bones and I threw myself in on one side and found myself on the opposite one, totally busted . . . *but happy to be!*" (*DogEatRobot Fanzine* 2013d, 24; emphasis added).

When I interviewed Craig Brackenridge, he smiled as he recalled his first show at the Klub Foot and how he—and other first-wave psychobillies—now had more than thirty years of wrecking experience on their side: "It was wild, that first time. I was just dumbfounded. It was carnage. That's why it's funny now—because you tend to get a lot of young guys that are quite healthy and got stamina, and then you get old guys like me that are like tree trunks, like rocks, because we've been doing it so long. So it's a crazy mess." However, he admitted that it *is* a little different now that he is in his fifties: "Now I don't have stamina for forty minutes so I'll stand around the pit and then dive in if it's a song I really like. And then, ooff! The past few years I've come out and I just feel like I've walked up a mountain or something and that's after three minutes in. Last time my watch came off and I went back and it was still strapped together. It just flung off!"

A watch is not all he has lost; during our interview, he took out his dentures and pointed out to me how many teeth he had lost in the pit. I was not surprised. Just before interviewing Craig, I had read the memoir he wrote about his experiences in the psychobilly subculture, *Let's Wreck: Psychobilly Flashbacks from the Eighties and Beyond* (Brackenridge 2003). He opens his book by describing the ecstasy he typically experienced while attending shows in the late 1980s. Generally he achieved this ecstasy by completing surrendering control of his body, giving in to the violent chaos of the wrecking pit. He describes one show at which he fell backward, was then propelled forward, and finally fell and cracked his head on something hard:

My head was cold and wet. [I thought] "some dirty bastard has thrown beer on me." But it was not beer and as I wiped my head I noticed the blood. It was soaking me. My friends dragged me down to the toilet and I saw myself in the mirror. The prom scene in *Carrie* sprung to mind. I laughed out of bravado then dropped onto a chair and asked my mate if I was going to die. An ambulance took me to hospital. "He's been drinking—probably fighting" [they said]. No anesthetic. Thirteen stitches. BAM! Welcome to the wrecking crew! (Brackenridge 2003, 5)[14]

Craig's memory of being "inducted" into the subculture exemplifies how psychobillies revel in the pleasures of intrascene unity by abandoning their bodies to a community of others they identify with. He also expresses his pleasure in rejecting normative ideas about how one is expected to use—and protect—one's body. Numerous interlocutors listed the injuries they had sustained (bruised ribs or worse), treating these as "badges of honor" that demonstrate their commitment to the undisciplined use of their bodies. And they always emphasized the amount of fun they had in the process. Indeed, bodily injuries come with the territory of pursuing an ecstatic experience that allows psychobillies to get "out of their heads" and forget about everything outside of the present moment, indulging in the pleasure of hearing their favorite song and surrendering their bodies to the pit.

Thus for many psychobillies wrecking is fundamental to the attempt to experience an ecstatic state wherein they can forget about their problems. But by expressing their resistance to authoritarian attempts to discipline their bodies, wrecking also represents an *engaged* rejection of hegemonic culture. Their chaotic movements in the pit signify their rebellious desire to move as they wish to, and they gleefully abandon traditional values about the sanctity of the body, surrendering their flesh and bone to the pursuit of an ecstatic experience. As they relinquish control and put their bodies (literally) in the hands of other psychobillies, they enjoy feeling part of a community of outcasts, rebels who share an ideology of resisting normative values and expectations.

The pursuit of pleasure often involves a combination of wrecking and alcohol, with the latter sometimes motivating fans to join the energetic wrecking pit. Titch, a member of Klingonz, explains:

There was a bar right next door [to the Klub Foot], 'cause it was in a hotel, well an old hotel they turned into the venue. Outside on a Saturday afternoon the whole road, all the pavement, all of Hammersmith Palais, was just full of psychobillies, throwing cans at

passersby, giving people stick [the middle finger]. The pub would
open at five o'clock and everyone would pile in there. So by the time
the bands would come on, you just wanted to get in there and wreck.
Getting absolutely out of their faces and going in there and killing
each other. (Decay 2004)

Several of my interlocutors apologized to me for their fuzzy memories of
psychobilly events, as Craig Brackenridge does in his memoir: "Another
reason for some of the gaps and omissions has got to be my befuddled
memory as I was almost consistently pissed [drunk] and/or stoned through
my psychobilly days and far too fucked up most of the time to keep an
accurate record of events" (2003, 95). While some psychobillies do use drugs
such as marijuana, cocaine, and methamphetamines, alcohol is the intoxicant
consumed most frequently at events, allowing subculturalists to forget about
their everyday troubles and enjoy themselves.[15] For Titch, intoxication is an
essential part of the psychobilly experience: "Everyone just pissed out of their
minds. That's what psychobilly is about to me. People just going along and
getting fucked up, honest to god. Getting pissed out of your face and having
a good time. That, to me, is what it's all about" (Decay 2004). His comment
evokes what Deena Weinstein calls the "Dionysian significance" of alcohol
within subcultures, "aiding and representing release into ecstatic experience"
(Weinstein 2000, 209) and allowing psychobillies to forget their frustrations
and problems, at least momentarily.

While alcohol can contribute to the evasive experience of forgetting
about everyday life, it can also encourage sociality and a feeling of unity
with other psychobillies, fostering a sense of belonging in a subcultural
community. As suggested by Titch, alcohol may motivate people to join the
wrecking pit, where intrascene unity is enacted and embodied. Psychobillies
also feel a sense of commonality with one another due to their shared enjoyment of alcohol. At one show I attended, the singer announced: "This song
is dedicated to all the alcoholics. We wanna drink some more. We're gonna
drink 'til we die!" This elicited cheers from the audience, demonstrating the
shared tendency to use alcohol to feel pleasure and forget about their troubles. This compares to Karl Spracklen's observation that "drinking alcohol
is a mark of metalness" and a "central part of metal's identity and ideology"
that "brings the musicians and the fans together" (2018, 417). Moreover, as
demonstrated in many studies of substance use at subcultural events, alcohol can facilitate social interaction and help participants achieve a sense of
connection with others (e.g., Weinstein 2000, 32; Greener and Hollands
2006, 406; Spracklen 2018, 417). For instance, Jock Young suggests that
drugs and alcohol can function as an antidote to the alienating effects of

capitalism: "Alcohol, then, is a common vehicle for undermining the inhibitions built up by our socialization into the work ethic" ([1971] 2005, 154–155). Thus alcohol, like wrecking, represents both a way to escape the normative world and a way to engage and identify with the subcultural and nonnormative one.

Bakhtin argues that during carnival, bodily experiences of pleasure and rebellious abandon are privileged as people are allowed a liberating escape from the conventions and responsibilities that mark day-to-day life ([1936] 1984). Psychobilly events encourage participants to use their bodies to achieve ecstasy, pleasure, and release from the worries that characterize their everyday lived experience. The surrendering of one's body to wrecking, the opportunity to forget about everything other than the pit, and the intoxicated freedom produced by alcohol are indicative of the ways psychobillies "turn to excessive bodily consciousness to produce this *jouissance*-like evasion" of social discipline (Fiske 1989, 51). For John Fiske, jouissance, "translated variously as bliss, ecstasy, or orgasm, is the pleasure of the body that occurs at the moment of the breakdown of culture into nature" (50). He uses this concept to suggest that "the orgasmic pleasure of the body out of control—the loss of self—is a pleasure of evasion, of escape from the self-control/social-control by which, in Foucault's telling phrase, 'men govern themselves and others'" (50–51). In other words, the ecstatic experience of "getting absolutely out of their faces," to use Titch's phrase, allows psychobillies to leave behind the world in which they and their bodies are subject to the controls and expectations of others.

But while the ecstatic experience helps psychobillies forget their everyday concerns, it is also important to remember that their subversion of normative expectations about the "proper" use of the body also makes visible their resistance to systemic forms of power. They evade the attempted social discipline of their bodies by moving as they want to, creating chaos, rejecting the "sanctity" of their bodies by sacrificing their skin and bone to the pursuit of the ecstatic experience, and overindulging in alcohol. They indulge in the grotesque body as blood and sweat from wrecking and vomit from intoxication unveil that which is normally hidden inside. Moreover, through the embodied pleasures of wrecking and drinking alcohol, psychobillies enact and manifest a sense of community, recognizing themselves as part of a subculture of other rebels who defy normative values and behaviors. In this space, they can enjoy doing so together. Psychobilly events thus provide attendees with an alternative world where they construct their own opportunities to achieve pleasure, bliss, and ecstasy, a hedonistic carnival that allows them to forget about their concerns while simultaneously rebelling against authority through the counterhegemonic use of their own bodies.

Transgressive Style: Scaring the Straights
by Looking Subcultural

> Their style has been termed "Mutant Rockabilly" and it is an apt
> description—with cartoon quiffs sometimes dyed green or purple
> and always thrust out far beyond the expectations of gravity,
> aggressive studded belts and Doc Martens, shredded, bleached jeans
> and leather jackets painted with post-nuclear-holocaust imagery.
> (Polhemus 1994, 102)

Ted Polhemus's description of the psychobilly style reflects how the
subculture's fashion, as defined at venues such as the Klub Foot, embraces
the carnivalesque: it revels in the excessive, the forbidden, the profane, and
the alternative. In this final section of the chapter I briefly consider how the
style that spread through first-wave subcultural spaces was designed to
challenge normative fashion standards and gender norms, reject commercial
mainstream culture, facilitate a communal identity, and manifest a refusal
to be disciplined by society's expectations and regulations. This is not by any
means an exhaustive summary of psychobilly's style culture;[16] my focus is
specifically on the effects of the performance of these carnivalesque transgressions of style.

As the subcultural style was codified at venues such as the Klub Foot,
the quiff quickly became its most unique marker. Like a Mohawk, the sides
are shaved, and like a flattop, most of the back of the head is shaved. But
instead of shaping what is left into a Mohawk that stands straight up, psy-
chobollies shape the hair into a point several inches in front of the forehead
and then mold it into place with vast quantities of hair spray. Because of the
way the hair is cut, the top of the angular wedge remains flat, like an exaggerated 1950s flattop crossed with a Mohawk and pompadour (see Figure
2.3). The psychobilly quiff celebrates the rejection of mainstream British
hairstyles in the 1970s and 1980s, transgressing cultural expectations. As
Alan Wilson pointed out to me, he and many of his peers were forced to
have military-style buzz cuts in school. When he became interested in rockabilly, he rebelliously started to grow out his hair into a full-bodied pompadour. He was chastised by school authorities, and like his bandmate Steve
Whitehouse, he usually ducked into bathrooms to comb and style his pompadour in secret. Later, when Alan discovered neo-rockabilly and psychobilly, he expressed his rejection of Teddy Boy culture by shaving the sides off
his duck-tailed pomp. Pulling what was left of his long hair forward, he was
able to fashion a slightly exaggerated flattop quiff, a feat that would have
been impossible had he still had a short buzz cut. Influenced by punk, Alan

Figure 2.3. Examples of psychobilly quiffs on members of The Quakes in 1987. (*Used with permission from Paul Roman [The Quakes].*)

and others often dyed their quiffs various colors, further expressing their countercultural inclinations.

The carnivalesque implications of the quiff are reflected in "Take a Razor to Your Head," by The Sharks (from *Phantom Rockers*, 1983), a song Alan Wilson wrote about the transition from Teddy Boy to neo-rockabilly and psychobilly style:

> *When your Mom says you look really nice*
> *When you're dressed up like a Ted*
> *It's time to follow this cat's advice*
> *Take a razor to your head*
> *When you feel it's time to move along*
> *And you feel like somethin' new*
> *Just follow the trail of discarded drapes*
> *Here's what you must do:*
> *Take your old man's cut-throat*
> *With the stains where he has bled*
> *And take a razor to your head*

The song underscores how Teddy Boy fashion had already lost its rebellious connotations. As discussed in Chapter 1, the rise of newer "threatening" subcultures, such as punk, and the widespread mainstreaming of the rock 'n' roll revival caused a shift in the public perception of Teds. They came to be associated with a quaint and innocent nostalgia, causing mothers to interpret their style as "really nice," as reflected in this song. By shaving the sides of their hair, psychobillies could continue to express their rebellious tendencies, rejecting both the buzz cuts that had traditionally represented institutional

Figure 2.4. The first all-female psychobilly band, Dypsomaniaxe, circa 1993. The band members' androgynous psychobilly wedge quiffs, with shaved sides, convey their rejection of traditional feminine hairstyles. (*One Too Many, by Dypsomaniaxe [Tombstone Records, 1993].*)

authority and the full pompadours that represented a Teddy Boy scene, which, stripped of its resistant potential, psychobillies now distanced themselves from. Moreover, by advising the listener to use an old bloodstained razor, the song celebrates the "grotesque," the vile, and the disgusting, further reflecting the transgressive and carnivalesque nature of the psychobilly style.

In short, the quiff was a new nonnormative hairstyle that signified psychobillies' total rejection of institutional and mainstream culture. If it was considered inappropriate for boys like Alan and Steve to reject the traditional buzz cut, it was even more transgressive for young women who adopted the psychobilly quiff. For instance, the quiffs on the women in the band Dypsomaniaxe signified their rejection of normative feminine hairstyles (see Figure 2.4). Psychobilly women, like female punks, often cultivated the same subcultural style as the men, refusing gender norms. As Lauraine Leblanc suggests, "In order to resist the gender games of the dominant culture, punk girls turn to male models of subcultural rebellion and create or adopt forms of dress and behavior that subvert the norms of female propriety" (1999, 159). I consider how women negotiate ideas of femininity with an androgynous style and how they cultivate "alternative" identities through their fashion choices (Holland 2004) in more detail in Chapter 4.

Over time the psychobilly quiff became more exaggerated, more "grotesque," as Brackenridge recalls: "The flat-top itself then mutated from a one inch table-top of hair to something increasingly longer. It also began to appear at an exaggerated gradient, moving from an inch long at the back to 4–5 inches at the front" (2007, 145). O'Prez told me that when he was seventeen, during the first wave of psychobilly, his quiff was fourteen inches long. I was surprised he could remember such an exact number, and I bemusedly imagined the teenage version of himself standing in front of a mirror, measuring his hair. He explained that he recalled it so clearly because it caused such a commotion in his small town: "In secondary school, that did not go down well. So they actually brought in new rules around my image. The wording of the rules: 'No fancy hair. No fancy shoes.' All this shit." Thus, as already discussed in terms of wrecking and other transgressive performances, psychobillies' stylistic defiance of conventional norms was often policed because of the challenge it posed to the traditional social order.

The subculture's stylistic culture is also carnivalesque in terms of its resistance to commercial consumer culture; it represents a rejection of the hegemonic imperative to participate in the capitalist economy. It has always been motivated by a DIY, working-class strategy that repurposes what one already has access to. As several of my interlocutors pointed out, they already had Dr. Martens boots and an appropriate jacket from their standard work wear. All they had to do to identify themselves as psychobilly was shave off the sides of their hair, buy a band T-shirt (directly from the band, not from a mainstream outlet), and throw some household bleach on their jeans. O'Prez, for instance, put bleach on some jeans he already owned and kicked them around in the yard to give them a distressed look. If they wanted to add some interesting elements to their wardrobe, psychobillies scoured secondhand rag markets. As Angela McRobbie has shown, these offered British working-class youth during the recession the opportunity to experiment cheaply with fashion while expressing their rejection of the conventions of normal apparel (McRobbie 1988). Today's psychobillies, still economically marginal, continue to creatively appropriate the materials at their disposal while circulating capital among themselves or through secondhand businesses. For instance, to make his patch jackets, Aaron uses an old jean or leather jacket passed down from a friend or something inexpensive he has found in a secondhand shop. He described his latest patch jacket to me: he had cut off the sleeves that didn't fit him, borrowed his sister's sewing kit, and figured out how to tack on his coveted band patches himself, patches he had bought or traded directly from the bands or other fans. He was able to express his individual interests and identify himself as a psychobilly fan without participating in the mainstream economy. Thus, psychobillies reject popular fashion norms through their stylistic choices and refuse to participate in the capitalist systems that have marginalized them, "underfucking the system" as Shane Greene suggests (2012).

Quiffs, bleached jeans, band T-shirts, and patch jackets characterized the subcultural style found in spaces such as the Klub Foot during the first wave of psychobilly. As many scholars have observed, a relatively consistent

and distinct style allows subculturalists to identify one another and identify *with* one another, signaling and affirming a collective subcultural identity (see, e.g., Hall and Jefferson 1976; Hebdige 1979; Hodkinson 2002). For
instance, Kim Nekroman remembers his excitement upon arriving at the
Klub Foot for the first time: "I came down from the tube, went down the
street, and there was this huge line of people. And I came closer and everybody had a quiff and it was an amazing sight" (Decay 2004). The exaggerated psychobilly quiff is particularly useful as a way of identifying like-
minded, nonnormative individuals outside a performance setting. Fergus
described how quiffs helped psychobillies identify each other when they
were wearing work gear and unable to express their subcultural identity
through their clothes: "If I was working [painting houses] and I'd see a guy
walk past with the sides of his head shaved, I'd go, oop! [He motions as if
trying to fix his quiff.] I was trying to get the remnants of the hair spray and
pull my quiff forward because that was how you were going to know each
other. That was your trademark. When I was dressed in my painter's overalls, that'd be the only way." This was even more true in America during the
1980s, when psychobilly was incredibly rare. Being committed to such an
underground style of music meant that two psychobillies would probably
have very common experiences, interests, and values and thus be particularly excited to meet each other. The best way to find like-minded psychobillies was to express oneself through the unique sartorial style in the hopes of
being identified by another subculturalist. Al, who was committed to the
extremely obscure psychobilly scene in California during the 1980s, remembered clearly the excitement of finally seeing another psychobilly: "I was
driving down Highland. I see this girl in bleached-out overalls with a shaved
head and a huge quiff. I'm like [gasp]. . . . And I saw her. I was like: 'I got to
park!' Highland has no place to park, so I turn around the first corner, wherever it was, there was an empty space. I park, jump out of the car, run up
behind her. Stupidly, [I shouted at her], 'Excuse me, are you into psychobilly?'"

Joey told me a similar story about seeing a psychobilly—recognizable by
his quiff, his sleeveless denim jacket with psychobilly patches, and Creepers—on the street in Austin, Texas, in the 1990s, when there were only about
five psychobillies in town. He pulled over and ran after the stranger to introduce himself. Both Al and Joey then played in bands with other psychobillies they chased down. The unique and subversive sartorial style has thus
been instrumental to the development of local psychobilly scenes by allowing subculturalists to easily identify one another.

While specific stylistic elements such as the distinct quiff have defined
the psychobilly look since its development, the subcultural style was, and

continues to be, diverse. Fergus pointed out: "You could go to a psychobilly festival dressed as a fairy, or a pirate, and nobody'd bother. You could turn up in anything." David Muggleton has called this "diverse unity," noting that members of a group share an underlying ideology even while they strive to express themselves individually (2000, 59). Indeed, while the expressive culture of psychobilly is somewhat heterogeneous, it is driven by the same ideology: a shared carnivalesque desire to resist norms, reject mainstream commercial fashion, and refuse to be disciplined by rules about appearance. Psychobillies may choose elements from a variety of sources to fashion their particular sartorial style, but whatever they choose will generally shock non-subculturalists. Individuals assemble their own style through syncretic bricolage, drawing on the expressive elements of Teddy Boy, rockabilly, punk, goth, and skinhead subcultures, mixing and matching brothel creepers, drape suits, pegged pants, Dr. Martens boots, fishnet stockings, bleached jeans, flight jackets, Fred Perry shirts, Mohawks, pompadours, quiffs, studded belts, plaid suspenders, miniskirts, overalls, band T-shirts, piercings, tattoos, and more. The resulting mix, though heterogeneous, nevertheless represents a type of "anti-fashion" that is "explicitly contrary to the fashions of the day" (Fischer 2015, 48). Psychobillies trouble hegemonic expectations, refuse commercial fashion, and defy societal restrictions as they pierce, tattoo, and express their subcultural identity through their bodies. As Kat told me, "I started to dress as I felt comfortable because I liked very strange and very exotic things. Colored hair is an important part that makes you 'different' from the rest. I enjoy it, and of course it is a form of expression, because although psychobilly has no social or political ideology, it is a form of rebellion that has to do with being free and living or doing whatever you want."

One of the most illuminating experiences of my fieldwork was watching the upper-class tourists—who had come to vacation on the beautiful beach in Pineda de Mar, Spain—encounter thousands of psychobillies who flooded into the small resort town for an annual weekend festival. I could sense the anxiety and apprehension of the tourists as they held their purses tight, crossed to the other side of the street to avoid the psychobillies, and turned away from restaurants when they saw too many unconventional people inside. They had nothing to worry about; over the twenty-five years that the festival has been held in Spain, there has never been an incident between members of the subcultural community and the tourists vacationing there. But the tourists' reactions served to remind me that "squares" are still threatened by psychobillies' subcultural style, and that this makes psychobillies particularly happy. Their commitment to testing society's expectations about normalcy may not be framed as a "political" goal, but they nevertheless derive a sense of pleasure from expressing their difference from the mainstream. Indeed, Steve Young encouraged fans to come to a Surfin' Wombatz gig by posting to Facebook: "It's not a psychobilly club, so you might get to frighten some straights too! *Now* don't you want to come?!"

Concluding Thoughts: Psycho Therapy

In *Resistance Through Rituals*, CCCS scholars suggest that subcultures "win space for the young: cultural space in the neighbourhood and institutions, real time for leisure and recreation, actual room on the street or street-corner" wherein they can enact a response to the material conditions of their lives (Clarke et al. 1976, 45). This chapter has focused on how psychobilly venues, such as carnival festivities, have provided spaces for subculturalists to perform their rejection of hegemonic culture and have fun while doing so, momentarily escaping their frustrations and anxieties. But some scholars have wondered whether subculturalists ever really "win" that space. For instance, Sarah Thornton argues that venue owners are the ones who win once they identify certain groups as "profitable markets" and "promote and advertise to both 'rebellious' and 'conforming' youth" (1996, 25). She points out that "marketing is most successful when youth feel they have 'won' it for themselves" (25). This recalls Eagleton's (1981) and Stallybrass and White's (1986) critiques of Bakhtin's idealistic celebration of carnival's transgressive potential. Are subcultural venues like carnival merely spaces of "licensed rebellion"? Are the elite "allowing" the working class to release their tensions and momentarily *feel* powerful, so that the status quo can be restored after they have "worked rebellion out of their system"? Even those CCCS theorists who so celebrated the heroic resistance of subcultures worried that rebellion would be incorporated into the popular market and that styles would become only "symbolically" resistant, doing nothing to change the class system that subordinates the working class (Clarke et al. 1976, 47–48; Hebdige 1979, 94–96). As Keith Kahn-Harris notes, many scholars have argued that transgression can effectively "be assimilated to the point where it is no longer transgressive" (2007, 158).

Are subculturalists duping themselves, believing they are agents of their own lives, actively resisting hegemonic culture, while in actuality their dissent is commodified and/or prescribed? Do psychobilly events sequester away working-class expressions of resistance to the dominant paradigm and allow for their release in small doses, preventing the possibility for "real" revolution? These questions seem to suggest that anything less than a full revolution is false consciousness and that the containment of transgression is accomplished. However, as noted in the Introduction, Shane Greene

(2012) and Ross Haenfler (2016) encourage rethinking our understanding of subcultural resistance. In this paradigm, psychobillies' refusal to obey hegemonic expectations disrupts the system, demonstrating that hegemony is not complete as long as subculturalists find places to enact their own alternative values and reject dominant ones. They construct a counterhegemonic world in which they resist the norms, expectations, and regulations of dominant culture. They break taboos through their celebration of the grotesque body, refuse rules of self-control and bodily discipline through their wrecking and drinking, and reject commercial fashion and conventions about the body through their pastiche of subcultural styles and alternative body modifications. And these transgressions do threaten the social order, as we have seen: authorities have attempted to censor and ban their performances, the press has labeled them as folk devils, and "squares" are visibly frightened by their shocking appearance.

While it is important to recognize the resistance to hegemonic culture that psychobillies express, we should not dismiss the significance of carnivalesque performances as vehicles for improving the *personal* lived experiences of marginalized individuals. Letting themselves go from norms of social control and self-control through alcohol, wrecking, and celebrations of the body's grotesque realities can produce feelings of ecstasy, or jouissance. As Simon Frith writes, "A party matters most, of course, to those people who most need to party" (1981, 245). Having fun is therapeutic, as suggested by the names of one radio show, *Psycho Therapy*, and P. Paul Fenech's and Nigel Lewis's first band, Rock Therapy. The fostering of a sense of community—as participants revel in their grotesque bodies, surrender themselves to the communal wrecking pits, and identify with one another subculturally through their style—can further heighten feelings of well-being, inclusion, and acceptance, antidotes to the alienation or frustration they feel in the everyday world.

These joys are ultimately why psychobillies participate. As an example, one day Dawn posted an update on her Facebook status that she was "feeling tired," "trying to remain positive in a world of negativity has me feeling like I've been put through the ringer and hung out to dry." I saw her at a local show that weekend and asked how she was feeling. With a huge smile on her face she replied, "Oh, I'm great now, of course!" She jerked around the wrecking pit, laughed as her boyfriend showed off his silly take on psychobilly style (a nonconformist among nonconformists if there ever was one), drank several tall cans of beer, and took several shots with her friends who were on stage. Radarmen, one of the bands that night, dedicated a song to the crowd, shouting, "Tough week at work? Here's one for the working class!," and the wrecking pit came to life. Later that month I touched base with another interlocutor, Richard, a soldier who had returned from Afghanistan and was struggling with post-traumatic stress disorder. Via Facebook messenger, I listed the bands that were coming through town to see if he would be interested in attending any of the shows. Richard responded that he was interested in seeing Rezurex and wrote back, "I try to make it to town weekly for therapeutic reasons, and this looks like as good of therapy as anything!" His response seemed to get at everything at once: the physical exertion in the wrecking pit, the drinking, the over-the-top performances on stage, the social identification with like-minded individuals, and the expression of resistance to norms were all therapeutic. By seeing Rezurex, he himself would feel resurrected.

Psychobilly events allow Dawn, Richard, and many of my other interlocutors to release some of the frustrations they feel as members of the social and economic underclass. In that carnivalesque space where "anything goes," they can abandon themselves to feelings of ecstasy and indulge in a sense of freedom. In this alternative world, they escape attempts to control their bodies, behaviors, interests, and choices. They defy "normative" expectations and enjoy momentarily inhabiting a world where they are not constantly reminded of their position on the lowest rung of the social order. Events are important not only as an *expression of* psychobillies' defiance of the bodily discipline and socioeconomic hierarchies that frustrate them about the world they live in, but as a way of *coping with* those frustrations. As Frith argues, we should not ignore the meaningful significance of the "politics of pleasure" that "defies the mundane, takes us 'out of ourselves,' puts us somewhere else" (1996, 275). Rather than representing a "helpless flight" from reality, as Adorno and Horkheimer suggested ([1947] 2002), there is value in the creation of an alternative space, a utopia, where subcultural parameters are defined, anxieties are released, and pleasure is embodied through playful transgression of mainstream norms. Perhaps this is why one festival was advertised on Facebook with the line: "Buy your ticket to paradise!"

The Klub Foot served as a home for experimentation with these transgressive practices and therapeutic parties for six years. Having withstood years of psychobilly wrecking, the Clarendon Hotel was demolished in 1988, ironically by a *wrecking* ball. Given the impending destruction of the building, the final Klub Foot events took carnivalesque abandon to an extreme. Nigel Lewis of The Meteors reminisces:

> Basically the atmosphere was anything goes. It was complete chaos in there. It was brilliant. People running around spitting fire, especially when King Kurt were playing. You know it was just madness, but

because nobody cared because it was going to get knocked down anyway. You didn't even have to like anything that was going on, as long as you liked getting drunk and seeing people make fools of themselves or making a fool of your own self. That was great. (Decay 2004)

The destruction of this space where subculturalists were able to break taboos and resist hegemonic norms dealt a significant blow to the developing psychobilly subculture. Many British psychobillies were left without a central place to express their transgression of normative culture in person, but they found other ways to subvert hegemonic expectations. As the next chapter explores, lyrics became increasingly carnivalesque during the "second wave" of the subculture's growth, providing fans with ways to *imagine* transgressing norms that they could not cross in real life.

THE POWER AND PLEASURE OF FANTASIZING ABOUT MONSTERS, MURDERERS, AND MADNESS

He was born with an error in his brain
A little devil lives inside his head
Some people call him mad, some call him insane
He can only be satisfied by the sight of blood and dead
He was born with an error in his brain
He was only nine when he bought his first knife
And that the end of his brother's life
He killed his sister because she called him mad
Two years later he killed his mom and dad

—NEKROMANTIX, "Brain Error," *Hellbound*, 1989

As Adam and I sat down to enjoy our pizza at a bustling Italian restaurant, I asked him about his favorite psychobilly songs. He immediately recalled the first time he heard "Brain Error," a song released on Nekromantix's debut album, *Hellbound* (Tombstone Records, 1989). "It just clicked," he said. "At that point, I fell in love with Nekromantix." He explained: "As a kid, I fucking loved zombies. I loved all the spooky shit, you know?" For him, psychobilly lyrics about horror-related topics were "fun and campy, if done right." After we finished our pizza, we walked down the block to a Halloween-themed store in Burbank that is open year-round. It was one of Adam's favorite stores, and he knew I would love it. He was not wrong. Like many of my interlocutors, I look forward to October all year, and my attic is stuffed with boxes upon boxes of Halloween decorations. It was probably because of my obsession with Halloween that I was intrigued by the subculture when I discovered it, like many of the psychobillies I interviewed. As demonstrated in Chapter 1, The Meteors established the subculture's association with macabre lyrics when they rebelled against rockabilly clichés (cars, clothes, dancing on Saturday night), singing instead about science fiction and horror themes borrowed from B movies, literature, and folklore. As the subculture spread, few bands strayed from the "psycho-standard themes such as horror, graveyards, getting pissed [drunk] and mental patients," as Craig Brackenridge notes (2007, 28). Lyrics today are still replete with references to the undead, serial killers, and characters from a variety of horror and science fiction movies, and the sartorial and graphic style is characterized by devils, bats, rats, skeletons, skulls, spiders, and coffins. Band names such as Torment, Coffin Nails, Nekromantix, Skitzo, Coffin Draggers, Spellbound, Bloodsucking Zombies from Outer Space, Zombie Ghost Train, The Hellbillys, and The Mutilators reflect the genre's fascination with dark topics.

Almost without exception, my interlocutors suggested that they liked psychobilly specifically because of their interest in horror movies, particularly classic ones from the 1950s or campy B movies. The genre's horror-influenced lyrics drew Pammy to the subculture: "I love horror, B movies, sci-fi, usually the older stuff. I've always had a dark sense of humor and a fascination with horror and the macabre. . . . So, when I was introduced to psychobilly, it was instant fireworks. It just fit me. It was all my favorite stuff. Horror, humor, and rock 'n' roll, and for the first time in my life, I felt like I actually fit somewhere." When I asked Enid if she was drawn initially to the way the music sounded or what the songs were about, she replied: "I love horror stories and generally weird stuff. I was hooked on *Addams Family* reruns and stuff like that as a kid. So I love that campy-creepy element of the subculture. The overall sound, lyrics included, is still the main appeal for me. That's what keeps me hooked."

Why do psychobillies tend to be fans of horror narratives or macabre themes? And how are these topics reworked in psychobilly songs in ways that listeners identify with and enjoy? This chapter explores the emphasis on monsters, murderers, and madness, particularly during the "second wave" of the subculture's development in the mid- to late 1980s and into the 1990s, to understand the power and pleasure that psychobillies derive from listening to songs about these topics. I argue that these lyrics represent a response to disempowerment, providing a way to express their experiences of marginalization and imagine an alternative world, one in which they are in control. These lyrics extend the carnivalesque utopia that psychobillies construct and experience at events, but this one takes things even further by creating fantastical scenarios of counterhegemonic behavior. As Chapter 2 demonstrates, events allow psychobillies to rebel against the social order, resist norms, break taboos, and indulge in the grotesque body through performative behavior; here I consider how song lyrics allow listeners to *imagine* transgressing societal expectations in ways they cannot in real life. I draw on the work of scholars of horror films and heavy metal music to argue that psychobillies do not actually want to engage in the scenarios they imagine. Rather, the songs reflect their subcultural interest in shocking society's moral compass and resisting hegemonic culture by celebrating that which is normally considered profane, grotesque, repressed, disreputable, and nonconformist: both horror movies and the monsters featured in them.

The "Dark Ages" of the Second Wave: As Clubs Go Dark, the Lyrics and Music Get Darker

My interlocutors often described the late 1980s and early 1990s as the "dark ages" or the "ice age" of psychobilly. According to several of my British interviewees, the explosion of the rave scene in the late 1980s prompted widespread licensing legislation that made it much more difficult to foster a live-music-based subculture. Dan Sicko explains: "As the rave movement reached critical mass in the United Kingdom, . . . the British government . . . passed licensing legislation that in effect prohibited ravers' mass gatherings, forcing the remaining diehards to roam the countryside in nomadic packs" (2010, 82). This wave of new legislation triggered the closure of many struggling establishments, including the epicenter of the psychobilly scene, the Clarendon Hotel, home of the Klub Foot, in 1988. Like rave organizers, some enterprising psychobillies in the United Kingdom attempted to work around these restrictions and maintain the scene by producing festivals outside the city, all-dayers such as The Night of the Long Knives (which ran from 1988 to 1990) or weekenders like the Hemsby Psychobilly Weekend (which debuted in 1990 and was later renamed the Hemsby Big Rumble). These festivals were often hosted in relatively isolated vacation spots where fans could enjoy their loud and rebellious music free from the regulations imposed on live music in the city. Chip Waite and Craig Brackenridge remembered attending these weekenders, renting chalets and camping in trailers during the "off" season:

> Craig: First it was like chalets—they were more like bunkers, like concrete square blocks with just like two bedrooms and a lot of leg room and a toilet. And then you moved further down the

road to caravans. But that's the funny thing, there was so much more damage in the caravans because people went crazy. And you could get one for just about ten pounds and then just wreck the place.

Kim: So people would caravan to the Hemsby Rumbles?

Craig: It was a British thing. It was a camp. So everything was there. You didn't have to take anything. It was like static caravans.

Kim: And that's where they'd do those weekenders? In campgrounds?

Craig: It's an old British working-class thing. Normally, fifty-one weeks of the year it would be mom, dad, the kids. They'd go and play bingo. There would be like Tom Jones look-a-likes singing and maybe a magician or something. And then once a year they would clear them all out and just flood in psychobillies.

Chip: It was usually winter season. Dark.

Craig: Shit times of the year when normal people wouldn't go on holiday.

Chip: But they seem to have gone to the warmer parts now. Hemsby [now a rockabilly weekender] was like two weeks ago in the summer, right?

Craig: The rockabilly ones have always been a safer bet. They're always going to pull a bigger audience, so they can probably afford to pay for a summer weekend. Whereas psychobillies, what have we got? The shit when nobody wants to go. "October's free? OK, we'll take it!"

Kim: So the organizers would rent out the whole campground?

Craig: Yes, it was three days, it was just you and your mates.

While weekenders allowed psychobillies to see live performances in the United Kingdom a few times a year, the loss of regular, weekly gigs took a toll on the scene. Pip Hancox of Guana Batz remembers the dramatic decline in attendance at U.K. psychobilly shows in the late 1980s and early 1990s:

The scene had moved on, almost overnight it seemed to us, and there was obviously no place for psychobilly in a world where things like the indie-dance revolution and grunge were holding sway. Guana Batz stuck at it as best we could. We discovered we still had a lot of support abroad and toured in new territories like Japan, which gave us a second life of sorts. After we made our last LP in 1990, *Electra Glide in Blue*, we gave up on the UK. We'd pulled audiences of 2,000 during Klub Foot days but by then we could barely draw 200 in London. It was dead. (quoted in Peacock 2015, 38)

With fewer opportunities to perform, young British fans were not as likely to form their own bands. Why start a group if there was no place to play or no crowd?

According to many of my interlocutors, psychobilly was only saved from extinction by the enthusiasm of musicians and fans in continental Europe, an area that first-wave bands had been touring since the early 1980s. Steve Whitehouse, who toured mainland Europe first with The Sharks (whose members split up in 1983) and then with Frenzy, remembered how the subculture spread across the channel:

> We were doing gigs in Holland. That was the biggest scene outside of the U.K. in the early '80s. We occasionally tripped just into the border of Germany. One club in particular was called the Arrata Club in Moers, which was literally just inside the border. We noticed that people were coming in coach loads from the rest of Germany, so we knew that it was going to start to grow. We started to grow into France, and all those kinds of places. Obviously Switzerland, Italy, and then it was throughout the whole of Europe.

Germany's centralized location made it a hot spot for well-attended weekenders such as the International Psychobilly Festival in Hamburg, which debuted in 1985. As European youth were able to see the bands who had developed the subculture, they were inspired to create their own groups. *Psycho Attack over Europe*, a compilation that was issued annually from 1985 to 1993 on the Dutch label Kix 4 U, showcased the development of continental bands, including Batmobile from Netherlands, Voodoo Dolls from Sweden, and P.O.X. and Sunny Domestoz from Germany. By the end of the decade, Mad Sin from Germany (formed in 1987) and Nekromantix from Denmark (formed in 1989) had become leading figures in the European psychobilly scene.

Many of these bands borrowed more deeply from punk and heavy metal than first-wavers had done, exploring heavier sounds and faster tempos, while their lyrics amplified the genre's penchant for horror-based subjects. These aspects were typical of what came to be known as the "second wave" of psychobilly's development. Most fans feel that the second wave began with the release in 1986 of Demented Are Go's album *In Sickness and in Health*, which introduced breakneck speeds, louder volumes, insistent rhythms, heavy metal–influenced guitar work, and the increased use of distortion.[1] Due to lead singer Sparky's growling vocal style, fans thought he sounded like a "chain-smoking demon fighting laryngitis with whiskey" (Partridge 2015). He established an even more "depraved" style of singing, and the

Figure 3.1. Demented Are Go in a pose that fits the group's theatrical style, which many fans believe inaugurated the "second wave" of psychobilly and increased the genre's penchant for horror, gore, and sexual depravity. (*Used with permission from Dirk "The Pixeleye" Behlau [photographer].*)

band's songs about sexual perversion and mentally disturbed murderers took the genre's unconventional and shocking lyrics to new heights. Sparky's performances also established a precedent for gory and gruesome theatrics. Using prosthetics, stage makeup, blood (real or fake, it is difficult to tell), and props such as oversized hypodermic needles, Sparky often appears as a reanimated murder victim who has been committed to a mental institution, where science experiments are performed on him by Dr. Frankenstein (see Figure 3.1). Inspired by Demented Are Go's gritty and heavy sound; growling vocal style; over-the-top subject matter; and theatrical, horror-influenced performances, bands throughout Europe explored new directions. Some first-wavers disapproved of the changes in the musical style, feeling that psychobilly had lost some of its "billy" heritage. As one musician lamented to me: "It became more about that grunge rockabilly, gorebilly, and zombie makeup. Really, really heavy guitars. . . . Everyone wanted to sound like Sparky from Demented."

By 1990, when Nekromantix played a German psychobilly festival, the second wave was in full swing, as Kim Nekroman remembers:

> At that time, psychobilly had already existed for like, ten years. But this was like a kind of new generation, even harder than before. We had no taboos. We took everything from metal to whatever and somehow, people from different subcultures said, "Oh, this is cool. There's no rules here." People outside the scene, they enjoyed our music and came to our concerts and everybody was having a good time. ("Nekromantix" n.d.)

In 1992 Kim Nekroman debuted his first coffin bass, an upright bass made from a real child's coffin, further signifying the subculture's investment in the macabre, as also demonstrated by the titles of the albums Nekromantix released in the 1990s: *Hellbound* (1989), *Curse of the Coffin* (1991), *Brought Back to Life* (1992), and *Demons Are a Girl's Best Friend* (1996). Exemplifying the heavier sound of the second wave, *Brought Back to Life* earned a Grammy nomination for best heavy metal album. Thus, while many first-wave bands had already sung about monsters, murder, and madness, the second wave increased the subculture's association with these topics and included music that sounded darker, grittier, faster, and more growly.

Symbolizing Oppressive and Abusive Power

The predominance of horror narratives in psychobilly songs, both of the campy and graphic variety, raises questions about why listeners have been so fascinated with these stories, both in horror films and in the musical genre. According to many scholars, horror films entertain us because they allow us to reflect on evil in our world, cathartically working through our fears. Cynthia Freeland, for example, writes: "Horror films have appeal because they continue a lengthy tradition of making art, addressing human fears and limitations, forcing confrontations with monsters who overturn the natural order—of life and death, natural/supernatural, or human/nonhuman. They depict vivid threats to our values and concepts, our very bodily and mental integrity" (2000, 273). Like horror movies, songs can offer psychobillies a way to reflect on the things that they find frightening, fearsome, frustrating, and threatening in their lives. Narratives of feeling trapped, tortured, and terrified by monstrous creatures, for example, can metaphorically represent experiences of socioeconomic marginalization, oppression, stigmatization, and other challenges psychobillies face. Consider "Hellbound" by Nekromantix (from *Hellbound*, 1989), in which the narrator imagines being tormented by the evil Cenobites from Clive Barker's movie *Hellraiser*:

> *Night after night they were torturing me*
> *They were mean, bad, as cruel as they could be*
> *Hooks in chains tearing apart my skin*

The torment that the narrator is forced to endure could symbolize the struggles that many psychobillies face and the sense of powerlessness they feel. Similarly, The Creepshow's song "Buried Alive" (from *Run for Your Life*, 2008) expresses many psychobillies' sense of desperation:

Now it feels like I'm six feet underground
The ceiling's caving in
The walls are falling down all around me
I'm six feet underground
So suffocated it feels like I'm buried alive

Sarah Blackwood, the songwriter, told me: "I wrote the lyrics of that song about some friends that were going through a hard time struggling with drugs and addiction." The bleak tone and sense of desperation could resonate with psychobillies facing an array of challenges or frustrations.

Ryan Moore suggests that in heavy metal, "social forces of power and destruction are envisioned as inhuman or supernatural beings that cannot be comprehended, much less resisted, by ordinary human beings" (2009, 147–148). He argues that working-class heavy metal fans wanted to convey their sense of powerlessness but did not know whom to blame for their socioeconomic marginalization: "They knew they were screwed, but it was hard to articulate why" (156). Accordingly, they represented social power as monsters and evil creatures, expressing "the sense of being at the mercy of processes that are absolute and overwhelming in their consequences, yet invisible and impersonal in their origins" (147). Likewise, psychobilly songs such as "Hellbound" and "Buried Alive" provide a way for listeners to express their frustrations with life, identifying as the victims in these narratives (as in horror movies), oppressed by supernaturally powerful monsters or unseeable forces. Mark Robertson of The Meteors, for example, pointed out to me that the songs his bandmate Nigel Lewis wrote were often metaphors about real-life tragedies:

> Mark: Nigel has always had this thing about standing up for people
>   that get a shit deal in society. . . . "My Daddy Is a Vampire"—
>   which was the first Nigel song on the album—is about domestic
>   abuse because he had a friend, and the father would come home
>   at night and beat the wife up. My daddy is a vampire. He works
>   the night shift.
> Kim: So, it's metaphorical.
> Mark: It is. You know, the blood comes seeping through—he was
>   beating—so, Nigel is trying to tell a story about domestic violence.

These songs are thus not unlike horror movies that, as Freeland suggests, "offer hints of real-life, and not wildly fictive, kinds of evil: problems like child sexual abuse, scientific hubris, racism, or corporate greed" (2000, 3). In horror films, she argues, "modern evil is often characterized as indifference to suffering" (3). These narratives resonate with psychobillies, who re-create them in songs, personifying (or "monsterifying") the power structures and situations that inhumanely threaten their health, happiness, and sanity.

Ryan Moore suggests that one way of fighting back against such abuses of power is to imagine "harness[ing] supernatural forces as sources of resistance and empowerment" (2009, 148). He observes that Black Sabbath's song "The Wizard," for instance, offers a fantasy "about magical forms of resistance against demonic evil. The wizard causes the 'demons' to 'worry' and thus brings forth 'joy,' even making people 'happy'" (148). So, while heavy metal listeners might on the one hand express their disillusionment by identifying as the victims of a demonic beast, on the other they might also imagine using supernatural or superhuman powers to fight back against the evil forces that threaten their lives. In the same manner, while some psychobilly songs represent a sense of hopelessness and fear, other songs flip the narrative. In these pieces, psychobillies imagine being the perpetrators of violence; they have the power in these scenarios.

Identifying with Nonnormative and Deviant Characters and Monsters

Before looking more closely at how psychobillies fantasize about empowerment by imagining themselves as "undead, unfriendly, and unstoppable" (the title of an album by The Meteors), it is important to understand how and why they tend to identify with the villains in filmic and musical narratives. In "An Introduction to the American Horror Film" ([1979] 2004), film scholar Robin Wood suggests that our society is marked by "surplus repression": "the process whereby people are conditioned from earliest infancy to take on predetermined roles within that culture" (108). The repression of certain desires or behaviors is designed to make us "(if it works) into monogamous, heterosexual, bourgeois, patriarchal capitalists" (108). That which threatens the status quo—namely female sexuality, the proletariat, other cultures, ethnic groups, alternative ideologies, non-heterosexual relationships and identities, and children—is repressed through overt or internalized oppression (109). The monsters in horror films, Wood argues, represent these "Others" (111–115); in the traditional narrative, "normality is threatened by the Monster" (117).

Wood's theory helps to explain why many psychobillies are interested in horror movies: rather than wanting to preserve normality, they identify with the monsters, the nonnormative, the "Other," the threat to society. Having been labeled "deviants" (Becker 1963; Stanley Cohen 1972), psychobillies empathize with the stigmatized monsters featured in these films, as interviewees often told me. For instance, Aaron drew a connection between his "weird" psychobilly identity and the "freaks" in horror films:

Kim: Why do you think horror is something that psychobilly musicians, when it was starting, kind of latched onto?

Aaron: I think there's something relatable about monsters, like the
freaks of society, the misunderstood, the underdogs. A guy like
me can watch *Frankenstein* and it's like: "This guy who looks
weird and everybody's terrified of him," or whatever, and you're
like: "I'm kind of that guy. Nobody's gonna understand me."
They're going to have their preconceived notion of just like, "this
guy's a weirdo, try to avoid him," stuff like that. And you're not
really getting to know the person [the weirdo, Frankenstein's
monster], who is obviously learning and trying to understand
everything, but nobody's giving them really a chance. So with
psychobilly, it's like you've got these people who look really
weird. You're at work and you get all these people who are saying
stupid shit like "on fleek" and then you get this other guy, you
know like me, where I have an unusual haircut and I listen to
songs about dudes dressing up like zombie transvestite drug
users. . . . So basically, working in an environment where you
want to have tattoos or you want to have a haircut a certain way,
but people are telling you, "that's weird, you gotta be like us" and
everything. That's why I identify with psychobilly, 'coz there's all
these weirdos who are misunderstood like me.

He went on to explain that he was told to shave off his quiff at work, without
hot water, shaving cream, or a mirror, or else be fired immediately. He was
frustrated that he had to "play the game" in order to keep a job. He was not
allowed to "be himself" at work, and he felt he was punished and treated
unfairly for being different from the other employees. He explained that this
is why he often identifies with the monsters in horror films and in psychobilly
imagery: he feels misunderstood, different, "Other," abnormal.

Feeling like an alienated outcast is a topic frequently discussed on psychobilly Facebook groups. Several conversations have been initiated by a fan
who feels like the lone freak in their community, particularly in more rural
areas. One member posted, "Is anyone located in Wisconsin? I just moved
here and people stare at me like I'm an alien, lol [laughing out loud]." Another member responded with a similar experience: "I'm in Minnesota / North
Dakota and people stare/talk to me as if I came in a ufo [*sic*]." The original
poster replied, "I know, some lady stared at me the whole bus ride." As discussed in the previous chapters, psychobillies celebrate their nonconformity
and often revel in the discomfort that "squares" feel around them. The Facebook group users were not complaining because they wanted to be *less* dif-

ferent from the norm but because they wanted to find others who were as different as they were. This is further demonstrated by the regularity with which a particular meme appears on the Psychobilly Worldwide discussion board. A screenshot from *The Addams Family* shows a very bored looking Morticia and Gomez Addams with the text: "When you're forced to hang with regular people." Responses to the meme demonstrate how psychobillies identify, and proudly so, with this sense of "otherness":

> "I'm an expert at faking it now thanks to school events and work. Looking around at the other parents at school functions are [sic] the worst!"
> "This was me at my kids [sic] cross country meet yesterday. One of these things is not like the other!"

The terms "freak," "lunatic," "sicko," and "weirdo" are often used within the scene to address each other fondly, as a post about an upcoming festival demonstrated: "Can't wait to see all you lunatics next weekend at the Big Rumble!" Some psychobilly events are even advertised as "Freaks Night." One member of the Psychobilly Worldwide Facebook group posted, "I'd rather be a unique freak than a boring stereotype."

Psychobillies generally feel that their difference from the norm is stigmatized, like the "evil" creatures and characters in horror movies. Not surprisingly, they identify with songs that embrace and describe nonconformity. One Psychobilly Worldwide member posted a YouTube link to a video of The Sharks performing their song "Sideshow Freak" (from *Sir Psycho*, 1996) with the caption, "The Sharks playing a song about me." The song directly references the feelings of difference that many psychobillies expressed to me:

> *Well I travel around in a painted truck*
> *I'm three feet tall and short on luck*
> *I got tattoos all over my skin*
> *You gotta pay to get in*
> *I go from town to town, state to state*
> *Just gettin' by and workin' late*
> *Scaring kids, when I'm in the mood*
> *'Cause I'm a side-show freak with a bad attitude*
> *(He's just a side-show freak) I'm a side-show freak!*
> *(Yeah he's a side-show freak) I got a bad attitude*
> *(He's just a side-show freak) That's what it says on my passport*
>   *ma'am!*

Figure 3.2. The Surfin' Wombatz 2017 album, *Menagerie of Abominations.* The cover depicts psychobillies as monsters, reflecting their identification as the "freaks" of society. (*Used with permission from Alan Wilson [Western Star Records and Department X Publishing] and Steve Young [Surfin' Wombatz].*)

(Now don't you point your finger at him, it's rude) I'm just a side-show
*   freak with a bad attitude*
I drive a six inch nail in the side of my head
The kids all scream as my blood runs red
I'm your fire-eatin,' mother-fuckin' fantasy
but I'm sick of people staring at me

Similarly, The Quakes' song "Psychobilly Jekyll and Mr. Hyde" (from *The Quakes*, 1988) describes how the narrator turns into a radically different person when listening to psychobilly:

The guitar twangs and the drums it bangs
My teeth turn into long white fangs
I told you I was normal but man I lied
Cause I'm psychobilly Jekyll & Mr. Hyde

The cover and title of the Surfin' Wombatz 2017 album *Menagerie of Abominations* further reflect the identification with monsters and freaks (see Figure 3.2). Quiffs on a rotting zombie, deformed mutant, and swamp creature represent these monsters as psychobillies and thereby signify psychobillies' identification as "freaks of nature." These are just a few examples of how psychobillies identify themselves as various types of monsters, mutants, freaks, and weirdos, a metaphor for their subcultural nonnormativity.

Carnivalesque Fantasies of Empowerment and Jouissance

Monsters in horror movies are not just misunderstood Others, of course; they are *powerful* and *scary* Others who can threaten the social order. Michael Myers, Freddy Krueger, the gang of "lunatics" in *A Clockwork Orange*, vampires, a horde of zombies, even an unnaturally large flock of birds can threaten society and normality. Psychobilly songs often imagine what it would be like to be a menacing and frightening monster or murderer, allowing listeners to fantasize about having power, an antidote to their general feelings of powerlessness and marginality in real life.

In The Meteors' 1982 "Hills Have Eyes," for example, the narrator describes himself as a member of a group of forgotten people surviving in a postapocalyptic landscape. They become tall and strong mutants, surviving in the hills by eating rocks. They warn people passing through their land that trespassers who attempt to hurt them will pay the ultimate price; those who have already attempted to kill the mutants are now dead. In this narrative, loosely based on the plot of the 1977 Wes Craven film *The Hills Have Eyes*, the forgotten ones find a way to take control, surviving on their own and threatening anyone who comes close, a fantasy many psychobillies enjoy. Similarly, Batmobile's "Scum of the Neighborhood" (from the 1985 *Batmobile* album) imagines the Othered "scum" as violently powerful. The song describes psychobillies as a gang that terrorizes society at night, fighting with weapons and having no regard for people's lives.

This idea of a group of disliked rebels who band together to pose a threat to society is further symbolized throughout the subculture through ubiquitous references to rats, bats, zombies, "crazies," and sharks: frightening creatures that are even scarier en masse. We find these references in band names (Retarded Rats, Guana Batz, Zombie Ghost Train, The Lunatics, The Sharks), logos, songs, graphic designs, and more. Psychobillies have called themselves "The Crazies" since the early days of the subculture (Brackenridge 2007, 19). The wedge hairstyle has even been described as a "shark fin," further referencing how psychobilly style can be threatening. All of these creatures are generally hated, feared, or seen as disgusting by society, and they pose even more of a threat as a collective working together. Accordingly, psychobillies embrace these icons, not only reflecting the way they have been miscast or mistreated but also imagining the power these misfits could wield if they banded together.

Murder, specifically, is often imagined in many psychobilly songs as a way of enacting power over others. The character in "Brain Error," the song that opens this chapter, killed his entire family because he was psychopathically driven by an urge to kill. Similarly, in The Sharks' song "Charlie" (from *Phantom Rockers*, 1983), the main character uses a chainsaw to butcher a teacher who had punished him in class:

> *He ran back to the classroom, "I'll get you all," he said*
> *The teacher tried to stop him but he sliced off half his head*
> *He butchered all his classmates and just to make his day*
> *He smeared blood on the blackboard saying "Charlie rules, OK."*

The headmaster sends a note home instructing the parents: "You must point out to Charlie that what he did was bad." But we learn that "Charlie doesn't care because he's killed his Mum and Dad." Songs can also describe murderous plots of revenge against specific people who have rejected or made fun of the narrator. For example, in Nekromantix's "Graveyard of Your Memory" (from *Hellbound*, 1989), the singer addresses his ex-lover:

> *I hear you laughing, laughing behind my back*
> *but I'm following you, yeah, I'm following your track*
> *a long, long time ago you broke my heart and let me down*
> *I searched for love with you, but bitterness and hate was [sic] what I*
>   *found.*

He warns his ex: "Once you let me down, but I returned and now I'm what you ought to fear / 'cause I'm the graveyard in your memory and I wanna see you die." All of these songs convey the murderous character's need to kill and utter lack of concern for the victim. Just as The Meteors expressed in "I Don't Worry about It," as described in Chapter 1, the characters in these songs are nonchalant about their acts of violence; they show no remorse and seem unaffected by the morals that most people live by. Recall that Cynthia Freeland suggests that horror films present evil as an "indifference to suffering" (2000, 3). In these cases psychobillies imagine themselves as the perpetrators of indifferent violence, for once, rather than as the subjects of suffering.

These examples, and countless others, provide ways for psychobillies, normally quite powerless, to imagine being in power. In these fantasies, socioeconomic success and authority are meaningless. The one with the most power is the chainsaw-wielding psychopath or the ravenous zombie looking for a satisfying meal. Presented with limited opportunities to achieve success and rarely finding themselves in the position of being respected or taken seriously, psychobillies can imagine monstrous and extreme ways of feeling powerful. Consider, for instance, the responses of the members of one band I interviewed:

Kim: What type of monster do you most identify with?

Band member 1: I have to say Freddy Krueger because I'm obsessed with '80s horror movies, and Freddy Krueger is one who really scared me when I was a kid. I finally watched it again a couple years ago and I loved it. He's so twisted and has such a unique way of getting to people.

Band member 2: Maybe werewolves. That's a generalization, but they're animals, creatures, they're animalistic, and I like that.

Band member 3: I would say Nosferatu because he was such a monster. He was truly evil and wicked and quiet—because it was a silent movie—and I think that just adds to the allure. And he also has that power to make people come to him and do his bidding.

Each of the answers touched on some ability of monsters or murderers to take control of others—through their "twisted" way of scaring people, their animalistic nature, or their mysterious power over people. The band members relished the idea of turning the tables, so that they—as the Othered, the marginalized, the stigmatized—would have some way of experiencing a rush of power and control over others. It is not surprising, then, that psychobillies often post a meme on the Psychobilly Worldwide Facebook page that asks others: "You are on a psychotic killing spree. What song is playing during the slaying?" The diverse responses attest to the number of psychobilly songs that envision narratives about killing people, reversing the feelings of powerlessness psychobillies generally experience.

Torben Grodal (1997) considers how horror narratives allow people to express their "concerns about autonomy in the face of threats from within or without" (Freeland 2000, 8). Given our desire to remain in control, horror films scare us precisely because they show us what it could be like to lose control, to be the victim who is turned into a zombie, attacked by a giant monster, murdered by a serial killer, or possessed by something terrible. Most viewers watch from the perspective of the victim, Grodal argues, reinforcing our desire for control: "Fear and terror caused by cognitive dissociation and/or violence have the morally dubious advantage of creating high levels of arousal and strengthening the viewers' wish for emotional autonomy and control by aversion" (1997, 252). Many psychobilly songs reinforce this desire for control by allowing the listener to identify as the perpetrator of violence rather than the victim. Already marginalized and oppressed, psychobillies want to imagine what it would feel like to be in charge. This perspective corresponds to Robert Walser's analysis of dark fantasies in heavy metal: "In their free appropriation of symbols of power, and in their material enactments of control, of hanging on in the face of frightening complexity . . . heavy metal bands suggest to many that survival in the modern world is possible, that disruptions, no matter how unsettling, can be ridden out and endured" (1993, 159). Horror—whether in film, heavy metal, or psychobilly—reflects a desire for control.

Since psychobilly songs often imagine control through the perspective of the monster, these fantastical songs turn the world upside down, just as carnival does, as the limits and behavioral expectations by which we normally bind ourselves disappear or are flagrantly ignored. Recall that in carnival, as Bakhtin ([1936] 1984) suggests, the lower classes can pretend to have power for a day, mocking and parodying the elite while pretending to be them. By listening to these songs, psychobillies can likewise invert the normal hierarchy, momentarily imagining what it would be like to have all the power. As the characters in these songs threaten society, they break society's most sacred moral codes and expectations of civility. Listeners can imagine acting with gleeful abandon in this free-for-all, hyperfantastic carnival in which "anything goes," where they can express their repressed desires, do whatever they want, and get away with anything.[2] Envisioning a world in which monsters, murderers, and mad people do as they please allows psychobillies to resist, albeit through fantasy, hegemonic codes of behavior and social control. Through fantasies of running rampant and breaking all the rules of society, psychobillies indulge in the "evasive pleasure," or jouissance, of escaping social and self-control (Fiske 1989, 51), just as they do when wrecking, drinking, and indulging in the grotesque body at carnivalesque events. They derive pleasure from this idea "of evasion, of getting around social control, of dodging the discipline over self and others that those with power attempt so insistently to exert" (69).

The Pleasure of Undeath as a Zombie

Because zombies are such an integral part of psychobilly's canon, it is worth taking a closer look at this particular monster. Philosopher Cynthia Freeland describes the monsters of horror films as "beings that raise the specter of *evil* by overturning the natural order, whether it be an order concerning death, the body, God's laws, natural laws, or ordinary human values" (2000, 8). Zombies, especially, overturn these assumed truths, reversing death through their "undeadness," defying the natural laws of the body by continuing to "live" while decaying, and refusing to obey ordinary human values. As philosophers Richard Greene and K. Silem Mohammad point out, zombies show no trace of their former humanity:

Zombies are generally depicted as unthinking corpses that have somehow retained the ability to walk around and perform basic motor functions. They are subverbal and largely without powers of reason. When they encounter former loved ones, they register no recognition of fondness. The resemblance between the zombie and the person who occupied its body in life would seem to be only an external appearance. (2006, xv)

Thus, as Shawn McIntosh puts it, they "represent a monster that can be killed guilt-free. . . . It becomes essentially a no-brainer—zombies are evil, and we are good" (2008, 13).

Accordingly, zombies are the perfect scapegoat when people are panicked or worried about world events. Annalee Newitz notes that increased production of zombie movies "always seems to [occur] slightly after a huge political or social event has caused mass fear, chaos, or suffering" (2008). For instance, the zombies in George Romero's *Night of the Living Dead* reflect cultural anxieties that emerged out of the turbulent war and conflict of the 1960s and 1970s. As Flint argues: "The zombie . . . spoke directly to audiences who felt that civilization was collapsing around them. The apocalypse seemed close, and zombie movies, with their unstoppable, expanding army of monsters who couldn't be reasoned with or who acted without feeling or emotion, seemed to capture a feeling of mass helplessness" (Flint 2009, 7).

Many scholars have suggested that we derive cathartic satisfaction from the human survival narrative in these films: zombies are out to destroy our world as we know it; they threaten our social and economic stability; and we must survive against all odds, shooting or bashing out the brain of any zombie who stumbles our way[3] (W. St. John 2006; McIntosh 2008; Newitz 2008; Bishop 2010). Popular culture typically promotes a narrative of human victory over the zombies, symbolizing our own survival of the things we may be scared of. And if we cannot survive, most people would rather die than reanimate as a member of the dead, as philosopher Richard Greene notes:

The Undead are evil, or, at minimum, perform acts that we tend to view as evil. Vampires and zombies do unspeakable things: they eat human flesh, they drink blood, they destroy property, they maim, they kill, and they cavort with the dregs of hell. The fact that people don't like to imagine themselves doing such things serves to explain why Undeath is generally regarded as being worse than death. Most people would rather be dead than to become some monster that might potentially kill a loved one. (2006, 12)

This, he explains, reflects our philosophical understanding of the "badness of undeath." Not surprisingly, then, when he conducted an unofficial poll of his university students about their favorite monsters, he discovered that there are "a number of students who think it would be cool to be a vampire. Pretty much nobody, however, wants to be a zombie" (4). Zombies are typically understood to be the rejects of the monster world, the monsters nobody wants to be.

Except psychobillies. As *Washington Post* journalist Carrie Donovan puts it: "Take an average rockabilly song about falling in love and add a verse about how that same girlfriend happens to be undead. That's psychobilly" (1998). Zombies are among the most commonly represented monsters in psychobilly's material culture (event flyers, album covers, shirt designs, band logos, arts and crafts) as well as in song lyrics. My interlocutors talked at length about how they identified with zombies. They pointed out that zombies do not have magical superpowers or abilities; they are not portrayed as smart or elegantly dashing like vampires; and they are ugly, slow, unintelligent, disheveled, dirty, and grotesque. These characteristics of zombies mirror the ways psychobillies sometimes perceive themselves or are perceived by others (Sklar 2008, 146–147). It is no coincidence that many illustrations of psychobilly zombies show a creature with its middle finger raised to the viewer; psychobillies identify with zombies' rejection by, and of, society (see Figure 3.3).

Moreover, psychobillies reverse the normative zombie narrative: rather than reinforcing the "badness of undeath," they imagine "the *goodness* of undeath." They depict zombies as rockin' and rollin' beings who enjoy a hedonistic apocalyptic or postapocalyptic world. They do not want to kill the zombies; they want to *be* zombies. As depicted in song lyrics or artwork within the subcultural community, zombies have the time of their lives—or rather, the time of their undeaths. They do not have to deal with the disappointments, frustrations, and responsibilities that psychobillies face on a day-to-day basis. They are unconcerned with paying bills or going to work; in an apocalypse, none of that matters (Sklar 2008, 147). And they can continue to indulge in the things that psychobillies enjoy. As represented in psychobilly songs and visual culture, they dance, drink, fall in love, have sex, become rock stars, and so on. Many of my interviewees embraced the subculture's particular representation of a zombie "life" (or undeath):

Jose: "It'd be awesome to be a zombie. It's a party, a world without responsibilities, a world without rules. You can do what you want. If the bartender tries to make you pay your tab you can just eat his brains!"

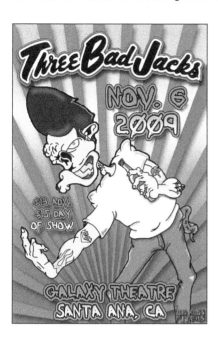

Figure 3.3. A Three Bad Jacks event flyer featuring a psychobilly zombie with middle finger raised at society. The image depicts the subculture's rejection of a society that rejects them. (*Used with permission from Rob Fatal of Big Rob's Flyers [graphic designer] and Three Bad Jacks.*)

Ben: "Zombies are badass! They are like punk rockers from hell, or rock 'n' rollers from the grave! I think we all want to be immortal. Why not live it through these sick creatures?!"

Consider the ideal afterlife described in "Dead Moonwalkin'" by Nekromantix (from *Dead Girls Don't Cry*, 2004). The protagonist stumbles upon a party of undead creatures in the graveyard and finds them dancing around a skull that has been used as a disco ball. He slowly begins to enjoy the way that female zombies and vampires interact with him and is convinced to join in on the fun. The song begins with him, alive, describing the dead moonwalkers that he sees. But by the end of the narrative, he describes himself as one of the dead moonwalkers. The character abandons his life, joining the ecstatic festivities, the fun-filled party that the dead seem to be enjoying. As is often the case in psychobilly songs, the character discovers how much more satisfying it is to be undead than alive. This narrative is explored repeatedly in psychobilly, imagining undeath as much more fun than life. After all, as Richard Greene muses, "Typically people don't desire death, unless life is bad (or at minimum, life seems bad)" (2006, 8). Why would psychobillies subscribe to the survival narrative described previously, trying to preserve life as they know it now with all its disappointments, frustrations, and limitations? Instead, they imagine a world in which they can embrace an undeath that is better than life.

Psychobilly not only romanticizes the zombie afterlife; it sexualizes it. There is a subtle sexual subtext in "Dead Moonwalkin'" as the lyrics use euphemisms to describe the narrator's sexual excitement: he's "going off" as the zombie "pulls on his leg," and the vampire drags him by "the bone." The subculture's lyrics and art often depict the pleasures of sex with or as the undead, fantasizing about a grotesque Bakhtinian carnivalesque hedonism that defies social restrictions, breaks norms of discipline, indulges in the excesses of the body, and abandons and rejects the codes of behavior expected of living people. "Nekromantik Baby" (from *Hellbound*, 1989), for instance, at first glance appears to be a song about a couple who enjoy making love in the graveyard, already reflecting a transgressive desire and sexual practice. We find out, however, that one of them is already dead, making this a much more transgressive fantasy:

Walking through the graveyard
Late at night
She's holding my hands
Oh so tight
She's making love to me
On top of the grave
There in my arms
She feels so safe
She puts me back in my grave
And goes home before daylight
But she'll be back again
For more another night
Cause she's my nekromantik baby
And she loves me so

In The Mutilators' song "I Fucked a Zombie" (from *She Put the Baby in the Microwave*, 2009), an undead girl is so alluring that a living person gives up his life to be with her. The protagonist goes to the cemetery with the intention of stopping the zombie apocalypse and putting "those god-damn zombie bastards back in the ground." After his friends are eaten, he finds that he is attracted to one of the zombie girls and "could not resist when she said 'your grave or mine?'"

Ooh, I fucked a zombie
Ooh, baby don't be sad [he apologizes to his living girlfriend]
Ooh, I fucked a zombie
She was the best I ever had

The sexy stench of rotting flesh
The grinding sounds as our bodies meshed
I "came" so quick but had to have another taste
When I saw the look of lust on what was left of her face
For a dead girl she gave me one hell of a ride
But somehow I was still not satisfied
Until I realized she could be trained
To suck my dick the way I seen her sucking on those brains

After having the best sex of his life, he decides, "She's the perfect girl for me; we're gonna settle down even though I'm six feet underground, and start a zombie family."

The sexualization of female zombies raises questions about the objectification of women in psychobilly more generally (explored further in Chapter 4), but here I use these songs to draw attention to how the subculture imagines the pleasures afforded by undeath, pleasures never depicted in mainstream zombie narratives that portray the undead as rotting, mindless bodies in search of their next meal rather than fantastic sex. Moreover, the glorification of necrophilia expresses psychobillies' nonnormative beliefs and behavior. While I never encountered anyone who actually admitted to being interested in necrophilia, many of my interlocutors *pretended* to be, enjoying the way their supposed morbid fascination shocked the squares and celebrated taboo desires. They wanted to appear to be so unencumbered by normative views about behavior and bodily control that they could enjoy sex with a member of the living dead. This contests hegemonic values, intentionally disrupting traditional norms and expressing their rejection of accepted modes of conduct.

The fantasy of an ideal zombie afterlife/undeath is not only explored in lyrics. Psychobilly events regularly invite attendees to dress up as zombies, and those who do are usually given a discounted admission price. In 2010 I attended a psychobilly show advertised as "Pub of the Dead." Riffing off the tagline from the *Dawn of the Dead* movie (1978)—"When there's no more room in hell, the dead will walk the earth"—the event flyer advertised: "Psychobilly night returns! When hell is full, the dead shall drink at Old Town Pub!" Attendees smeared their faces with white, grey, green, and black paint and artfully dabbed fake blood around their mouths. Scabby bits of prosthetic rotting flesh dripped from their faces. Band members were fully in character as well. Their makeup started to run down their faces as they sweated under the bright stage lights and from physical exertion, but that just added to their disheveled, soiled, undead appearance. This role-playing allows psychobillies to perform their version of the zombie afterlife, one in which they can hedonistically forget about their obligations, drink, flirt, and enjoy rock 'n' roll.

It is no surprise, then, that after leaving a Nekromantix show one night, I found myself following a car with the license plate "BZOMBI." By embracing this grotesque monster, psychobillies express their antimainstream sensibility and celebrate nonnormativity in carnivalesque ways. Zombies refuse to allow their bodies to be controlled and disciplined: they invert life and death, they rot away, they eat brains, and they reject human values. Just as psychobillies try to shock people through their defiant modification of their bodies, using tattoos, wild hair, and eccentric styles to express their rejection of "acceptable" fashion, they enjoy the idea that as zombies their eyes might just slip out of their skulls as they rot away, disgusting and offending "normal" people. They indulge in the thought of not being confined to rules, of being zombies stumbling around society without obeying any natural or social orders. They imagine a utopia where, as zombies, they can be everything that society rejects and represses, and they indulge in the taboo-breaking fantasy of having sex with those grotesque monsters. In short, psychobillies fantasize about how life/undeath would be so much better as zombies that subvert and transgress every societal expectation.

Celebrating Taboos, Embracing the Grotesque, and Shocking Society's Moral Compass

In her study of death metal, Natalie Purcell notes that "lyrical content should not be assumed to correlate with the beliefs of fans" (2003, 123). Death metal fantasies about gruesome scenes of murder and gore are not an indication that fans actually want to engage in these extremely transgressive behaviors. Similarly, Helen Farley points out that the members of Black Sabbath were surprised to find that some people thought they actually worshipped Satan (2009, 80). As Purcell (2003), Farley (2009), Walser (1993), and Weinstein (2000) argue, heavy metal songs about gore and perversion fundamentally serve to "shock and disgust the mainstream" (Farley 2009, 82) by *pretending* to celebrate taboo behavior. Heavy metal provides youth with a way to rebel against authority figures by embracing that which society disapproves of. As Ross Haenfler puts it: "What better way to alienate and offend adult society than to flaunt satanic images? Just as punks who wore swastikas were not necessarily Nazis, metalheads who sport inverted crosses or pentagrams are likely not actually Satanists. Satan is a symbol of rebellion and open disdain for mainstream society" (2016, 72). Natalie Purcell adds that satanic and nihilistic imagery is "simply another means of flouting a tradition, of embracing a taboo to the shock and horror of many conservative adults. Sometimes, taboos are violated simply because it is fun to shock one's parents and others" (2003, 168).

For psychobillies, part of the appeal of participating in a subculture associated so strongly with songs about murderers, monsters, and deranged individuals is that it offends many people. They embrace what society rejects, whether it is the grotesque body and its natural processes, as seen in Chapter 2, or the "evil" deeds of zombies, serial killers, and lunatics. And as also demonstrated in Chapter 2, psychobillies often derive pleasure from the transgressive nature of their carnivalesque behaviors and fantasies: it is fun to revel in that which disgusts the rest of society. This sort of "dark leisure," as Karl Spracklen argues, is representative of counterhegemonic resistance because it embraces that which has been "forbidden and controlled" (2018, 481). It is only considered "deviant" because it has been designated as such by an authority and thus "needs to be understood as being a space or activity shaped by a communicative rationality to transgress and rebel, and by the instrumentality that constrains it: the conservative, morality of the major religions of the West" (419).

Moreover, by glorifying monsters and murderers, psychobillies also validate and empower themselves, for they too are marginalized, stigmatized, and excluded. Just as the low becomes high during carnival and at carnivalesque psychobilly events, horror movies and psychobilly songs invert the natural order and critique traditional values. This negation of normative values, as Greil Marcus argues, is inherently political: "It assumes the existence of other people, calls them into being" (1989, 9) by making visible other norms, lifestyles, attitudes, personalities, and so on. Like punk, psychobilly represents "a reversal of perspective, of values; a sense that anything was possible, a truth that could only be proven in the negatives. What had been good—love, money, health—was now bad; what had been bad—hate, mendacity, and disease—was now good" (67). Some horror film scholars have suggested that the genre's humorous play with the grotesque, particularly in what William Paul calls "gross-out movies," reflects a progressive politics akin to the carnivalesque celebration of that which society represses and shuns:

> I would argue there is something creative in the desire to break down inhibitions, to move away from the repressions of our traditional society. . . . There is an underlying intent to make the private public property, to bring out into the open "closeted" prejudices as a way to destroy them. At the least, gross-out also functions as a way of bringing out into the open precisely those things we have most been inclined to repress. (Paul 1994, 45)

This corresponds to Robin Wood's theory that "central to the effect and fascination of horror films is their fulfillment of our nightmare wish to smash the norms that oppress us and which our moral conditioning teaches us to revere" ([1979] 2004, 119). For Wood, the "return of the repressed" that is symbolized by the monster allows the viewer to question normality and consider a world in which traditional values are completely upended rather than reaffirmed (128). Psychobilly songs, like horror movies, offer an opportunity to imagine a different utopia, a carnivalesque alternative that turns the world upside down, in which normative values are abandoned and all that is typically repressed or oppressed is allowed out to play.

Since horror films indulge in those things that society shuns, hides, and represses, they have been considered taboo themselves. They have been shunned and stigmatized, as Robin Wood points out: "Horror film has consistently been one of the most popular and, at the same time, the most disreputable of Hollywood genres. . . . [Films] are dismissed with contempt by the majority of reviewer-critics, or simply ignored" ([1979] 2004, 202). Horror movies and the psychobilly subculture thus both have "shock value": they are seen as a threat to society and social mores and are often condemned as low class or low quality. Of course, this taboo reputation generally only increases a fan's devotion. As Andrew Tudor puts it: "Some horror fans relish and rely upon the stigma that attaches to such officially undervalued culture" (1997, 461). For psychobilly musician Brian, the stigma of horror movies made them more appealing:

> Kim: Many of your songs revolve around horror or comedy-horror themes. Why? What's your inspiration or interest in this come from?
>
> Brian: Horror movies for me were always "off limits" by my parents. I had to get friends who had seen *Nightmare on Elm Street* to tell me what happened in the movie because I wasn't allowed to see it! So for me it was always the forbidden fruit, which only made me want to see horror movies MORE than normal. So that's definitely where the interest came from.

Thus, not only do psychobillies relish their fascination with the taboo subjects of horror movies, they also flaunt their interest in the "forbidden fruit" of the films themselves.

Further expressing their deviant and nonnormative interests, psychobillies especially celebrate nonmainstream and obscure horror movies, privileging the particularly campy and low-budget films. I conducted many interviews at a very psychobilly-friendly bar in Austin, Texas. While I waited for interviewees to arrive, I usually sat in the back where I could watch the horror movies being played on two small screens. The bar never screened big-budget films or anything I would ever have seen in a mainstream movie theater. Instead I watched low-budget Italian grindhouse movies such as *Burial Ground* (1981), "splatstick" films from the 1980s such as *Braindead* (*Dead Alive*) (1992), and cult classics such as *Return of the Living Dead* (1985) and *Army of Darkness* (1992) that may have initially achieved some commercial success but are now lambasted by many for being cheesy. Once my interviewees arrived, we would chat about the films they liked as they rattled off encyclopedic knowledge of obscure B movies of both the gory and campy varieties. Their interest in the low-budget, unpopular movies further reflected their resistance to normative and mainstream trends and identities, as suggested by my interview with Aaron and Dawn:

> Aaron: Like a cheerleader type girl, she's only going to watch the big horror movies with a bunch of her friends. She's not going to be like, "Oh have you seen this fucking movie called *The Brain*."
> Dawn: She's not going to be like a nerd who knows about the lesser known stuff . . .
> Aaron: You know, that's how psychobilly kinda goes full circle with, you know . . .
> Dawn: Just part of not being like cookie cutter, you know?

Aaron and Dawn did not *want* to like what others liked, whether music or movies. They delighted in knowing that they liked films that are generally too screwball, odd, gory, or campy to have earned mainstream success. Their specialized knowledge of movies—and music—completely beyond the average consumer's radar signified their subcultural identity. Psychobillies relish this sense of difference from "the squares," which they express through their consumption of off-beat, unpopular, and unknown movies.

In fact, it was a desire to distance themselves from the norm that inspired psychobillies to incorporate horror movie topics into their lyrics in the first place. As noted in Chapter 1, first-wavers wrote about topics from the B movies they watched as a reaction or response to the cliché stereotypes found in rockabilly music at the time. Aaron underscored the ways that the horror-based lyrics developed by original psychobillies such as The Meteors helped them express their difference from the "squares":

> Aaron: When The Meteors started, they were basically saying: "I like old school rockabilly. I love it so much. I want to [play that style

of music]. But you know what? The rest of the bands doing all this bullshit—people are talking about their nice suits, their pink Cadillacs, and my girl, and all this. We don't like that. We don't identify with that. We think it's stupid. We're working class and everything. What could we do to kind of piss these guys off and kind of stand out? What do you think we should do? Oh, we should write about how we feel this way so we're going to fuckin' be like we're teenagers from outer space, just say Zorch. You know? Like that would trip people out. So we're going to be different. We want to be like the opposite of what rockabilly is about now." That still happens, where you'll have a psychobilly band singing about horror. They'll be singing about something wacky or zany. And then you'll get like a rockabilly guy that's like "Well, I got my blue suede shoes, and I got my stuff, I got my things, and my girl."

Kim: So, like the horror themes in psychobilly help set it apart from the more traditional rockabilly purists?

Aaron: Yeah, it's like, "We're going to play these really classic [rockabilly] riffs that we grew up with it and are very influenced with, but I'm going to [sing] 'my daddy is a vampire, and my mom's a mummy.' We want you to say 'what the fuck,' but then we want all these other people to say 'hey, how's it going?'"

Kim: So it helps to sort out like who's going to just want the cliché rockabilly thing and who's down with something weirder?

Aaron: Yeah.

Thus, psychobillies' fondness for disreputable horror movies and the grotesque characters in them reflect their nonconformist, rebellious identities as well as their feelings of alienation, monstrosity, stigmatization, marginalization, and disempowerment. Since the beginning of the subculture, they have used these film references and song lyrics to mark themselves as different, shocking, and profane, expressing their rejection of mainstream trends and norms, a reaction to having been rejected by society in the first place. As M. Selim Yavuz, Samantha Holland, and Karl Spracklen argue in a special journal issue devoted to "dark leisure," a fascination with death and other taboo subjects can serve importantly, then, to express the "transgressive, liminal, and alternative" inclinations of nonconformists (2018, 391). Thus, it is necessary to emphasize "how communicative and constructive this type of [dark leisure] activity can be for individuals' and communities' lives" (393).

Concluding Thoughts: Not to Be Taken Seriously, but Still Seriously Important

Time and time again, members of the subculture reminded me that the lyrics in psychobilly songs are not meant to be taken seriously but rather as overtly, excessively, and outrageously over the top, with tongue placed firmly in cheek. Mark Robertson from The Meteors told me: "The horror side of [our lyrics] was very cartoon. 'Coz if you've seen *We're Going to Eat You* and *Madness*, both from 1980, it was all B movie." The movies they were influenced by were very campy, so the lyrics they wrote were "all very, very tongue in cheek." In an interview with a psychobilly fanzine, one of the members of Bang Bang Bazooka responded to a question about the horror references in their songs: "Well don't take it all too seriously. When writing a song you need a subject, a story to tell. The devil, demons, booze, cars, women, monsters, lunatics, clothes, shoes, etc. are always fun to write about. It's just like the movies" (*DogEatRobot Fanzine* 2013c, 9). Several of my interlocutors agreed that one of the most important things about psychobilly, including the horror aspect that defines the genre, is that it is supposed to be fun:

> Stuart: It's tongue in cheek, totally. All the songs that we write, it's never serious.
>
> Steve: Stop taking everything so seriously. Psychobilly is a lot of things but serious ain't one of them. We're all hellbound sinners, so let's have fun!
>
> Pammy: I feel like I relate to the content in the shared love for horror, humor, just wanting to have fun, saying "fuck politics, this is a song about drunk mummies" or something like that, and being different, rebellious.
>
> Dawn: The campy horror of psychobilly definitely drew me in, because I've always been a fan of horror movies. When I was growing up, my mom was always at the video store and we'd always be picking out something. It could be like the shittiest movie and she'd just talk so much shit about it, but we'd still watch it. It was fun. That's how we spent our weekends, you know, and, so hearing songs about things like that was like fun. It's really great to be able to escape from reality. And yeah, maybe it's about a horror movie or maybe it's like something stupid, you know, but it's still fun and it's still something you can relate to. I'm not a serial killer, obviously, but it's something that

you're interested in and it's something that's kinda fun and out of reality.

My interviewees' responses reminded me of Iain Chambers's theory that subcultural participants reflexively and specifically consume popular culture for their own enjoyment: "In contrast to the anonymous drudgery of the working week, selected consumer objects provide the possibility of moving beyond the colourless walls of routine into the bright environs of an imaginary state" (1985, 17). The fantasies about monsters, murderers, and madmen allow psychobillies an escape from their real lived experience, one marked by disappointments, frustrations, and limitations. As during carnival, they can momentarily suspend reality and instead indulge in the idea of being a responsibility-free rockin' and rollin' zombie, a murderer getting revenge, or an unleashed lunatic unburdened by norms of "acceptable" behavior. The joy they derive from imagining these taboo scenarios makes the drudgery of work worthwhile.

The CCCS's tendency to romanticize only the "heroic" total revolution of the subculture's "semiotic guerilla warfare" continues to influence those who all too easily dismiss or disqualify the importance of escapist entertainment. Critics of alternative music styles often fall back on this argument when bemoaning those subcultures that lack political substance, as discussed in Chapter 2. As explored throughout this book so far, many contemporary scholars, however, consider how hedonistic escape represents a sort of "everyday politics" (Riley, Griffin, and Morey 2010). For instance, Ryan Moore "contradicts the prevailing view of heavy metal as escapist fantasy" by demonstrating that heavy metal lyrics thoughtfully critique the power bloc (2009, 148): "Heavy metal's search for mystical sources of empowerment also speaks to a profound sense of disempowerment in the social world, for it can only imagine fantastic and otherworldly methods of resistance to power" (148). Similarly, though they feel unable to change the system, psychobillies can at least imagine resisting the power structures by running wild, shirking responsibilities, and terrifying others when they are holding a chainsaw or looking for some tasty brains to munch on. These fantasies should not be written off as meaningless and merely escapist. The construction and expression of these fantasies is an important way psychobillies take control over their own lived experience. They work around the system, breaking boredom on their own terms and providing themselves with relief from oppressive circumstances. Rather than wishing to change the status quo or fight for improvement of their conditions in a system that has already failed them, they take matters into their own hands and create their own pleasure, not unlike the carnivalesque experiences at performances described in Chapter 2.

Moreover, the active process of selecting precisely how they want to create that pleasure—by consuming disreputable horror movies, seemingly identifying with and glorifying the monsters and murderers that mainstream society shuns, and imagining taboo activities such as having sex with zombies or murdering scores of people—is a further pleasure itself, the joy of distancing themselves from the "squares." By expressing their non-normative interests they refuse to become "boring." If they have to "play the game" (participate in the workforce) to afford their own leisure, at least they will consume and construct an identity that is as diametrically opposed to the norm as possible. Making their lives just a little more enjoyable, participants delight in these evasive fantasies, indulging in fun, camp, and silliness that rejects normative ideas of social discipline and embraces the unregulated behaviors associated with carnival.

I end this chapter by underscoring how many of these psychobilly fantasies about monsters, murderers, and madmen are ultimately about survival. While the normative "survival horror" narrative champions human victory, psychobillies imagine their own survival as monsters, murderers, or carefree zombies. Ultimately, these narratives are just one more example of how the subculture values the reanimation and survival of all that is rejected and discarded by mainstream society. Psychobillies have reanimated aspects of midcentury culture by reviving rockabilly, cars, and campy B movies. They keep bringing vintage culture back from the dead, just as Frankenstein's monster or a zombie comes back to life, demonstrating that these forgotten relics of the past are still capable of providing pleasure (not unlike a zombie girl in some psychobilly songs). And most important, they reanimate and resurrect themselves, the unwanted and abnormal, by participating in a genre that quite literally helps them survive. They are "Brought Back to Life," as the name of a Nekromantix song (1992) implies, by the psychobilly subculture.

MALE DOMINANCE AND FEMALE EMPOWERMENT

The Complexities of Gender and Sexuality

She's a pale looking hooker and a new shooker
That hot and sticky night
Walking down the street flashing off her meat
Trick number 69
Got her in the bed and made her give head
Was ain't no faking here
Cause she brought up back, got up my jack
The time was nearly here
I slapped her once, and slapped her twice
Put a razor right down her side
Watched the blood soak in the sheets
One less girl 'cause of me
Well trick is over, work is done
Really got off, I've had my fun
One dead hooker on my bed
Sexy bought tail is 15 per head

—Frantic Flintstones, "Necro Blues," *Take a Hike*, 1991

I n 2007 Raucous Records released *Psycho Vixens*, an album featuring only psychobilly bands that included women, such as Empress of Fur, Speed Crazy, The Creepshow, Formaldebrides, Deadutantes, The Hatchet Wounds, Thee Merry Widows, and Hellsonics. The description on the back of the record pointed out, as if it were surprising, that women were as "wild and crazy" as the men: "The international Psychobilly scene is red hot, and the girls are leading the way, showing that they can rock out just as wild and crazy as the guys. Check out *Psycho Vixens*, a killer collection of some of the best female fronted and all-girl groups on the Psychobilly scene old and new." It was only by the mid- to late 2000s, during the "third wave" of psychobilly's development, that there were enough bands with female performers to fill an album. This is why DJ Trash could say in 2010: "Psychobilly and Rockabilly has always pretty much been the domain of men. Face it, this is a fact! Songs are generally written about women and not by women or women were hangers-on in the scene and generally regarded as groupies. However, over the years there have been some notable female fronted bands rocking the scene just as good, if not better than their male counterparts" (DJ Trash 2010). The genre had been conspicuously lacking female performers throughout the 1980s.[1] It was not until more than a decade after the development of psychobilly that a female psychobilly band—The Dypsomaniaxe—moved from the wrecking pit to the stage, releasing their only album in 1992 (see Figure 2.4). Beginning around 1997, bands with female performers began to emerge at the rate of about one per year. A high point occurred in 2004, when at least four bands formed,[2] likely inspired by the commercial and crossover success of the female-fronted band HorrorPops, who released their album *Hell Yeah* in February of that year. Over the course of ten years of fieldwork, I saw only nine bands perform that featured at least one female member,[3] and, as described in this chapter, many of those bands were considered "tangential" to psychobilly. At the time of writing, I am aware of only sixteen bands that include at least one woman and still perform in psychobilly contexts.[4] While women make up about 30–50 percent of the audience at most of the shows I have attended, they are rarely found onstage performing.

This book has shown how psychobillies have found in this subculture a variety of ways to imagine and realize a better world for themselves: by rebelling against the clichés of other subcultures and creating one that is more relevant to their unique interests, by reveling in the carnivalesque escapism they enjoy at events, and by singing along with songs in which they fantasize about exerting power over others. In this chapter I explore how men have imagined and realized a better world for themselves by performing and enacting their own privilege within this subcultural context, representing women as disempowered objects for male pleasure through discourse, song lyrics, and graphic art. At the same time, I consider how women have engaged in the subculture to imagine and realize a better world for themselves by disrupting traditional performances of femininity on the one hand and expressing an empowering female sexuality on the other.

"The Boys' Club": The Exclusion of Women

There are a number of reasons female psychobillies are not commonly found onstage performing. First, there are challenges involved in learning to play instruments that have been "designed for men, by men," as Mavis Bayton observes (1997, 45). One reason for the low numbers of women in rock, she argues, is the shape and positioning of the electric guitar, which physically makes it a difficult instrument for women to play; for example, some find it uncomfortable to hold against their breasts. In psychobilly, we can apply this observation to the upright bass, the dominant instrument. The upright's bulky size and unwieldiness make it difficult for women to master. One needs to be fairly tall and strong to hold the bass steady with the left hand while standing off to the front right side of the instrument. During my first informal upright lesson, my male instructor told me: "You might have a difficult time pressing down hard enough and reaching across the neck since your hand and fingers are much weaker and smaller than a man's." While I was taken aback by his comment, I could tell he thought he was stating an obvious fact; he wasn't purposely trying to offend me. When I indicated that I wanted more lessons, he paused and finally answered that yes, he could try to teach me more, but he had never taught a woman before and might have to think up new methods designed specifically to teach a woman to play the upright.

Furthermore, many male musicians think of the curvy upright bass as having a feminine identity, and most bassists personify their instrument by giving it a female name. One member of a band posted a photo to Facebook of a bass that had been painted to look like the front and back of a woman in a bikini, with the words "I want a big fat mama" and "Slap me!" written on the side. His comment read, "Yes! This is what I want!" One bassist I know even sleeps with his bass in the bed, hugging the curves of the instrument. The physical way men slap and straddle the bass mimics a man's sexual domination of a woman. Kim Nekroman often licks the strings of his bass, straddles it on the floor and rides it, or rubs himself against it. Male musicians often simulate masturbation by running their hands up and down the neck of the electric guitar as well. Indeed, as Bayton points out, "It is not only the [guitar's phallicentric] shape which is symbolic, but also the sheer volume and attack of the instrument which connotes phallic power" (1997, 43). This sexualized symbolism may discourage women from taking up such instruments.

If women successfully struggle against these odds to learn an instrument and attain musical expertise, they often "find that the lines of exclusion are now elsewhere" (Straw 1997, 15) when they are not given entrée into the "inventories of knowledge" that are maintained by men (Whiteley 1997, xviii). Explaining the overwhelming exclusion of women from rock, Sara Cohen argues that men often control necessary resources and knowledge bases, limiting access for women, who cannot break into the "guy's club" (1997). During her observation of the Liverpool music scene, Cohen discovered that women were not encouraged to seek out rock music lessons or become involved in rock music production (1991). Rock music studios and performance spaces were male zones, often deliberately made uncomfortable for women through the pervasive use of male banter, sexual references, and chauvinistic attitudes (Sara Cohen 1991). As Sheila Whiteley points out, "the bonds which produce particular cultures (whether rock or rockabilly) are primarily homosocial, and that knowledge is highly male-centred and serves to reinforce gender boundaries" (1997, xxv).

Psychobilly men have often told me that women are really there "just to meet guys" or "show off their vintage fashion." Women internalize this exclusionary attitude and take it for granted, assuming they should not be concerned with the genre's music and history, and limiting their participation to the social realm. When I approached women for formal interviews, more often than not they responded along the lines of: "You should really talk to my boyfriend about that stuff. He's the one that knows all about the history and music of psychobilly. I don't know that much about it." As a result, as mentioned in the Introduction, all but fifteen of the interviews I conducted were with men. Women seemed to think that they were not "worth" interviewing, despite my attempts to encourage them and validate their insider knowledge.

This coding of men as the keepers of knowledge and women as mere auxiliaries or fashion accessories perpetuates gender-defined roles and barriers, making it difficult for women to include themselves in rituals of information sharing that normally take place during homosocial rites of bonding, as Will Straw suggests (1997). I personally experienced this at the Viva Las Vegas festival when I approached a U.K. record vendor to pick up a few rare rockabilly compilations. Even though I told the male vendors that I was a fan of one particular label known for its informative liner notes, they did their best to ignore me, perhaps assuming I was just there to buy clothes and meet guys. While I lingered, many male customers engaged in conversations with the vendors that lasted ten minutes or longer. Despite my attempts to interact with them, it was all I could do to get them to take my money and hand me a couple of albums. They excluded me from their boys' club, keeping privileged information out of my grasp. I sent a male friend over to the booth, and he had a cheery thirty-minute conversation with the vendors about the best bands, records, re-releases, rare covers, and so on, talking about the same record label I had tried to talk to them about.

The difficulties psychobilly women face when trying to participate on equal footing with men correspond to Robert Walser's analysis of the "exscription" of women in heavy metal. He observes that metal attempts the "total denial of gender anxieties through the articulation of fantastic worlds without women" (1993, 110). In other words, by excluding women from music videos and performances, men are allowed to breathe easy and forget about the insecurities and anxieties they have about women and relationships. In psychobilly, too, the subculture seems constructed to prevent women from being too noticeable in performative contexts; a woman-free space is ensured when only men are allowed access to privileged realms of knowledge and performance. But as previously mentioned, women make up a significant portion of the audience (I return to this later) and even some of the bands, so I now turn to a consideration of these female performers.

Female Performers as "Inauthentic" and "Pop"

If a woman manages to successfully learn an instrument, form a band, and participate in the circulation of musical and historical knowledge among men, she then faces another difficulty: the struggle to be considered "real" or "good" by members of the subculture. Female singers are often considered too "poppy" just because they are women, regardless of their individual musical style, approach, and talent. As one interlocutor told me during an interview: "I think sometimes a female voice can make the band sound too 'poppy.'" A particular thread on a WreckingPit.com discussion board (Wrecking Pit n.d.) remained active for four years as people responded to the following post: "So far I have only encountered 3 female fronted or all female psychobilly bands that I can actually enjoy listening to at any given time. It seems like alot of them don't have that great of a voice or the music just all around [sic] sucks." Respondents criticized almost every band that was suggested by users—including HorrorPops, The Creepshow, Mad Marge, Dypsomaniaxe, Kitty in a Casket, and Empress of Fur—for not being "authentic" psychobilly. For instance, one person argued that HorrorPops "are not psychobilly. It's just some bubblegum trendy ass shit. The Creepshow is the same as well as Mad Marge and the Stonecutters. There are not many *real* psychobilly bands with girls around." A female user wrote: "HorrorPops, Mad Marge and the other ridiculous stuff is just crap. I don't know which genre they play, but I'm sure that it's not psychobilly." One user finally called the critics out for not being specific about why they did not consider these bands to be "real" psychobilly. She pointed out that people might be excluding them from the psychobilly label because of the sex of the band members rather than their musical style: "I don't understand what your criteria for Psychobilly is??? Maybe they are punk bands? Or pop bands? I think the upright bass makes them fit the psychobilly genre in a lot of people's eyes. People should like a band if they like the music, not dependent on the sex of the members. I happen to respect any female artist who can take on the boys!" Another echoed this concern: "I love The Creepshow and Mad Marge. But if this isn't psychobilly, please tell me: what do you think real 'female fronted psychobilly' is?"

When HorrorPops appeared on the late-night television show *Jimmy Kimmel Live!*, the comments posted underneath the YouTube video of their performance further revealed what many psychobillies thought about the "psychobilly-ness" of the female-fronted band:

> "The band sounds too normal to be called psycho. I fell asleep while listening."
>
> "Too pretty sounding to be called psychobilly. It can maybe be called pop music with a stand up [*sic*] bass."
>
> "Oh wow, a wannabe pin up [*sic*] girl jerking off an upright bass."
>
> "This band is an embarassment [*sic*] to psycho!"
>
> "Fuckin' hell. This is NOT PSYCHOBILLY . . . this is POPA-BILLY!"
>
> "Horror*Poops*. This is pure fashion-a-billy . . . without the 'billy' word; this isn't 'billy' at all. These poops are just crappy horror-pop crap for kids."

Adjectives such as "normal," "pop," "pretty," "fashionable," and "bubblegum" act as terminological gatekeepers that critics use to prevent women from attaining the "authentic" status of male musicians, yet they make no reference to specific musical features that disqualify the band from fitting the generally acknowledged definition of psychobilly: some twangy guitar riffs, a little bit of shuffle to the rhythm, and a slappin' upright bass from rockabilly; a little speed and volume from punk; some horror themes; and an exciting and energetic performance. The performance on Jimmy Kimmel's show included all of those characteristics. These types of responses—and the lack of such heated debates about male bands' authenticity (with one exception, Tiger Army, as is discussed later)—suggest that the inclusion of women is at odds with the overwhelming masculinity of the genre.

This has resulted in the words "female" or "girl" acquiring an inherently negative connotation. When Retarded Rats, a band from Germany with two female members, was asked to close an interview with any final thoughts, they took the opportunity to tell the psychobilly community:

"Mark this well folks: we're no girlie band!" (*DogEatRobot Fanzine* 2014, 25). In 2017 a member of the Psychobilly Worldwide Facebook group started a discussion by posting that he liked the female singer Lilit Clockwork because "she does not sound like a typical female singer. She does not sound super clean and has a powerful sounding voice." In these examples, "girlie" or "female" were understood to imply "poor," "weak," or "poppy."

Debates about the psychobilly authenticity of female performers have led many to hope that fans will assess them according to their talent, rather than their gender. An interviewer asked As Diabatz: "Do you feel that people mention that you are an all-girl Psychobilly band rather than simply a Psychobilly band?" One of the members replied: "I think the fact of us being an all-girl Psychobilly band can draw more attention than normal because there are no Psychobilly bands of girls today. But we are here to make music, and this is what really matters" (Brackenridge 2008). Likewise, a contributor to the WreckingPit.com discussion on female-fronted bands observed that female musicians were doomed to be treated differently because of their gender: "Has anyone else ever noticed that most people's attitudes towards all-girl bands seem to be skewed? From my experience, it seems people think most bands tend to fall either into the "Special Olympics" camp, where they get extra credit because no one has a penis, or the "get back in the kitchen" camp, where no matter how talented a band is, they can never be good enough."

This comment reflects Bayton's findings about women who play the electric guitar: "The most general problem is simply not being taken seriously. The status 'woman' seems to obscure that of 'musician.' Female guitarists are expected to be sexy and incompetent and these expectations form a hurdle which must be coped with or combated in some way" (1997, 47). Many female psychobilly performers are aware that they will be identified first and foremost as women and may be recruited by bands as exotic female props. During my trip to the Pineda weekender, I met a female performer from Canada. While we were eating lunch one day, I talked to her about what it was like to be a female performer in the scene. She replied that she was always treated exactly as that, a woman first and a musician second: "I've been invited to be in a bunch of different bands just because I'm a girl. It's like they want me to be their token girl so that they stand out as different. But I don't want to be a puppet."

Female musicians have suggested to me that they also feel unfairly stereotyped. Sarah Blackwood, the lead singer of The Creepshow from 2007 to 2012, described to me how she faced stereotyping and felt a need to overcompensate so that the men in her band would have no reason to make fun of her:

Even if I am trying to tough it out [when I'm sick and on the road],
it still makes me seem wimpy if I complain, 'cause I am a girl and
that automatically puts me in a DIVA category. Like if the guys all
ask for no tomato on their burgers and their fries not to touch their
ketchup, it's all good. If I ask for that–which I fucking wouldn't–then
I am demanding and bitchy. So there are some challenges, but
nothing that isn't easily handled.

The Canadian performer I met at Pineda pointed out another stereotype
about female performers: "I can write music, but if you're in a band with
guys, people automatically assume the guys are writing the music." She
eventually released a solo album just to prove that she was the one writing
and performing the songs. She also found that club managers did not take
her seriously because she was female: "They always talked to the guys in the
band directly, and never even looked at me."

The preceding examples point to the various ways in which women are
not taken seriously and are considered to be "inauthentic" or "pop" on the
basis of their gender alone, regardless of their musical style or merits.
Women likely receive this treatment because underground music cultures
often "construct and maintain genre boundaries through gendered behavior
and expectations," as Ben Hutcherson and Ross Haenfler argue (2010, 117).
They explain: "Participants continually seek to establish and maintain their
authenticity, framing legitimacy in gendered terms that cast masculinity as
authentic and femininity as inauthentic. They construct authenticity by
comparing EM [extreme metal] to other genres, classifying underground
scenes as masculine and "real" and other, often more popular, scenes as
feminine and 'fake'" (117–118).

As documented by the examples already given, many psychobillies necessarily equate femininity with "pop" or commercial music, regardless of
the women's actual musical style. The subcultural tendency to code authenticity as masculine makes it particularly difficult for female players to be
taken seriously in their own right. Hutcherson and Haenfler also note that
increased participation of women in subcultural scenes often results in the
fragmentation of the genre, as veteran participants construct a space that
re-excludes women and preserves the "purity" of the original scene by reinforcing masculine ideals: "For example, soon after women became increasingly visible in the early punk scene, 'hardcore,' a stripped-down, hypermasculine punk subgenre, gained widespread popularity. Likewise, as
women's participation in rap music grew in the 1980s, gangsta rap emerged
to dominate the genre for over a decade, framed as more 'real' or 'street.' EM
[extreme metal], of course, arose alongside glam metal" (2010, 118). As glam

metal attracted women and became commercially viable, extreme metal developed as a hypermasculine alternative that excluded women. One wonders if psychobilly will fragment if more women become visible participants and performers in the scene, more than the "eye candy" they are often assumed to be today.

In her study of Balinese death metal and punk, Emma Baulch finds that participants "frequently conflated commercialization with feminization" (2007, 9). Like Hutcherson and Haenfler, she observes that bands that had too many female fans were rejected, considered to be too mainstream. Similarly, psychobilly bands that have many female fans, such as Horror-Pops, The Creepshow, Tiger Army, and Nekromantix, are accused of being too commercial. Baulch does not read this response as motivated by an "intent to subjugate women," however, but rather as "an attempt to root themselves in preexisting and stable identity discourses, such as those of masculinity (which necessarily contain discourses of domination) while they experimented with others" (9). These Balinese death metal and punk fans were already Othered, themselves, as marginalized, subcultural participants; they wanted to hold onto the one way they could feel powerful, using the dominant, hegemonic frameworks of masculinity. As I consider next, the subculture is indeed a space for marginalized male psychobillies to reinforce feelings of power by relying on traditional discourses of masculinity.

Sexualizing Women in Music, Lyrics, Art, and Discourse

Since men generally control the production of music, lyrics, and visual media, it is necessary to understand how they construct gender and desire in the psychobilly subculture before we can contextualize women's responses to such representations. One of the most common tendencies is to represent women, on stage or in lyrics, as sex objects.

Nekromantix's song "S/M" (from *Curse of the Coffin*, 1991) describes how women only exist to fulfill men's fantasies. It begins with the sounds of a woman being whipped, her sexual groans growing louder and more orgasmic over time. Then Kim Nekroman (a male performer) sings in a throaty growl over a one-bar guitar riff that repeats throughout the entire first verse, musically symbolizing the relentlessness of the flogging:

Leather sitting tight to your skin
This game we are playing is a game none of us will ever win
Woman, you're my playmate, you're my toy
I get rid of my frustrations in a way I enjoy

When the chorus begins, the guitarist chugs out chords in a sharp, staccato manner on each downbeat to evoke spanking as Nekroman cheerily chants:

> *I am a sadist with a whip, I get my kicks*
> *I like the slap beat, well yeah, I tie up chicks*
> *You're a masochist, a victim of my sexual fantasy*
> *You are my sex slave begging for orgasm*

The "slap beat" has a double meaning, for it references both the slapping of the bass and the spanking of the submissive woman.

Austin-based band Pickled Punks (now defunct) always included their crowd-pleasing cover of the children's song "Do Your Ears Hang Low" during live sets. Their version substituted "lips" for "ears," as lead singer Spike gestured to his crotch and acted out these lyrics, referring to the supposed sagging of a sexually experienced woman's labia.

> *Do your lips hang low? Do they wobble to and fro?*
> *Can you tie them in a knot? Can you tie them in a bow?*
> *Can you throw them o'er your shoulder like a Continental soldier?*
> *Do your lips hang low?*

The second verse substituted "tits" instead, while Spike cupped his hands to support imaginary breasts that hung down to his knees. Both verses imply that these are the negative consequences of being too sexually active and "used-up," ultimately making the woman undesirable. At the same time, the singer seems to enjoy the woman's sexual experience. Since only physical traits are described, the song suggests that a woman's sexuality is her main asset; once she becomes unattractive, there is nothing left for her to offer a man and she becomes fodder for mockery. He can use her up and discard her.

Like these songs, the Frantic Flintstones song "Necro Blues," which opens this chapter, conveys the narrator's quest to have sex with, and then kill, a prostitute. The woman described in the narrative is one-dimensional; her only value is as a sexual commodity. These songs are indicative of the trend within psychobilly to portray women as the objects of the male gaze and as vehicles for the release of male sexual desire. "Wake Up, Get Up, Get Out" (Frantic Flattops), "Get You into Bed" (The Ghost Storys), "Love Whip" (Reverend Horton Heat), "Clitoris Bite Boogie" (Demented Are Go), and "Don't Put Your Clothes On" (Liquor-N-Poker) are just a few more examples of the oversexualization of women in songs (note the last band's name is a play on the words "lick her and poke her").[5]

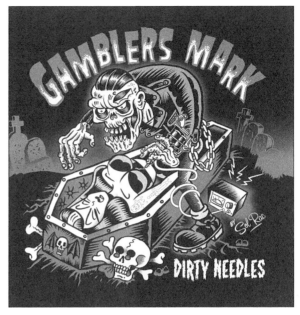

Figure 4.1. (above left) An event poster portraying a voluptuous zombie, as part of the common theme of women as willing sex objects. (*Used with permission from Robert "Nix" Nixon [graphic artist] and Koffin Kats.*)

Figure 4.2. (above right) The cover of a Gamblers Mark album showing a disempowered woman at the mercy of a male monster wielding a tattoo gun. (*Used with permission from Sol Rac [graphic designer] and Gamblers Mark.*)

Visual media further reinforce the sexualization and objectification of women in psychobilly culture. It is common to see images of hypersexualized female bodies on concert posters and album covers. Whether the woman is represented as alive or undead, she is usually portrayed as a willing sexual object, with her legs open, decked out in lingerie or naked, with a flirtatious smile and ample cleavage tempting the viewer. Alternatively, the woman is often disempowered or distressed, usually being attacked or sexually assaulted by a monster or science fiction creature (see Figures 4.1 and 4.2).

The representation of male domination over women reveals a desire for control in a world that has defeated and subjugated psychobilly men. This correlates with Robert Walser's (1993) assessment of heavy metal as a space in which men reclaim, through musical performances of patriarchy, traditional roles of masculinity that have been compromised by postmodernity. He argues that "gender constructions in heavy metal music and videos are significant not only because they reproduce and inflect patriarchal assumptions and ideologies but, more importantly, because popular music may teach us more than any other cultural form about the conflicts, conversations, and bids for legitimacy and prestige that comprise cultural anxiety" (Walser 1993, 111). Similar to many heavy metal fans, most psychobilly men fall into the lower economic strata of the working class or are unemployed, yet they still want to support a family with a "blue-collar" job. Having lost self-confidence due to their economic instability, men can claim control over an even more subaltern group—working-class women—through fantasies of empowerment and sexual domination. Similarly, in her study of death metal, Natalie Purcell explores the extreme violence of the sexual fantasies portrayed in song lyrics, drawing parallels with the graphic pornographic gore depicted in horror movies. Drawing on film theory, she suggests that these images may serve to reinforce patriarchy through the objectification of women, bringing men's anxieties about women under control (2003, 180).

In his study of South Texas folklore, José Limón finds that homosexual, scatological humor among men is used to negotiate experiences of marginality. In their joking, they reverse "the sociosexual idiom of *chingar* [to screw] as practiced by *los chingones* [the screwers, the Mexican American and Anglo upper classes] that continually violates the well-being and dignity of these working-class men" (Limón 1994, 132–133). Limón argues that through sexualized verbal play, Chicanos invert the negativity and aggression elites foist upon them; they are normally "screwed" by gringos, but when hanging out by themselves, they joke about "screwing" each other. They become *los chingones* for once. In the same way, psychobilly men "negate the alienating constraints of the historically given social order . . . and affirm the possibilities, at least, of a different social order. The participants momentarily overturn the alienating effects even while reminding themselves of the real aggressivism in the world" (135). By appropriating a narrative of dominance over women, psychobilly men symbolically and momentarily place themselves in a position of power: they can screw women instead of getting screwed by those who already marginalize them.

Just as Chicano wordplay does not imply an actual or fulfilled homoerotic desire to "screw each other," male psychobillies' expressed aggression toward women is not necessarily an accurate reflection of their personal treatment of women, nor does it represent a tendency toward sexual violence within the subculture. As Baulch (2007) notes, Balinese metal and punk fans did not intend to subjugate women when they reproduced discourses of masculinity. Rather, the production and enjoyment of such lyrics reflects a pretend imagining of domination over women and sexual satisfaction that allows men to momentarily and symbolically cope with the relentless subjugation they face, as described in "S/M":

Won't you come along with me
Into this world without problems
To this paradise of ecstasy?
This is my way to escape reality

This is how psychobilly men *imagine* a better world for themselves, a world in which they feel both in control and out of control (in this case, in a state of transcendental ecstasy), similar to the fantasies of killing people as murderers, madmen, or monsters described in Chapter 3.

It is important to remember that psychobilly is a genre defined by a tongue-in-cheek play with both horror and sexual fantasies. Note the female psychobilly's response in this interview:

> Kim: A lot of songs have some pretty violent and/or sexist things to say about women. For instance, I was listening to the lyrics of the Frantic Flintstones song "Necro Blues" the other day. Do those types of lyrics ever bother you?
>
> Pammy: Lol one of my favorites! I am a strong proponent of feminism, but I still enjoy the music, I still let it make me laugh. You can't [take] this stuff too seriously!

I asked Enid the same question by email, and she responded:

> Yeah I take a lot of those things as tongue-in-cheek as you say. It comes across to me as part of the horror-fantasy aspect of it all, just like zombies and vampires, and really about as serious as campy movie monsters. And, going out on a bit of a limb here, but misogyny being an entrenched part of '50s culture, including rockabilly and horror movies, I think it can be a good thing to play with those ideas; I feel like making them ridiculous and over the top takes a lot of the power out of those ideas. My circle of psycho friends is pretty small, but the women I do know are very quick to stand up for themselves, and they don't take any crap. They're certainly in on the joke if you ask me! I think a lot of them, myself included, are making it into our own thing, playing with these '50s-era ideas about femininity, toying with them.

There is something to be said for how the "ridiculousness" and "over-the-topness" of these sexual fantasies means that these examples of sexual degradation are merely that: fantasy. Fantasy fulfills its purpose; men are able to momentarily indulge in the idea that they could have power over someone else, reversing the feelings of marginalization they experience, and women are able to interpret the fantasies as ridiculous and pretend, as Enid suggested, just like a horror movie. As Purcell notes, "If innate desires for violence and sex must be expressed, it is far better for society that they be expressed only in art such as songs and movies . . . to help process repressed fears" (2003, 179). Deena Weinstein argues that the power that male British heavy metal fans express is a "triumphal . . . response against repressive social organization" (2009, 28). It allows them to play with power: "Their response is an affirmation of forceful individuality and chaos that they rarely act out in their lives outside the play-forms of the subculture" (28). In psychobilly these fantasies allow men to momentarily indulge in fantasies of control that serve as an antidote to their general feelings of powerlessness.

At the same time, the values reflected in psychobilly lyrics and art *do*, to some degree, extend beyond fantasy to real instances of female objectification, stereotyping, exclusion, and disempowerment. One male performer said in an interview: "When I'm on stage looking out across a sea of faces, some of the females in the audience seemed to be in some form of a trance! Perhaps they are just writing their shopping list inside their heads, thinking about decorating the house, taking the kids to school, who knows?" (*DogEat-Robot Fanzine* 2013b, 12). Clearly the performer had internalized the idea that women had little to think about other than shopping lists, housework, and kids. I have also noticed that men who write reviews of psychobilly shows pay particular attention to the appearance of female performers, whereas they focus on the musicianship of male performers. For example, a reviewer of the sixteenth annual Bedlam Breakout described the performance of two contemporary psychobilly/horror-rock bands with female singers:

> The Wolfgangs took to the stage and certainly stopped many male psychobillies in the venue dead in their tracks. Female lead singer Cha Von Wolfgang is quite simply a knockout French sexpot with the powerful wail of a banshee and unfortunately I didn't spend much time looking at the rest of the band. . . . Another treat [was] in the form of Hungarian horror-rockers The Hellfreaks with female vocalist Crazy Sue [*sic*; the singer was actually Shakey Sue] giving the punters another eyeful of raw sex appeal while they were still frothing at the mouth after seeing The Wolfgangs. I know it is unfair to define a band by their singers va-va-voom but with Sue roaring and writhing as she does on stage it is hard to focus much on the rest of the band. (Brackenridge 2014a, 20, 22)

This review seems to assume that the crowd was mostly composed of heterosexual men. The reviewer never commented on the "sex appeal" of the male performers in similar fashion. As in heavy metal, as Ross Haenfler notes, even when female performers attempt to "defy the stereotype of women as groupies, asserting their power in a male-dominated subculture, . . . still, their beauty, as much as their musical talent, is often center stage" (2016, 69). Standing behind a group of men at one show, I clearly heard them comment on the female singer's breasts multiple times, apparently not noticing her powerhouse voice. One performer gave me the nickname "Legs" the first time we met because I was wearing shorts that hot June night when I saw his band perform on an outdoor stage in San Antonio. After that he always introduced me to friends as "Legs," never as "Kim."

The objectification of women as willing sexual bodies reinforces the assumption that women come to psychobilly shows only to meet men, as previously mentioned. The first night I met Bobby, I took out my phone to type some ethnographic fieldnotes, and he joked as he looked over my shoulder: "That's 714–599 . . ." He didn't finish his phone number, laughing at his attempt, but he had hinted that as a woman in this scene, I was surely interested in getting his number and hooking up that night. He kept it up, telling me his self-admittedly bad pickup lines: "I must be a UPS guy, because I see you checking out my package." He later admitted that he thought I was making up a story about being a researcher in order to talk to him; after all, he had never heard of an ethnomusicologist.[6]

As a female ethnographer, I struggled to navigate the various ideas about masculinity, femininity, and sexuality that psychobillies have internalized from lyrics and visual representations. This reflects Foucault's (1978) idea that discourse produces and reproduces conventionally held understandings of gender and sexuality. The lyrics and images within the subculture perpetuate the idea that women are first and foremost sexual objects that fulfill male desire, reinforcing dominant gender norms. The marginalization and exclusion of women in subcultures often mirrors the marginalization of women in the dominant culture, as many scholars have noted (Walser 1993; Thornton 1996; Weinstein 2000; Goodlad and Bibby 2007; Brill 2008; Hutcherson and Haenfler 2010; Haenfler 2016).

The Contradictions of Female Sexuality

Having explored how men, who control much of the subculture's creative content, construct representations of women, I turn now to a consideration of how women interpret and participate in these representations and how they perform their own sexuality and gender to express nonnormative, subcultural identities. I find this particularly important given subcultural studies' historical weakness in addressing women's perspectives (as noted by McRobbie and Garber [1991] 2000; McRobbie [1991] 2000; Brake 1985). As Samantha Holland explains, the masculinist bias of early scholarship led to a false understanding that girls did not participate in subcultures:

> The fascination with male subcultures and gangs led McRobbie and Garber (1991) to examine the ways in which male researchers identified with their male subjects, adopting their attitudes and colluding with them to exclude girls. They question the absence, or marginalization, of girls in subcultural literature and suggest a rereading of the "classic" texts: a new analysis of subcultures to find out where the girls were. They sought to understand whether the invisibility of girls meant that they were not active in subcultures, or whether the ways in which the research had been done and where it was done had rendered them invisible. (2004, 21)

Since "the distinctive types of activities that females engage in, and the parental supervision they are subjected to limits subcultural participation," early scholars often did not see many girls "in the field" (Baron 1989, 209). Accordingly, "McRobbie and Garber sought to illustrate how these differences in ways of participation did not necessarily mean that girls were automatically not participants in subcultures but instead that they participated in other ways than boys were able to do" (Holland 2004, 22). Though I have already highlighted to some degree the way that women participate in psychobilly despite the barriers they face, this section more fully engages with how women produce their own representations of gender and sexuality within the subculture.

In "MissFit" (from *Kiss Kiss Kill Kill*, 2008), Patricia Day of HorrorPops points out that she is marginalized not only because of her subcultural tendencies, but also because of her gender. She observes that she is understood to be mediocre, a "MissFit." However, she warns that she will defend her right to do what she wants and will fight for her independence. She describes her rebellious streak, her straightforwardness, and her adoption of subcultural fashion: in short, her nonnormativity. Since psychobilly is a subculture that embraces all of these rebellious and subcultural traits, "MissFit" seems to suggest that psychobilly women might not be the submissive sexual objects that psychobilly men have portrayed in many songs. In this anthem, they stand up for themselves.

In "Psychobitches Outta Hell" (from *Hell Yeah!*, 2004), Day demonstrates how psychobilly women can be subcultural while manifesting sexual confidence for their own benefit. She paints a picture of a psychobilly woman that is at odds with the image of powerless damsels in distress who only serve to satisfy male sexual desires; in this case, the women are the ones with sexual agency, and they actively fulfill their own desires. She also disrupts gendered stereotypes, suggesting that these "psychobitches" enjoy the same subcultural activities that men do and noting that not all women fulfill the expected domestic roles; some prefer driving vintage cars and working in garages to cooking and cleaning. With a subtle use of upright bass played by Day, a barely there, two-note surf guitar riff played by Kim Nekroman, and an assaulting rhythm pattern that evokes the "primitive" drumming style used during burlesque performances, Day describes independent women who confidently express their own sexual desires and pursue their own leisure activities. Even the changes in her vocal register express multiple femininities, as her voice changes to a faux Marilyn Monroe accent in the last verse, soft, feminine, and sultry, just before she returns to a deep growl, an expression of female masculinity (Halberstam 1998). This portrayal complicates the narrative of women that we find in songs and visual culture created by men. In this case, "psychobitches" do what they want.

Patricia Day's assertive lyrics indicate that psychobilly women refuse some hegemonic values about femininity. As Day argues in her songs, psychobitches don't cook or clean, and MissFits can be loud, aggressive, and annoying. At the same time, Day's lyrics show that psychobilly women also embrace feminine aspects that have traditionally appeased the male gaze: red lips, curved hips, and short skirts. But her lyrics suggest that psychobilly women actively utilize these tools to reflect their femininity in an empowered, rather than submissive, way. They are as sexually driven as men are typically understood to be; they have a "masculine" interest in sexuality. They do not exist solely for men's sexual fantasies and entertainment, as many psychobilly songs and concert posters imply; Day suggests they are just as interested, involved, and in control of their sexuality as men are.

As Ross Haenfler notes, scholars have observed that many subcultural communities offer women a space to assert an empowered sense of "active" sexuality that contests hegemonic standards of "passive" femininity:

The goth scene provides women with a space to resist "passive" femininity and engage in "active sexuality" (Wilkins 2004). As with straight edge women, goth women believe their scene affords them greater independence from men and control over their sexuality. They feel sexy despite looking and dressing somewhat differently than what is typically seen as sexy. . . . Although girls are typically believed and expected to have less sexual desire than boys, goth women tend to be more open about their sexual desires and enjoyment of sex. (Haenfler 2016, 105)

Some psychobilly women project this assertive sexuality through their fashion choices, wearing "sexy" outfits that show off their hips, cleavage, legs, and buttocks. Many draw heavily from burlesque, pinup, and rockabilly culture, relying on dresses with A-line styles from the 1950s, high heels, and form-fitting, curve-hugging, and cleavage-revealing dresses and tops. They know that the rockabilly pinup look intrigues the men in the subculture and drives them wild.

But do these open expressions of sexuality and femininity really reflect self-empowerment and a rejection of hegemonic ideals, or are women still pleasing the male gaze? Are they reproducing the sexual objectification of women that is constructed by men in the subculture by catering to male sexual desires, despite Day's assertion that she is driven by her own sexual urges, rather than those of men? Some scholars have noted that subcultures that offer spaces for women to express a sense of female sexual empowerment may simply be reaffirming patriarchal values that objectify women. For example, Amy Wilkins argues that in goth dominant feminine roles are reinscribed through "the compulsion for women to dress sexily and to be sexually available, the continued objectification of women as recipients of predatory and critical male and female gazes, and the maintenance of gendered double standards in individual sexual relationships" (2004, 329). Similarly, Dunja Brill observes that goth men are allowed to subvert gender norms by playing with androgyny while "the subculture espouses an extremely feminine look, a hyperfemininity" that created a "cult of femininity for both sexes" (2008, 41). In other words, while men could resist gender norms, women could not break free from them. Women were still expected to look feminine, and "sexiness" was still understood to be a performance of "feminine" norms. Haenfler argues:

> The women may feel as if they are making a "free choice" to wear corsets to clubs, choosing to perform femininity in their own way. But the fact that many, if not most, women perform a "sexy" femininity shows that choosing how we perform our gender is not truly a free choice and sexual freedom for women may benefit men more as they have greater access to women without having to relinquish any power. . . . All of this shows how male privilege and sexual double standards are deeply embedded in our culture and, yes, our subcultures. (2016, 105)

He concludes by wondering, "So is their resistance meaningful or illusory? Is the freedom to dress sexy really freedom? This is a very difficult question, and one that other subcultures have wrestled with as well" (2016, 105). John Fiske asks a similar question about Madonna and her female fans who imitated her: Do we read their confident projection of female sexuality as a liberating move away from patriarchy, or are they reifying it by dressing in a way that men find sexy (1989, 124)?

These contradictions cannot easily be resolved. Brill argues that many "subcultural practices can be seen as both reactionary and progressive, both fettering and liberating at the same time, depending on the (sub)cultural positions and individual perspectives of the subjects concerned" (2008, 181). She finds that for some, "gothic male androgyny puts pressure on them to embody an even more ornately styled image of femininity, and thus restricts rather than enhances their potential to experiment with gender in style" (181). On the other hand, one of her interviewees saw androgyny in male fashion as "a general relaxing of gender norms and barriers, encouraging her to engage in sartorial practices of gender play herself" (181). Likewise, Fiske suggests that Madonna "is so full of contradictions—she contains the patriarchal meanings of feminine sexuality and the resisting ones that her sexuality is *hers* to use as she wishes in ways that do not require masculine approval. Her textuality offers both patriarchy and ways of resisting it in an anxious, unstable tension" (1989, 124).

Some popular music scholars have drawn on Judith Butler's theory of "the foundational illusions of identity" ([1990] 2007, 46) to consider how traditionally "feminine" performances can reflect subversive, feminist reconstructions of gender identity. For instance, Jacqueline Warwick argues that Motown girl group singers, trained by their male managers to perform femininity, adopted a highly self-conscious and artificial presentation of girlhood. She demonstrates how the "putting on" of femininity called attention to the already constructed nature of gender and sexuality: "When girl group singers and their fans willingly took on the restricted movement, prissy posture, and elaborate makeup foisted on them, they put on girlness with a vengeance and thereby could undermine assumptions about what is natural and appropriate for girls" (Warwick 2007, 86). Their display of femininity was recognizably artificial, but that was exactly the point: "The parodic gestures of girlness . . . could signify all the stereotypes of girlness writ large, showing their audience how to play with these clichés, . . . and point to the artifice of behaviors believed to be natural and inevitable" (87).

This is similar to Fiske's point about Madonna's parodic undermining of patriarchal sexuality: "Madonna knows she is putting on a performance, and the fact that this knowingness is part of the performance enables the viewer to answer a different interpellation from that proposed by the dominant ideology, and thus occupy a resisting position" (Fiske 1989, 105). Fiske argues that Madonna excorporates the defining features of female sexuality and "exaggerates and mocks them, and thus mocks those who 'fall' for its ideological effect" (105). She emphasizes not only the stereotypes themselves but also how they are constructed by calling attention to "herself as the one who is in control of her own image and of the process of making it. This, at the reading end of the semiotic process, allows the reader similar control over her own meanings" (105).

Thus we can see how the self-conscious performance of an overly sexualized femininity can resist patriarchal structures. By drawing attention to the construction of gendered expectations in the first place, women "make gender trouble . . . through the mobilization, subversive confusion, and proliferation of precisely those constitutive categories that seek to keep gender in its place" (Butler [1990] 2007, 46). Consequently, by acknowledging the constructed nature of gender performance, women can "put on" femininity when they choose to, as Mary Russo and John Fiske argue: "To put on femininity with a vengeance suggests the power of taking it off" (Russo 1997, 318); "Madonna's excessively sexual pouting and lipstick can be read to mean that she looks like that not because patriarchy determines that she should, but because she knowingly chooses to do so" (Fiske 1989, 105).

It is with this in mind that I consider performances of female sexuality in a heavily male-dominated subculture, understanding how psychobilly women choose of their own accord to project femininity, when and how they choose to do so. They "put it on" and "take it off" according to their own motivations, knowing, like Madonna, "the importance of the look" in three different senses: what she chooses to look like, how she looks at others, and how others look at her (Fiske 1989, 112). Liz, one of the few psychobilly women I have known to openly call herself a feminist, posted this astute comment underneath an article I published online about female sexuality in the psychobilly community: "I'm a pretty active feminist. I've felt the tension between my feminism, my enjoyment of getting dressed up, and my own feelings of power when I look sexy. At times, the pressure to be 'hot' bothers me. This is when I throw on an old band t-shirt, cuffed jeans, and creepers. And that's fine. If I'm wearing a skin-tight dress and bright red lipstick, I'm asking to be seen. And then I am. And I dig that too" (Kattari 2009). This comment alludes to the conflicting feelings many women deal with when deciding what "appropriate feminist activity" looks like. But like other psychobilly women, Liz ultimately concludes that she can *choose* to look sexy and *enjoys* doing so, reflecting an empowered feminist identity;

women's "control of the look (in all three senses) is crucial to their gaining control over their meanings within patriarchy" (Fiske 1989, 112).

Bettie Page, the famous pinup model from the 1950s, has had a tremendous impact on psychobilly women's ideas of their own performance of sexuality, as well as on men's ideas about female sexuality within the subculture. Psychobilly women are often called "psycho-betties" because of the pinup model's strong influence on the scene; many imitate her hairstyle by carefully curling their "Bettie bangs" across their foreheads, and I have seen Bettie Page tattoos on scores of both men and women. The idea among psycho-betties that women can look sexy without reinforcing female objectification derives from their feminist interpretation of Bettie Page (even if they do not explicitly call it a "feminist" interpretation). Page is perhaps most remembered for her "unconventional bad girl" image: photographers documented her in bondage gear, tied up, being spanked or paddled, being whipped or whipping someone else, or even strung up between trees with her legs dangling in the air. In 1955 she was one of the most iconic sex symbols; she won the title "Miss Pin-up Girl of the World" that year and also posed for the centerfold of the January issue of *Playboy* magazine.

On the one hand, Bettie Page seems to have represented the silent, submissive female: mouth gagged, arms and legs tied, a woman that men could control, fetishize, and consume. In *The Female Eunuch* (1970), Second Wave feminist Germaine Greer condemns the masculine shaping of stereotypes that prompted women to wear restrictive clothing, plaster their faces with makeup, shave their legs, and perform any number of other bodily modifications to fit the image of the ideal woman that men desire. Page seems to be exactly what Greer criticizes, manipulating her body in extreme ways as she offers herself to the male gaze, sucking in her stomach and wearing six-inch heels.

Others credit Page with ushering in the "sexual revolution" of the 1960s with her relaxed attitude toward nudity and sexuality. Page recalled that she "was never one who was squeamish" about being nude (Page 2010). She once said that she wanted to "be remembered as the woman who changed people's perspectives concerning nudity in its natural form" (quoted in Sahagun 2008). Olivia De Berardinis, who painted iconic portraits of Bettie Page, points to this unabashed self-confidence as evidence of "a certain sensual freedom and play-acting . . . part of the fun of being a woman" (quoted in Sahagun 2008). She also pushed sexual boundaries, openly representing and catering to alternative sexual fetishes such as S&M and role-playing fantasies.

Can Page have been the feminist groundbreaker Greer was looking for, a woman who was comfortable in her own skin, a woman who thoroughly enjoyed her own sexuality and body? Greer points in her work to the repression of sexuality that has rendered women eunuchs: "Women have somehow been separated from their libido, from their faculty of desire, from their sexuality. They've become suspicious about it" (quoted in Weinraub 1971). Popular culture supports the view that women in the 1950s were not permitted to enjoy or express their own sexual desires. Movies such as *Pleasantville*[7] and *Far from Heaven*, and television shows such as *Masters of Sex*, suggest that women during that era felt they were not supposed to be concerned with their own pleasure, only their husbands'. Whether or not this generalization is accurate, today's psycho-betties believe it to be true, making Page's embrace of her body and her sexuality seem that much more radical and groundbreaking.

Bettie Page used her body to fuel a successful career, the profits of which continued to support her for the rest of her life. Perhaps without being conscious of it, Page stood at the forefront of Second Wave feminism, which stemmed from an awareness that the political and economic equalities gained during World War II were lost afterward: "Especially after World War II, women seemed to be retreating from active participation in the wider society" (Mead and Kaplan 1965, 4). The perceived post–World War II equality of economic power, educational opportunities, and employment options for women was a myth, as Betty Friedan points out in *The Feminine Mystique* (1963); more often than not, suburban housewives lost social agency and fell victim to complacent consumerism tailored to women. Given this, one might redeem Bettie Page as an emergent Second Waver, an industrious career woman who found an alternative space for herself within a post–World War II America that male soldiers came back to reclaim. Sierra, a model for Bettie Page Clothing, expresses this sentiment: "I think Bettie was beautiful and ambitious, but most important of all she did what she wanted. I admire her quality and courage" (Bettie Page Clothing n.d.).

My intention is not to settle the debate once and for all, but rather to point out that psychobilly women view Page as a woman who confidently embraced her sexuality and achieved financial independence by taking charge of her own sexual agency and body. Inspired by Page's attitude and style, Tatyana created a retro/vintage fashion line that caters to the swing, rockabilly, and psychobilly subcultures. Bettie Page Clothing specializes in past-the-knee retro dresses rather than S&M lingerie, yet the products reflect a pride in female sexuality that stems from Page's legacy. As noted on the website, model Karla Joy feels that wearing these clothes "makes a woman feel sophisticated and seductive at the same time" (Bettie Page Clothing n.d.). Myya echoes this feeling: "I love wearing Bettie Page Clothing because it makes me feel like a classy woman who still loves to have fun!

Bettie Page Clothing hugs every womanly curve and flaunts a sexy flirty style" (Bettie Page Clothing n.d.).

Moreover, Bettie Page's own confidence in her body has contributed to a sense of self-esteem among psycho-betties, who express body confidence even (or especially) when they do not conform to mainstream expectations. The female singer of one psychobilly band I interviewed told me how her fascination with Bettie Page developed: "I was in love with her. I wanted to buy everything I could find with her on it. I think I liked her so much because she wasn't like everybody else. I didn't know her whole story at first. I just like the way she looked, because she was like me. She wasn't little. Like Marilyn Monroe, too. They were bigger, curvy girls but they were so beautiful and there was nothing wrong with their physique."

In addition to serving as a role model for large-figured psycho-betties, Page also functions as an example of how women can overcome abuse. Page's personal struggles are well-known to fans through biopics such as *Bettie Page: Dark Angel* (2004) and *The Notorious Bettie Page* (2005). Page's father and several of her husbands abused her sexually, physically, and emotionally; she turned to modeling, and eventually religion, as a matter of survival. Melissa told me that during some particularly dark times, she spent one night watching all the documentaries she could find about Page:

> I was crying my eyes out because a lot of the shit that happened to her was a lot of the shit that I went through. I didn't know that part of the story. That's when I wrote that song about escaping my demons. It's heavy stuff. Like her, I was saved for a while; a year ago, I was at church three, four times a week. I got religion just like her. But she stayed with it, while I missed beer and all the fun stuff. But still, she helped me to change and fight my demons. She helped me realize that even if that's how things are, you can still change and move on.

My conversation with Melissa reminded me of Patricia Day's HorrorPops song "Emotional Abuse" (*Hell Yeah!*, 2004), wherein the vocalist refuses to be told how to act and realizes that she deserves more than an abusive relationship. Day, who one journalist noted "looks like a voluptuous, tattooed Bettie Page" (Cray 2009), is known for her own iconic Page-style black bangs, pinup girl tattoos, leather fetish, confidence in her full-bodied figure, and "take-no-shit" attitude. In short, Bettie Page and Patricia Day have both served as role models for psycho-betties who embrace their sexuality, strive for economic success, project body confidence, and achieve emotional independence.

Psycho-betties also admire Bettie Page because she enjoyed using her sexuality to tease and intrigue men: "Whether entirely bare or decked out in garters, stockings and heels, a ball gag tucked in her mouth, she always appeared to be having a swell time. With her encouraging smile, she didn't just look as if she enjoyed being photographed; she looked as if she enjoyed your looking at her too" (Dargis 2008). One burlesque dancer who performs at psychobilly events credits Bettie Page with creating "fetish with a smile." She shifts the "gaze" back upon the camera, acknowledging the viewer who has just been caught looking at her and delighting in her ability to provoke his desire.

By adopting a sexy Bettie Page–inspired look, psychobilly women enjoy looking sexy while deriving a sense of self-esteem from knowing that they are being looked at. This recalls Fiske's ethnographic research among teenage Madonna "wanna-bes": "When asked why they dressed like [Madonna], they replied 'It makes people look at us' or 'When I walk down the street, people notice.' . . . [T]he self-assertiveness evidenced here is more than mere posturing, it is, potentially at least, a source of real self-esteem" (Fiske 1989, 100). The girls notice Madonna's "pleasure in her own physicality and the fun she finds in admitting and expressing this pleasure" (100). Fiske argues, then, that the teens derive a sense of empowerment by aligning themselves with a source of power. Sharon Lamb observes a similar trend among preadolescent girls who play dress-up at home: "Today we might assume, as many feminists do, that makeup and heels are a male invention to make women objects for their viewing, to make them ridiculous and powerless. Regardless, many girls see these items as having special power. . . . There are two kinds of power in being an object. In one sense, the power is in the gaze of the other" (Lamb 2001, 44). By adopting Page-inspired pinup fashion, psychobilly women derive a sense of self-esteem and a certain power over men, gazing back at those who look at them and complicating hegemonic power relations by suggesting that they too enjoy the dialectical performance of feminine sexuality.

Some psychobilly songs and videos express the self-esteem that women derive from using their sexuality to project power over men. Miss Alpha Mantis produced the music video for "Killing" (*Rise of the Undead*, 2005), a song by The Rocketz. Her chosen name hints at the desire of women to control and even devour men with their sex appeal, just as a female praying mantis consumes her mate after reproduction. The video dramatizes the story of two innocent men (bassist Tony "T-Mac" Macias and drummer Andrew Martinez) who experience car trouble and wander into a dilapidated shack to find help. Unfortunately, a "psychobilly madman on a killing spree" (played by lead singer and guitarist Tony "Slash" Red-Horse) and his sexy female sidekicks are inside, ready to attack. Dressed in tight leather bodices, lacy underwear, thigh-high fishnet stockings, high heels, and heavy makeup, the women bind and torture the confused, helpless men. The facial expressions of the bound men and the orgasmic guitar soloing suggest that the men enjoy being dominated by these women, as if this is a sexual fantasy come true (minus, of course, the psychobilly madman on a killing spree). The women, too, enjoy using their sexuality to dominate the men. They are not simply catering to men's fetishes, but clearly relishing a reversal of power relations as they bind the stupefied men while the singer screams "I love to watch you bleed / I love to hear you scream." Chaining up the men, they invert the role Bettie Page played in most S&M photos, in which *she* was the one bound and gagged. While portraying an extreme fantasy of sadomasochistic domination over men, this video reflects the self-esteem many psycho-betties derive on an everyday basis from looking sexy, from being looked at, and from knowing that they can use their sexuality in empowering ways.

Finally, this "putting on" of femininity is also self-satisfying and provides a homosocial function: women enjoy looking nice for themselves and for other women, not just for men and not just for the power they feel when seducing men. As Jen told me, "I like dressing up this way for shows. Yes, it's nice that guys think I'm hot when I dress up, but I mostly do it for me. It makes me feel sexy and confident." Sharon Lamb's study of playtime among preadolescent girls suggests a similar fulfillment: "When girls dress up and dance in front of the mirror, as they do, they also become the looker, the one with the eyes, the one desiring and approving of themselves" (2001, 44). This also becomes clear through the standard arrival procedure at psychobilly shows: couples arrive together but typically separate to their own gendered social groups and spaces. Men greet each other with bumps of the fist and head over to the pit together to wreck, while women welcome each other with hugs and kisses, compliment each other on their hair or their outfits, and share information about where they purchased their shoes or dresses. It is common for unacquainted women to flatter one another in the restroom, a gendered space I had access to, admiring each other's clothes or hairstyles. By creating bonds through the appreciation of how they look, the subculture fosters a sense of female companionship and solidarity with one another. A firm believer in the importance of women forming homosocial bonds, Dawn posted a cartoon on her Facebook page on International Women's Day about the internalized misogyny that so many women embody when they say things such as "I'm one of the guys" or "I'm not like other girls" because "girls start so much drama" and "feminists make me embarrassed to be a woman." With the cartoon, she posted: "Stop distancing and belittling women because you think your gender is inferior. Just stop. It's not cute."

The production of feminine identity, centered around a Bettie Page–inspired attitude and fashion style, is thus at least triply motivated: (1) psycho-betties derive confidence from Bettie Page as a physically full-figured, emotionally resilient, and economically savvy role model who embraced her sexuality; (2) like Page, they find pleasure in the projection of their sexuality, relishing their ability to control and satisfy male desire; and (3) they enjoy being looked at by other women too, forming important homo-social bonds in the subculture. By means of such strategies, psycho-betties retain some control over representations of female sexuality, even within the heavily male-dominated psychobilly scene. As Warwick (2007) suggests in her analysis of girl groups, psycho-betties can "put on" femininity with a vengeance, consciously, highlighting the constructed nature of this performance.

On the basis of her anthropological studies of a variety of world cultures, Sherry Ortner (1974) suggests that women are often not allowed to participate in cultural production because they are viewed as having only "natural" roles related to reproduction. These observations led anthropologists Michelle Rosaldo and Louise Lamphere to conclude that women "have accepted, and even internalized, what is all too often a derogatory and constraining image of ourselves" (1974, 2). Since men dominate the production of psychobilly and represent women primarily as sex objects, it would seem at first that the psychobilly scene reproduces these same divisions and limitations.

But if we consider how women utilize their bodies and their clothes to represent an empowered feminine sexuality, by reclaiming Bettie Page as a symbol of self-confidence, resilience, sexual freedom, empowerment, and independence, it becomes clear that psycho-betties also participate in the construction of female identity and derive feelings of self-worth from their projection of it. This can be likened to Fiske's understanding of how Madonna fans "actively choose to watch, listen to, and imitate" Madonna and "make meanings that connect with *their* social experience" (Fiske 1989, 97; emphasis in original). Situated in a context in which they are dominated by masculine representations of women as sexual objects, psycho-betties find empowerment and solidarity through their interpretation of, and identification with, Bettie Page. They see her as an assertive sexual figure, aware of her own body and willing to use it. They respect her as a woman who transcended conventional 1950s gender roles that traditionally placed women in front of the stove, June Cleaver style, not in front of the camera, with a whip. They attempt to transcend the objectification of women that is expressed in songs and graphic art by performing and using their sexuality with confidence and assertiveness, unlike the disempowered damsel in distress or sex object that is depicted by men.

Blending Feminine and Androgynous Elements

The previous section considers how traditionally feminine performances reflect the empowered way women choose to construct their own sexual and gendered identity. But psychobilly women have also contested traditional norms of femininity by adopting masculine fashion elements. As in punk (Leblanc 1999), early female members of this subculture often assumed the same fashion style that male psychobillies did. They bleached their jeans or overalls with Domestoz, shaved the sides of their heads, wore band T-shirts, made DIY denim or leather jackets that featured their favorite band patches, and wore Dr. Martens boots or Creepers (see Figure 2.4).

Jane Dipple considers the androgyny of psychobilly a way for women to be accepted in a "genderless subculture" in which everyone wears the same thing: "Psychobilly could be read as a progressive move towards greater equality for young females" (2015, 98). The androgynous or nonnormative fashion choices that many subcultural women make can be interpreted, on the one hand, as a transgression of heteronormative feminine ideals. As Samantha Holland suggests in her study of "alternative femininities," many self-identified "alternative" women use fashion styles and body modifications to "resist" conventional gender roles; "participants felt they had escaped from what they saw as the restrictions of a traditionally feminine appearance" (2004, 158). Lauraine Leblanc found that many other punk girls, like herself, choose to adopt "masculine" elements of the subcultural fashion, "celebrating displays of toughness, coolness, rebelliousness, and aggressiveness" and rejecting some of the hegemonic norms of femininity (1999, 8). One of her research interviewees suggested that the subculture "gave her a place to be assertive and aggressive, to express herself in less 'feminine' ways than other girls" (6).

On the other hand, the fact that masculine fashion choices were "the subcultural norm" reflects how authenticity is often framed as masculine in underground subcultures, as discussed by Hutcherson and Haenfler (2010) and Baulch (2007). As Leblanc notes, subcultures tend to valorize working-class masculinity: "Masculinity becomes codified in these subcultures, rendering them 'masculinist' in their value orientations and norm construction" (1999, 108). Accordingly, as noted previously, while subcultures "oppose the norms and values of mainstream culture . . . in practice, punks adopt many of the gender codes and conventions of mainstream adolescent culture" (110). Even as subcultures subvert some hegemonic cultural values, they reinforce others, reproducing patriarchal discourses as marginalized men attempt to exert and reaffirm their empowerment. In psychobilly, since the "authentic" look is based on masculine characteristics, girls who adopt an androgynous style are often taken more "seriously" by their male counterparts and thought to be more "real." I routinely noticed that men preferred socializing with women who adopted the masculine psychobilly look, hanging out with them "like one of the guys," befriending these "real" psychobillies but not viewing them as potential romantic partners. For flirting and sex, they preferred women who adopted a more feminine approach, women whom they did not expect to be completely devoted psychobilly fans.

In short, just as overt performances of femininity can be interpreted in contradictory ways—understood to be progressive representations of empowered female sexuality by some and reaffirmations of the misogynist gaze by others—overt performances of masculinity by women can also be analyzed in multiple ways. Some may read androgyny among women as a subversion of dominant gender norms for women (see, e.g., Dipple 2015), while others see the subcultural authenticity of masculinity as a perpetuation of gender inequality (see, e.g., Baron 1989; Krenske and McKay 2000; Hutcherson and Haenfler 2010). As Walser suggests in his analysis of heavy metal, subcultural gender practices can both affirm and subvert dominant gender norms. Ultimately, as Brill (2008), Leblanc (1999), and Holland (2004) observe, the meanings are individual: each subcultural participant interprets gendered sartorial performance differently.

Most psychobilly women play with their sartorial choices, expressing their femininity while also subverting dominant gender norms by performing androgyny or masculinity. To present a feminine touch, they use makeup, add accessories to their hair, leave a long strip of hair in front of their ears, or fashion their hair into a rounded pompadour instead of a sharp wedge, as depicted in Duck Plunkett's representation of a typical psychobilly woman (see Figure 4.3). They may combine clothes that would be seen on any psychobilly man with a few "feminine" elements, as exemplified by Adriana Pérez Palacios, the bassist of the Mad Skeletons (see Figure 4.4).

The diversity with which psychobilly women cultivate their unconventional look corresponds with the various approaches to "alternative femininity" that Samantha Holland encountered in her research. She found that many of the women she interviewed "did not see femininity as some overarching and rather menacing orthodoxy but, instead, as something which they had a right to and constantly sought to integrate with their appearance" (2004, 158). Similarly, Leblanc observed that most punk girls accepted some aspects of femininity while rejecting others, constructing their own mixed-gender style (1999, 134–165). She argues that their "blendings of

Figure 4.3. (above left) "Old School Psycho Girl," a sketch by Mr. Duck Plunkett, demonstrating androgynous elements of psychobilly style. (*Used with permission from Duck Plunkett [graphic designer].*)

Figure 4.4. (above right) Mad Skeleton bassist Adriana Pérez Palacios from Mexico City playfully combining feminine and masculine elements of psychobilly fashion. Her head is shaved at the sides, and she wears a jean vest with patches over a band T-shirt. But her nails and lips are painted, her eyes are winged with liner, and her accessorized pompadour-style hair leaves a feminine strip in front of her ear. (*Used with permission from Adriana Pérez Palacios.*)

punk and femininity subvert both the norms of the dominant culture and those of the subculture" (160).

In short, as Leblanc notes, "girls must accommodate female gender within subcultural identities that are deliberately coded as male" (1999, 8). For girls, she argues, "'doing gender' in punk means negotiating a complex set of norms, reconciling the competing discourses of punk and femininity" (140). They redefine certain feminine qualities as "punk," making their adoption of traditionally feminine elements valid within the subculture, without having to outright reject their femininity, similar to the alternative women Holland interviewed (2004). In doing so, they "expand the parameters of what is permissible" (Leblanc 1999, 165), calling attention to the arbitrary constructedness of expected gender norms and establishing their own ways of playing with the rules. As Hodkinson puts it, "the parodic transgression of gender roles is deemed to have the potential to expose the constructed and performative nature of the dominant notions of male and female which form their target" (2002, 48). By adopting both masculine and feminine sartorial elements, psychobilly women are not acquiescing to the dominant narrative that privileges male fashion but rather "doing gender" on their own terms.

Concluding Thoughts: Women in Subculture

Influenced by Angela McRobbie's observations of the effects of "postfeminism" on popular music scholarship, Susan Fast notes: "As gains [of the feminist movement] became visible [by the early 1990s] they began to be taken for granted, considered to be a given" (2008, 47). As a result, scholarly attention to women in music has actually decreased over the last few decades. Fast continues: "We might ask whether there exists any urgency about 'recovering' women musicians from the obscurity of dominant historical narratives anymore or to put those women who are currently making music into the discourse. Do many of us think this is now being sufficiently taken care of?" (47). It is with this in mind, as well as the ways in which subcultural studies have historically tended to erase, ignore, and misinterpret the voices of women, that I use this chapter to specifically address the role of women in the subculture.

Women have to carefully negotiate complex gender assumptions and norms when they choose to participate in traditionally male-dominated subcultures in which authenticity is framed as masculine. Songs and discourse perpetuate male supremacy and allow men to imagine fantastical narratives of empowerment over women while constructing spaces that serve to exclude women from the stage. Some women embrace the masculine aspects of the subcultural fashion, rebelliously transgressing hegemonic values about femininity while simultaneously reifying the value and power of masculinity within the subcultural space. While some men (and women) find empowerment through performances of hypermasculinity, some women find performances of female sexuality empowering and personally satisfying. They control the way they project their own sexuality, how they use their bodies, and how they respond to lyrics or images that sexualize and objectify women by performing themselves and their sexuality in powerful ways. They find subcultural ways to express themselves that both contest and affirm traditional gender norms. As Helene Shugart and Catherine Egley Waggoner point out, spectacular performances of gender that may appear to conform to conventional discourses can also be interpreted as postmodern resistance:

> In this context, the outlook for resistive potential in female spectacle appears bleak. If indeed prevailing discourses can adjust themselves to absorb, reconfigure, and thus redefine resistive performances in ways that ultimately reify dominant ideologies, then it would appear that spectacle is simply another hegemonic strategy to this end. However, some critics afford a resistive potential to spectacle, citing

its proclivity for disrupting normative gender assumptions via the denaturalization of gender (Judith Butler 1990, 1993; Mary Ann Doane 1987; Mary Russo 1986, 1995; Debra Silverman 1993). In their view, women who render themselves as spectacles may well be engaging in bold acts of transgression that appropriate the very dominant discourses that would constrain them. (2005, 65)

Thus, as Leigh Krenske and Jim McKay note about heavy metal (2000), there is evidence of both "multiple masculinities" and "multiple femininities" that can reify or transgress dominant norms, depending on individual motivations.

Accordingly, this chapter was the most difficult for me to write. I am frustrated that women have faced significant challenges in being taken seriously within the subculture. I initially was excited to see so many women embracing masculine aspects of the fashion, interpreting it as resistance against hegemonic gender norms. But after talking to many women in the scene, I came to understand how "looking just like one of the guys" reified the normativity and authenticity of masculinity within the subculture. And while I often talked to women who dressed more femininely about how they felt their appearance expressed confidence and empowerment over their own bodies, I also heard men "write off" these women as groupies or "arm candy," not "serious" or "authentic" psychobillies. Ultimately, I think it is important to underscore the different ways women choose to express their gendered and sexual identities: some women find it personally satisfying to transgress traditional norms of femininity, while other women reappropriate femininity as a tool for confidence and empowerment. Each of these strategies can be transgressive in its own way and allow women to take sovereignty over their own lives. It should also be pointed out that this chapter necessarily explores only some of the most common performances of masculinity and femininity in the community; there are more that I do not have the space to discuss here. As a community of self-identified "freaks," psychobilly is a subcultural space that embraces difference from the norm in many ways. While not every expression of gender or sexuality is granted the same authenticity, the subculture does allow for the performance of multiple identities. Accordingly, every psychobilly finds in the subculture a way to distance themself from the norm, reject hegemonic standards, and eke out a space in which to perform or imagine confidence and power, whether by expressing deviant fantasies about sexual empowerment, transgressing norms of femininity, or embracing hyperfemininity.

THE POWER, JOY, AND PURPOSE
OF SOCIAL AND ECONOMIC CAPITAL

Give me a little shelter
Give him a little too
I could do with a little help
Instead of a writ to sue
I don't mind variation
I don't mind ups or downs
But all we ever get
Is kicked down to the ground

—**TORMENT**, "Worse and Worse," *Hypnosis*, 1990

As it has been with other subcultures, the Internet has been increasingly utilized by psychobillies over the last couple of decades and has "highlighted an ever-increasing complexity in communication among people interacting in musical spaces" (Gardner 2010, 73). Subcultural theorists have shown interest in how the Internet has facilitated social and communicative bonds between members of a community that identify with each other. For instance, J. Patrick Williams and Heith Copes (2005) have studied straightedge Internet forums to understand how people express subcultural authenticity online. They find that Internet forums have been particularly significant to those who feel marginalized and nonnormative, as psychobillies do: "Our research explores how some youth use Internet-based subcultural forums to combat the liminal feelings that are widespread in the face-to-face world. This partially explains the growth of marginalized groups in cyberspace. Many individuals who feel marginalized in contemporary society search for others in emerging virtual spaces" (Williams and Copes 2005, 85).

Similarly, researchers have considered the translocal and global connections among various subcultures: Paul Hodkinson among goths (2002), Holly Kruse among indie alternative fans (1993), Keith Kahn-Harris in the extreme metal scene (2007), and Tracey Greener and Robert Hollands among members of the virtual psytrance community (2006). They all observe that global connections between fans of a particular musical style allow marginalized members of society to identify with each other and feel a sense of belonging that stems from their shared tastes. Greener and Hollands refute "postmodern conceptions that global youth styles are, by definition, depthless, transitory and internally fragmented" (2006, 395). Instead, they find that "connections between subculture members were not temporary, superficial connections as suggested by certain theorists (Bennett 1999), but were very strong" (414), allowing participants to identify with one another and support each other in many of the same ways that subculturalists traditionally do in local, face-to-face scenes. Moreover, scholars such as Kruse, Greener and Hollands, Hodkinson, and Kahn-Harris find that "translocal scenes also are tied together through *concrete* connections, especially travel, commerce, and media" (Haenfler 2016, 106).

Psychobillies have used the Internet to engage in virtual communication with fans all over the world. Independent from commercial record labels and deals, bands and event promoters rely on social media platforms to advertise their music and upcoming shows. News is shared throughout the international community. Friendships are formed—and sustained—online through Facebook group pages. This is particularly significant to those who live in areas without local psychobilly scenes, where they may be the only ones who know what psychobilly is. The Internet provides a way for them to not feel so alone and isolated; through online communication, they recognize themselves as part of a larger community of like-minded individuals. They then often meet up in person at festivals where members of the international subculture converge: Psychobilly Carnival in Curitiba, Brazil; Psychobilly Meeting in Pineda de Mar, Spain; Bedlam Breakout in Northampton, England; Long Beach Psyclone in Long Beach, California; and Psychomania Rumble in Potsdam, Germany, to name just a few. Fans communicate with members of their favorite bands frequently online, even (or especially) if they are separated by thousands of miles geographically. And when a band tours, fans host the performers in their homes and take them around town during their stay. Posts about bands or fans who need help for one reason or another circulate across social media platforms, resulting in the generation of both financial and emotional support.

In short, because psychobilly is such a small scene and so few people know about it, the expansion of Internet access since the beginning of the twenty-first century has helped to foster a sense of membership in a global subculture. Whether they live in Japan, Russia, or a tiny town in Montana, psychobillies feel as if they belong to a global community of others who share their nonnormative values and interests. And whether or not they have ever met face to face, they help each other out when times are hard. Their commitment to such a unique subculture confers upon them a number of social and economic benefits that improve their lives in measurable ways. I begin this chapter with an excerpt from my fieldnotes from a festival I attended that attracts psychobillies from all over the world, in order to point out not only the role of the Internet in fostering this global community but also the social and economic significance of the members of such a small and dispersed subculture being able to know (or know of) each other.

July 2015, Pineda de Mar, Spain

Psychobilly has now been around for thirty-five years. The average person has never heard of psychobilly, yet devoted fans exist everywhere, from Alaska to Brazil, Russia to Japan, France to Australia, Finland to Mexico. Here I am today in Spain at the twenty-third annual Psychobilly Meeting in Pineda de Mar. Fans of the subculture have been meeting here annually since the early 1990s, when the subculture spread out from London and started to be sustained by an ever larger audience of nonnormative "freaks" across Europe. And now they come from all over. I've never seen so many psychobillies in one place before . . . and speaking so many languages. In this beautiful beach resort town, thousands of tattooed psychobillies show off their freshly dyed hair, newly trimmed quiffs, and most eclectic outfits as they take over the town. They sell out the local hotels, fill the restaurants to capacity, lounge on beach chairs under rented umbrellas, and drink cold beers under the tent of Santi's Beach Bar. It feels odd to see so many psychobillies in the daylight (I'm used to nighttime shows) and to see them in their beach wear—swimming trunks, board shorts, bikinis, and retro 1950s bathing suits—rather than dark jeans and band T-shirts. Many do not even have their quiffs done up since they choose to swim in the ocean during the day. Before tonight's show at Can Xaubet, everyone will go back to their hotels to do their hair and put on their "show" clothes. But right now, as I look out the window at all the psychobillies in their beach wear, I still marvel at how "different" they look from "the norm." Even without their signature outfits and quiffs, their bodies give away their nonnormative identity through their tattoos, hair colors, and various body modifications. I've noticed that many of the tourists are extremely confused and shocked, not expecting their favorite beach to be taken over by thousands of subculturalists. Clearly they've never seen people that look like this before, at least not this many at one time. I overheard one couple at the registration desk ask the receptionist to cancel their reservation. They were going to go to the resort town further down the coast instead. The receptionist wasn't concerned. The event organizers had told me that they had a good relationship with the local businesses and chamber of commerce. Pineda de Mar welcomes the psychobillies every year, for they pour their money into alcohol and food, and never has there been any major violence or confrontation with the "squares."

When I left Santi's Beach Bar yesterday, I headed over to the hotel where most of the performers were staying. I had arranged to interview the members of one of the bands before they had to head over to the main festival tent for soundcheck. It had been very easy to contact many of the performers through Facebook Messenger to explain my research project and make plans to meet up for an interview. There was no sense of a "holier than thou, I'm a rock star" arrogance, and I didn't have to "go through" a manager or booking agent. Many of the musicians directly messaged me back within hours, happy to arrange an interview even while they were trying to enjoy a "working" beach vacation with their friends and family. While waiting for my interviewee at the poolside bar, I saw performers from bands that were crucial to psychobilly's success in the 1980s hanging out in the pool with members of contemporary bands who were half their age and with fans who took the opportunity to toss a beachball at their favorite musician. No doubt the fans felt as if they knew the musicians quite personally, having met their heroes several times at festivals and then sustained those connections through social media. In a few hours, the performers would be rockin' out onstage, and their fans would be wrecking in the pit. I thought about my bus ride back to the hotel after the concert last night and how Sparky, the lead singer from Demented Are Go and perhaps one of the subculture's most (in)famous icons, was sitting a few benches behind me casually chatting with fans. Meanwhile, I chatted with a psychobilly fan from Belgium who was excited to hear that an academic was interested in the subculture that had played such a meaningful role in his life.

After the poolside interview, I walked the mile back to my hotel, enjoying the fact that I could take a more casual approach to my fashion choices during the day, wearing shorts, flip-flops, and a tank top instead of the heels and dresses I sometimes feel inclined to wear to regular shows in Los Angeles. I was able to dress just as I would on a normal summer day. Back in my room, I attempted to style my hair and dress up a bit for the show, but the hours spent in the sun had made me lazy. Besides, after years of ethnographic fieldwork, I am less and less concerned with trying to dress like a psychobilly. It seems that psychobillies are a little more likely to talk to me when I am dressed in a way that represents my real identity anyway, rather than trying too hard to look "psychobilly" and risk being called a poseur or a "fashionbilly." After all, since I don't identify as a psychobilly myself, I'm not going to go the extra mile and shave the sides of my head to have a real psychobilly quiff. So, last night, I decided that a casual approach that more accurately represented my own identity was preferable. I chose my low-top Converse sneakers instead of heels, knowing that I might not want to wait for the bus to take me back to the hotel at the end of the night and would probably prefer the long walk home alone. The solitude would allow me to reflect on my observations and interviews. However, I knew that for the trip over I should catch the bus to Can Xaubet tent with the other psychobilly attendees and strike up some conversations. People would not be as drunk on the way there as they would be after the show, so I was bound to have slightly more lucid conversations, especially given that we were trying to understand each other in numerous different languages.

While waiting for the bus, I chatted with psychobillies of all ages who had come from Italy, California, Australia, Russia, Sweden, Japan, Brazil, Canada, and many other places. They told me that they looked forward to coming each year, making sure they saved their money so could attend. Sometimes their friends from their local scenes couldn't afford to come, but they hopped on a plane anyway, even if they had to travel alone, because they knew they would fit in, make new friends, and find old friends as soon as they arrived. Indeed, as we waited for the bus, people happily embraced fellow psychobillies from other countries whom they hadn't seen since the previous year's festival, although they *had* remained in touch on Facebook. As tourists crossed the street to avoid the mass of strange-looking people, psychobillies talked to each other about the shows they had seen recently, what their new favorite albums were, and whether their local scenes were dying or thriving. Some even brought their kids this year, eager to introduce them to the scene they identified so strongly with themselves. They discussed the latest gossip in the international psychobilly scene, topics that came up frequently on the Psychobilly Worldwide Facebook group, such as how the lead singer of a contemporary band had been accused of being a sellout by an OTMAPP supporter (someone who believes that Only The Meteors Are Pure Psychobilly). OTMAPP believers had posted to Facebook a photo of this singer with a target photoshopped on his head. That had actually frightened me and many others. Those at the bus stop lamented that they were tired of the hating and infighting within the community. They appreciated that the Internet made it easier to keep in touch with their friends in the scene, but it also brought out a bunch of "haters," "elitists," and "trolls" who felt safe taking shots at others as they sat behind their computer keyboards or phones.

On the bus, I introduced myself to the person next to me, Carlos, who had come by himself from a small town in Mexico where there were no other psychobillies. He had diligently saved up his money in order to attend weekenders in South America and Europe. He was excited to see some really "big" bands for the first time that had never toured through Mexico. Every now and then, he said, you get a band like Nekromantix, Tiger Army, or even Mad Sin that will play in Mexico City, but it's rare. He also travels up to Southern California quite often to see bands who tour there, and he loves the Psyclone Festival in Long Beach. We discovered that we had been to some of the same shows in Southern California, and he had met many of the performers I knew from Californian and Texan bands who sometimes cross the border to play in Mexico. We "added" each other on Facebook, and I told him to let me know the next time he was going to come up to a show in California. He reciprocally extended an invitation for me to head down to Mexico for an event. He said he would be happy to show me around and introduce me to the psychos he knew in the Mexico City scene.

The bus pulled up to the festival site, which had been constructed in a vacant lot over the past week or so. We passed through security, where we had to empty our pockets, be waved over with a security wand, and then be patted down if the darn thing beeped. Then Carlos went off to check out the band playing inside the large tent, while I headed to one of the merchandise booths located around the perimeter of the smoking patio. Since psychobilly is not produced by major record labels, it is important for bands to sell their albums and other merchandise at events, often earning just enough on the road to get to their next destination. After picking up for a friend a few T-shirts that are unavailable in the United States, I headed over to the Gamblers Mark merch booth to catch up with the members of a band from California that I had met many times since starting my research in 2007. As is typical, the members of the band were selling their merchandise themselves and hanging around to talk to fans. We commiserated about the long and multiple flights we had had to take to get there from the States, and I felt bad for them after learning that one of the airlines had lost some of their luggage. Since the bag they carried their own merchandise in was not lost, they were a little worried that they would be forced to wear their own band's T-shirts for their performance later that night. But other bands graciously gave them shirts from their own merchandise tables, saving the performers from having to make an embarrassing fashion faux pas.

As I worked my way around the merch tables, I joked with another band about the video they had shot of themselves in preparation for Psychobilly Meeting. The festival's organizers encourage bands to film short video messages to their fans, which are posted on the event's website and on Facebook to drum up excitement about the upcoming event. Attendees looked forward to these silly, personal messages from their favorite performers, who usually took the opportunity to be as ridiculous as possible. I then chatted briefly with another band about the donations that were being collected to help pay medical costs of one of the members of their local psychobilly community. Some friends had started a GoFundMe page to raise money to help the family, and the band had shared the link on the Psychobilly Meeting Facebook page. Festival attendees from all over the world had donated to the cause.

I eventually excused myself and told them that I had to track down my next interviewee, a performer who had been an original member of The Meteors. I had seen photos of Mark Robertson when he was about seventeen in 1981, but I had no idea what he might look like now. My cell phone wasn't reliable with international roaming, and I fretted about how I was going to find him in the sea of people. One of the vendors from a nearby booth happened to hear me describing my dilemma to the members of Gamblers Mark and offered to help me find Mark. My friendly assistant turned out to be Tobe, the organizer of one of the most popular festivals in England; it seemed he knew almost everyone in the scene personally. It took several laps around the patio, peering into the dense crowd, before he spotted my interviewee. We all settled down on the picnic bench and started to talk about the development of the subculture, listening with one ear to the familiar strains of Demented Are Go performing inside the tent . . . .

Communitas in Liminal Communities: Sameness among Performers and Fans

Within just twenty-four hours of arriving in Pineda, I had observed many of the aspects that most fascinated me about the social and economic dynamics of the psychobilly subculture: the importance of in-person gatherings at which members of this small but internationally dispersed community socialize with others who look and feel just as nonnormative as they are; the significance of forming and maintaining those relationships online because of the geographic distance that separates them and/or the lack of local scenes where they come from; the friendly and informal engagement between fans and their favorite musicians, often facilitated by online communication as well as in-person interactions; the way the scene is economically sustained entirely by its own fans, who buy tickets and merchandise; how those fans help each other emotionally and economically when members of the community are down on their luck, utilizing the Internet to collect donations or resources and express sympathy; how even the most "entrepreneurial" agents—such as those who organize the major festivals—identify first and foremost as devoted psychobilly fans who are committed to keeping their beloved subculture alive; and how they use the Internet to make the international psychobilly scene feel personal and intimate.

The psychobilly community privileges what Gary Alan Fine and Brooke Harrington call "small groups" or "tiny publics": "groups that depend upon personal (typically face-to-face) interaction with the recognition by participants that they constitute a meaningful social unit" (2004, 343). There is a local tiny public in any town big enough to support a psychobilly scene, but even the international community represents a tiny public, made intimate through festivals and the Internet. Both online and in person, this tiny public generates and distributes socio-emotional and economic capital that plays a meaningful and significant role in psychobillies' lives. Drawing on theories of communitas in liminality (from Victor Turner and Thomas Turino) and social capital (from L. J. Hanifan and Jean-Jacques Rousseau), I discuss in this chapter how the flow of social and economic resources allows psychobillies to build, nurture, and benefit from tight-knit personal networks. This allows members of this community, most of whom feel alienated by and marginalized from the general society, to depend on each other rather than on outsiders.

To understand why the socio-emotional and economic benefits of participation in the subculture can be so essential to its members' lives, I begin with a reminder of the marginal and liminal status of most psychobillies, who are attracted to the subculture in part because they feel displaced and alienated from society in general and identify with others who feel the same. As members of the social and economic underclass, they have not benefited from systems of support outside of the subculture, and they have learned from an early age not to trust elites, government agencies, social services, or generally anyone who either acts as an authority figure or comes from a higher socioeconomic bracket. Despite their experiences of marginalization, however, they do not want to engage directly with politics or attempt to change the root of the problem. They come to shows and socialize with other psychobillies to get away from their problems; to escape and forget; to forge an alternative, nonnormative community where they can transgress hegemonic cultural standards; and to have fun, making things better for themselves in this space.

When I met Armando years ago, during the economic recession of 2008, he had just been let go from yet another job. He had decided to make the most of his unemployment by devoting his free time to music. He packed a suitcase and his guitar and headed off to Los Angeles, where he spent the next several months crashing on the sofas of his friends and fans. He formed a new band there, recruiting a local upright bassist and drummer. He scraped by on the tips he made and the profit from the merchandise he sold, since the bulk of his unemployment check mostly went to paying child support, a fact he laughed about onstage as he requested free beers or gas money from the audience. He returned to Texas when his mother's declining health forced her to stop working, and he slept in her living room, taking care of her and his grandmother, who had dementia. To help pay his family's growing medical costs, he tried to keep a steady job. However, he was laid off time and again from jobs that have high turnover rates: stocking jobs, warehouse packing jobs, inventory and shipping jobs, and delivery. He earned some money here and there by staying active in the psychobilly scene, picking up gigs for any band that needed a bass or guitar substitute, but those gigs did not pay much. If he wasn't working on a Sunday night, he would hang out at the Jackalope, a psychobilly-friendly bar. The bartenders played psychobilly songs all night and showed gruesome B-level horror movies on the televisions mounted above the bar. Sunday was "service industry night," during which patrons who had a service job could purchase discounted beers for two dollars each, before heading back to work at their frustrating and often dead-end jobs the next day. I often joined him, threw back a few beers, and talked about the "good ol' days" when we were in California. We did not dwell on tough times. We just drank away our sorrows along with the rest of the psychobillies there, who were down on their luck but laughing and smiling as they forgot about their problems that night. There was a collective sense of carefree optimism in the air, as if together we could still have some good times before facing the reality that waited outside the bar. Armando managed to survive mostly due to the social and economic support of his psychobilly network. Years later he told me, "I'd never give this up. It's my bread and butter. It's what keeps me going."

Psychobillies are members of an underground subculture who are "liminal," in Victor Turner's words. He states that "liminal entities are neither here nor there; they are betwixt and between the positions assigned and arrayed by law, custom, convention, and ceremonial" (Turner 1969, 95). His initial observation of liminality refers to individuals in the process of a rite of passage—such as the initiation ceremony of a chief among the Ndembu of Zambia—who are momentarily between social classifications of status or identity. In such rituals, the chief must temporarily become the slave. But

Turner also extends his understanding of liminality to include people in Western society who likewise occupy social positions that are not clearly part of the social structure's established hierarchies: "They are persons or principles that (1) fall in the interstices of social structure, (2) are on its margins, or (3) occupy its lowest rungs" (125). He references the beat generation and hippies: "These are the 'cool' members of the adolescent and young-adult categories—which do not have the advantages of national *rites de passage*—who 'opt out' of the status-bound social order and acquire the stigmata of the lowly, dressing like 'bums,' itinerant in their habits, 'folk' in their musical tastes, and menial in the casual employment they undertake" (112). While psychobillies would not identify with beats or hippies, they have either opted out of or been excluded from many of the "normative" options for success and are members of a disadvantaged working class who feel or remain alienated from the mainstream. They make up the margins of society, if not its lowest rungs.

Turner suggests that transcendent feelings of solidarity and togetherness are fostered during liminal moments when members of the society are made to feel equal rather than socially stratified: "The second [major 'model' for human interrelatedness], which emerges recognizably in the liminal period, is of society as an unstructured or rudimentarily structured and relatively undifferentiated *comitatus*, community, or even communion of equal individuals" (1969, 96). In the liminal moment, the abandonment and sometimes inversion of the society's usual social order helps forge what Turner calls the "ritual powers of the weak" (109) and "a temporary travesty of the ruling order" (Schröter 2004, 46), providing a momentary sense of acceptance and equality for these "betwixt and between" individuals who normally feel rejected by or displaced from the larger social structure. This recalls the discussion of Bakhtin's and Turner's philosophical interpretations of carnival in Chapter 2, a time when "rituals of rebellion and inversion" give all members of society the opportunity to reject their everyday social status, to "play" as someone else. They can indulge in feelings of togetherness while they ignore their differences and perform their basest desires. In that moment, they are all simply just human.

While Turner initially focused on the purpose of *communitas* during ritualized moments of liminality, he also noted that some communities have tried to evoke a longer-lasting sense of social togetherness and equality. Susanne Schröter explains:

> Turner analyzed certain movements, some of them religiously motivated like the early Franciscans, others, like the Beatniks, more secularly oriented. All practiced communitas or were at least strongly

concerned about developing communitarianism in daily life. . . . The movements cited by Turner were mainly interested in changing the society. Communitas was considered to be more than a ritual stage; it became the final goal of all political and spiritual efforts. Here the members of such a movement created a model of society which was necessarily opposed to the ruling order. (2004, 46)

While psychobillies would explicitly reject the political goal of such a project, they do attempt to foster a communal spirit akin to that of the hippies or the beatniks. They reject the social differentials that characterize society at large, since they have never known any experience other than the social alienation and marginalization that result from such social stratification. Why would they want to (re)create those feelings of exclusion within the community they have constructed for their own enjoyment? Within their own community, they want to be on the same level. Applying Turner's conceptualization of communitas, Thomas Turino understands music-based communal gatherings as "the antidote to silence and to being alone" (1993, 251). In his discussion of music and dance festivals of the Peruvian Altiplano, Turino emphasizes the creation of communitas through music's potential to bond, arguing that communal participation in panpipe music festivals reflects strongly held views about the value of equality.

Turino's observations of communitas through music correspond to psychobilly's avoidance of social hierarchies between fans and performers, as illustrated by my vignette about the Pineda weekender. I have observed those types of casual and friendly interactions between fans and performers on multiple occasions. At one particular event I was standing in the entrance line behind one of the members of Guana Batz, a band that had helped to develop the scene in the early 1980s in England. He paid the $10 cover just like everyone else. And while people clearly recognized him and were excited that he was at the event, no one acted any different around him. He was like everyone else there: a sincere psychobilly fan who wanted to come out and enjoy some good music with good friends.

Perhaps the Guana Batz member was at this particular event because he felt a sense of connection and community with the promoter of the event. When I interviewed the promoter, Mason, he told me that he was surprised to learn that not all promoters have a well-developed rapport with the bands they book and the attendees at their shows:

I think the thing that makes me different is that I'm like everyone else. I want to get to know you and be your friend. Me and [a member from a band who plays frequently at the venue] were talking about this recently, and he said, "That's why I really like you, because I can talk to you on the phone. You'll call me and say, 'hey, how you been,' or we'll hang out." And I'm like: "Are promoters [in other scenes] not like this?" And I started realizing and noticing that they don't really make that bond with the bands or the fans. . . . [The promoter Mason learned from], he'd sit up there in the balcony by himself, real quiet, while I was the social butterfly, walking around. I was the face of production. I was there for the bands. They'd come to me for set times, for payouts, whatever. And I was the one hanging out backstage with them, partying, or whatever, smoking cigarettes. Or we'd go after the show to eat. . . . And I'm also out there on the floor, deejaying between sets and talking to the people at the bar. On a personal level, hey, the people in this scene are cool. Why wouldn't you want to talk to them? This is my community.

The "vibe" at this particular venue, one of those I attended most often during my fieldwork, was always welcoming. The promoter often greeted attendees by name as they entered the club or came outside to share a cigarette with them. I was always impressed that he found time to relax with the crowd and the band members, even though he clearly had many logistics to juggle and manage. But he never seemed stressed; rather, he seemed to be "in his element." He was happy to provide a service to the community he identified with by booking bands and providing a place for the community to gather.

The promoter's sense of communitas was infectious, as band members casually mingled with the crowd, drinking beer and watching the opening acts along with everyone else. After their set, they usually came out to the "merchandise booth," which was one of the dive bar's pool tables covered with a cloth, to sign albums and T-shirts, take photographs with their fans, provide them with plenty of free "swag," and genuinely get to know them. Although there will inevitably be exceptions to the rule, psychobilly musicians are widely recognized for being friendly and approachable.[1] After all, they identify first and foremost as fans of the genre and the subculture. They're no different from anyone else, as Dawn pointed out:

We're fans. That's what everything starts from. Everybody in this scene is a fan of psychobilly. It doesn't matter if you're The Meteors. It doesn't matter if you're a band no one's heard of, you know? The Meteors were fans of somebody, they got inspired by them, and they started their band. Somebody got inspired by The Meteors, started their band. Well then this other person likes seeing that band play so they're like: "I'm going to throw a show because I want to see this band play." So everyone—the bands, the promoters included—we're all here because we love psychobilly, you know?

This shared common ground in a very obscure and small subculture inevitably contributes to the ease with which performers and fans interact. Performers, even some of the most famous ones, are usually genuinely excited to talk to their fans because they all love a type of music that most people do not even know about. One of my interlocutors was pleased to discover this upon meeting Jimbo, the bass player for Reverend Horton Heat. Tyler remembered being extremely excited to meet Jimbo after being "blown away" by the bass player's spectacular and entertaining performance:

I waited for hours to talk to Jimbo, and I was so ridiculously eager and excited. He could've been an asshole. I mean, they were already famous, and I'm sure he had tons of people just like me wanting to talk him. But he was so cool. I told him how amazed I was by everything he did up there on stage, and how I basically wanted to be just like him. Jimbo told me everything I needed to know—what type of bass to find, what strings to get, how to learn, how to learn by watching every bass player I could . . . just everything I needed to know to get going. And I was so grateful to him for taking the time to tell me all that. I mean, he totally didn't have to do that. What a good guy. Amazing guy. That was how I became a bass player.

Several promoters in the scene arrange "meet and greets" so that fans can have more time to talk with band members without having to worry about set times or last calls, further establishing a sense of "communion of equal individuals" (Turner 1969, 96). These "meet and greets" become particularly important when bands from outside the country come to perform, when it might be a fan's only chance to see that band. For instance, one Brazilian fan posted a photo of himself with two members of his favorite band from the United States after meeting them at the Psycho Carnival weekender in Brazil: "Psychobilly, man, how this scene is important to me. Only in psychobilly can you get in touch with the people who make your life better with music." Having already become "Facebook friends" with the band members, he "tagged" them on the post and would inevitably keep in touch with them. When I asked Dan, an event promoter, to share the most satisfying aspect of his job, he responded: "Definitely the satisfaction of seeing the fans involved, happy, and excited to see and meet the bands. I take thousands of photos, and it's great to see everyone having such a good time,

Figure 5.1. Girls from the audience crowding the stage during Nekromantix's performance of "Subcultural Girls," a clear demonstration of the lack of distancing between psychobilly musicians and their fans. (*Photo by the author.*)

meeting people they never thought they'd get the chance to talk to, musicians that have had such an impact on their lives."

The enactment of equality and community between fans and musicians is also visible in various ways during performances. Performers ask for requests and immediately launch into the songs that fans shout out. They often invite attendees to sing into the microphone, and fans routinely reach across that invisible barrier to touch the upright bass, a guitar, or a band member. During one show, the singer of Three Bad Jacks invited women up onto the stage for his ballad number, and about fifty young women immediately leapt up and crowded around the band. Much to the chagrin of security guards and event managers, hundreds of young women rush the stage during Nekromantix shows when Kim Nekroman invites them up for the band's homage to the scene's female fans, "Subcultural Girls" (Figure 5.1). Musicians also frequently leave the stage, swinging from rafters, singing in the middle of the crowd, or wrecking with the fans. During the Psychobilly Meeting, I watched as members of The Sharks floated out onto the crowd on inflatable pool loungers and a member of Mad Sin moved into the center of the wrecking pit as sparklers shot out from the top of his upright bass.

The previous observations testify to how psychobilly musicians and fans erase the hierarchal difference or distance that typically characterizes the relationship between bands and fans in popular music styles that have a larger audience. This can produce a powerful sense of "sameness," as Turino points out, that I argue is particularly important to subcultural citizens who feel marginalized, disempowered, and disenfranchised:

> What happens during a good performance is that the multiple differences among us are forgotten and we are fully focused on an activity that emphasizes our *sameness*—of time sense, of musical sensibility, of musical habits and knowledge, of patterns of thought and action, of spirit, of common goals—as well as our direct interaction. Within the bounded and concentrated frame of musical performance *that sameness* is all that matters, and for those moments when the performance is focused and in sync, that deep identification is *felt* as total. (2008, 18; emphasis in original)

Interactions between the musicians and the audience during a performance disrupt the barrier between the crowd and the stage, creating what Turino describes as "participatory performance," "a field of activity in which stylized sound and motion are conceptualized most importantly as heightened social interaction" (2008, 28). He argues that "the quality of the performance is ultimately judged on the level of participation achieved" and "by how participants *feel* during the activity"; "this heightened concentration on the other participants is one reason that participatory music-dance is such a strong force for social bonding" (29). Because the crowd and the musicians interact *together* to create the total performance, fans feel involved in the process. They, too, are part of it.

Simon Frith, in describing the development of BBC radio, alludes to how fans want to feel *invited* to participate and that their engagement in the show matters to the performer:

> The enjoyment of the wireless came to depend on the processes of *flattery* and *familiarity*. BBC audiences were flattered by a tone of voice, by speakers, comics, singers, addressing them directly, as if each individual listener's pleasure mattered to them personally. . . . The BBC represented its listeners to themselves. What was (and is) enjoyable is the sense that you too can become significant by turning on the switch. (1988, 42)

Psychobilly performances foster this familiarity and significance among participants by even including them in the event planning process. For instance, many events hosted by Mason are linked to celebrations of important milestones in the lives of regular club attendees. He reaches out to his faithful and devoted attendees to ask which bands they would like to see perform for their birthdays or an important anniversary. The fan's name and the reason for the occasion are included on the main flyer that circulates across social media platforms. A special excitement fills the venue on these nights, as everyone celebrates the guest of honor together. The direct, participatory engagement of and recognition from fans contribute to the sense that everyone is significant, everyone matters to the community, everyone matters to the performance, and everyone is getting some pleasure out of it. The sense of communitas this creates is as integral to the show as the musicians themselves.

The active engagement between performers and fans has been crucial to the survival of a subculture that exists outside of corporate sponsorship. The bands depend on money collected from entrance fees and from selling merchandise to pay for gas to get to the next show. Performers are not likely to be compensated for luxuries such as hotel rooms or for transportation. Instead, they rely heavily on their fans and on event organizers when touring. Dawn and Aaron described how they helped out Batmobile when they performed in California, driving them around, taking them out to eat, and acting as tour guides:

> Aaron: The cool thing about psychobilly is that your heroes are completely approachable.
>
> Dawn: They're totally accessible. I've been a huge Batmobile fan for years. I've kept in contact with them, talked with them online. I met them in 2005 for the first time. I was completely starstruck. They came for Ink 'n' Iron [a weekender in Southern California] last year, and we drove them around, and even though we'd been in contact for this long, I was still really starstruck.
>
> Aaron: We were both really giddy *and* there's a language barrier [Batmobile hails from The Netherlands]. You're trying to translate to Batmobile! You know what I mean? But what was amazing, the most spectacular thing ever, was they were incredibly nice.
>
> Dawn: They were so kind and gracious. And, like, humble.
>
> Aaron: In the past we'd talk to them on the Psychobilly Online message board or on Facebook. Then I interviewed them once, and even then I was fanboy-ing. Then all of a sudden they messaged us, saying like, "Hey we don't have a driver or car or anything like that, and we really want to hang out. We have this day off and that day off. Can we hang out with you and can you drive us around?" And we're like trying to be all cool in the message, like, "Yeah, sure, no problem, that would be great."

Dawn: But of course we're like shaking each other, like, "Oh my god, we're going to be hanging out with Batmobile!"

Aaron: And we drove them around, and we took them to the Hollywood Forever cemetery, saw the Johnny Ramone statue, tried to look for Jane Mansfield, but we couldn't find her. They're telling us about how back in the '50s and '60s, Jane Mansfield went to the Netherlands and she kicked the soccer ball at this big stadium but she had her heels on. And we're just hanging out. It was just really cool. Look, I'm a nerd, and I've always read comics, and then I found out there was this band called Batmobile and they have songs about Batman. I found out they still read and collect old-school Batman comics, and I'm like this is amazing, I want to hang out with them, you know? And we did! That's such an amazing thing about this scene.

Like Armando, touring performers often rely on the fans and friends they have made all over the world. When Russian band The Squidbillies tours in the United States, for instance, they always stay with one particular event promoter who has welcomed them to his home many times. He takes them on sightseeing excursions and, as a fluent Spanish speaker, has even accompanied them to their shows in Mexico so that he can help translate.

Within the past decade, the Internet has further facilitated a sense of equality between fans and performers, as demonstrated by Dawn and Aaron's story of getting to know Batmobile first through online conversations and the special videos posted by bands before Psychobilly Meeting (described at the beginning of this chapter). Social media platforms such as MySpace (when I first started my research), and more recently Twitter, Facebook, and Instagram, have provided an accessible vehicle for band members and fans to communicate with each other and even to involve fans in the creation of the music. For instance, Santa Cruz–based band Stellar Corpses once reached out to fans asking for inspiration for new songs: "Thanks for sharing your nightmares with us. We are writing new songs as we speak so your input is appreciated ;) . . . Had any crazy dreams lately? Warning: anything you say may end up in a song!" They also utilized these platforms to encourage face-to-face relationships between their fans by asking them to arrange carpools for those looking for rides to the show. Fans themselves utilize online spaces to make their own connections. When one teenage fan proudly posted a photo on his Facebook page of his first car, with a Nekromantix sticker displayed on the back window, Kim Nekroman himself "liked" the post.

The Internet has also been utilized effectively to quickly get the attention of performers to ask them to contribute to a particular cause. At a recent international weekender, an American fan was involved in an accident and had to spend weeks in a hospital in a foreign country recovering from surgery. She missed out on the whole festival, which she had saved her money all year to attend, and faced medical bills she couldn't pay. Her friends quickly posted the news throughout psychobilly's various online communities. Within hours, performers from the festival brought her signed merchandise, agreed to sing to her in the hospital, and donated to a GoFundMe account, eager to do whatever they could to make up for the fan's disastrous experience. Rather than online media serving as a *substitute* for in-person connections, as often lamented by those who believe the Internet has destroyed face-to-face social communities, in the psychobilly subculture they have provided a way to reinforce and maintain social bonds that already exist and allowed new ones to materialize.

The Significance of Social Capital

Not unlike Torment's song "Worse and Worse," which opens this chapter, the lyrics of HorrorPops' song "Boot2Boot" (*Kiss Kiss Kill Kill*, 2008) evoke Turner's definition of liminality and the sense of communitas that can be fostered among marginalized communities. Patricia Day sings about subculturalists who have been rejected and abused by society and are broke, homeless, and discriminated against. But in the end, she reminds them, at least they have each other. "Boot2Boot" specifically references a flophouse in Copenhagen where psychobilly and punk misfits supported one another. Day describes the importance of the Youth House to alienated youth:

> It was the one and only punk rock venue and house. It was a place for kids to go, like punk rockers, you know, general outsiders. They have their own house. You can go stay there if you didn't have a place to stay, you know, they're always cookin' food, and it's like a little small community taking care of each other. And unfortunately we got a government that was, or still is, . . . not very nice to anybody that's different, so it got closed down. It got bought up by a Christian community and they tore down the building, not because they wanted to build but because they wanted to get rid of the people. (Blair 2009)

The emphasis on taking care of each other is an important aspect of liminal communities that foster a sense of communitas, of equality and sameness within the subculture, as opposed to the social order outside the subculture, which places most psychobillies at a disadvantage. By privileging a sense of equality or sameness in liminal psychobilly spaces, these communities satisfy a number of personal and group needs for their members through the distribution of social capital. In 1916 Lyda Judson Hanifan was among the first to refer to "social capital" to describe the benefits of social bonds. As state supervisor of rural schools in West Virginia, he insisted upon the importance of community involvement for successful schools:

> In the use of the phrase *social capital* . . . I do not refer to real estate, or to personal property or to cold cash, but rather to that in life which tends to make these tangible substances count for most in the daily lives of people, namely, goodwill, fellowship, mutual sympathy and social intercourse among a group of individuals and families who make up a social unit. . . . If he may come into contact with his neighbor, and they with other neighbors, there will be an accumulation of social capital, which may immediately satisfy his social needs and which may bear a social potentiality sufficient to the substantial improvement of living conditions in the whole community. The community as a whole will benefit by the coöperation of all its parts, while the individual will find in his associations the advantages of the help, the sympathy, and the fellowship of his neighbors. (Hanifan 1916, 130–131)

While Hanifan coined the term "social capital," the central idea that people have social needs, "relationships matter," and "social networks are a valuable asset" (Field 2003, 1–2) recalls Jean-Jacques Rousseau's notion of the "social contract." Disillusioned by the corrupting influence of modernity in the name of progress, Rousseau idealized a rural mountain community along Lake Neuchâtel, which believed was "a simple form of culture, a small state, a face-to-face society where everyone knew his neighbors and where all men were more or less equal" (Cranston 1968, 19). Two hundred years later, Beem echoed this same ideal of small interactive communities: "The concept of social capital contends that building or rebuilding community and trust requires face-to-face encounters" (1999, 20). The psychobilly subculture is a prime example of an extended community that has benefited from face-to-face (as well as online) encounters that sustain the scene and provide support networks for participants.

The need for social capital that can satisfy one's social needs is particularly important given psychobillies' alienation from the superculture; since they do not fit in with the mainstream, their sense of belonging within the subculture feels (or may need to feel) especially significant. A journalist who covered a psychobilly social event at Knott's Berry Farm called Camp Psycho began his article by pointing out that "psychobillies are used to being misunderstood" (Jackson 2017). The organizers wanted to host an event at which psychobillies could have a good time together outside of a nighttime performance context: "It's all about coming as you are, being comfortable and leaving your ego at the gate. We're just trying to make friends and bring people together" (Jackson 2017). One of the organizers, Tawney, told me that their intention was "to unite people": "You don't have to love each other. You don't have to go to each other's house every day. But you obviously have something in common with all these other people because you like the same music, and movies, and fashion, and everything else. So we want this event to make you feel like you're part of something that's much bigger than you. It's a safe place to celebrate the culture, the music, all of the above." The other organizer, Remy, added: "There's something for everybody to do at Knott's. Sometimes people can't go to shows because it's like, 'oh I can't get a babysitter.' But you can come to the restaurant for the pre-party. And we've had people bring their kids to Camp Psycho, and everybody had a really good time."

Tawney later elaborated further on why social interaction between psychobillies was so important. She suggested that "finding one's tribe" was incredibly significant to all of them, given their sense of alienation from, and marginalization among, others. She wanted to remind people that their shared interest in a unique and underground style of music meant that they automatically had something in common with other psychobillies:

> We all found our tribe, 'cause psychobilly is not mainstream. So when you find it, it's special because you're like: "I *finally* found what I like." It's unique, and it's not like everybody knows about it, so you get excited that you found your thing. Whether you're a lone wolf or you have like your big group of friends, either way you're at some psychobilly event because you're like: "OK, I didn't fit into this [other thing], but this is where I belong, this is what I'm into, this is what I love." And it's a really small world, it's a tiny scene, but it's out there everywhere. So it makes you feel like: "OK, cool, I have something in common with this forty-five-year old man that lives in the U.K., or Japan, or Brazil, or whatever."

Psychobillies' feelings of nonnormativity, which initially attract them to the subculture, result in their having common experiences that they can relate to one another about. A member of one of the bands who developed psychobilly in the 1980s described to me how he was *like* the other psychobillies because they were all so *unlike* the norm:

You've got a kind of link [with other psychobillies], a kind of connection 'cause I always see myself as an outsider. I always was as a kid. I was the kid who never got invited to any parties, I was the kid, the kind of freak in the corner who sort of wasn't popular with everyone, you know? And I think—I'm not trying to say that the psychobilly scene is a place, like a magnet for rejects or anything—but I think probably every single person out there today [at this psychobilly weekender], I think they kind of revel in the fact that they're not normal. I wouldn't really want to be shopping in the Gap—that's good for those people, but it's not for me. I don't want to be the same as everyone walking down the street.

Face-to-face interactions are thus important to psychobillies as a means through which to generate social capital and alleviate their feelings of alienation. They eagerly look forward to seeing one another at shows, even spending lots of money to travel to weekenders in other countries to enjoy not only the carnivalesque experience of the music and the wrecking (as described in Chapter 2) but also the forging of social bonds with others who are just as nonnormative as they are. As one member of the online Psychobilly Worldwide Facebook discussion board posted in anticipation of heading to the Psychobilly Meeting: "Can't wait to see you lunatics and weirdos soon!" A band member playing at the same festival posted the event flyer on Instagram with the comment: "I might not make it back alive but I'm ok with that because I'm going to die a happy man!" Fed up with debates about what type of music and fashion should or should not be considered "authentic psychobilly," another member of the Psychobilly Worldwide group suggested that the real ethos of psychobilly is the sense of belonging achieved by attending shows with others with similarly unique and nonmainstream tastes:

Back in the day, there were so many bands that sounded different that there really wasn't a clear definition of "psychobilly" music. For me it was about "belonging." I needed something to relate to that took me away from the turgid shit force fed to the youth via "top of the plops" and radio etc. Being brought up in a sleepy shitty Northern town you had one of three career paths to follow after school—Burglar . . . Tarmacer . . . or smack head! None of the above appealed to me and my mates. Instead we worked all week to make the pilgrimage 200 miles via coach to The Clarendon and Sir George Robey and various other meccas that allowed us to be with like minded individuals and escape the drudgery of life. For those precious hours we were individuals together and it felt fucking good. THAT to me is how I'd define psychobilly—not a certain style of music or a certain band. It was (for me anyway) a sense of belonging and I fucking loved EVERY second of it ;-)

In reviewing the Bedlam Breakout Festival for *DogEatRobot* fanzine, Craig Brackenridge writes:

Every Bedlam Breakout is different but two things never change: good times are guaranteed but so are the famous Post-bedlam come down blues—that horrible feeling when you realize you were back among the squares and the next hit of bedlam is almost 6 months away. A few pubs in town seem to get taken over by the psychobilly hordes during Bedlam but even after all these years the townsfolk still don't seem to understand what is happening as waves of rockers descend on them, drink heavily, then move on. These bars are an essential part of the bedlam experience though as they offer the rare chance to catch up with old mates that you usually only see twice a year before the rest of the weekend is drowned in loud music, shouting and a sea of booze. Entering the Bedlam venue for the first time of the weekend is always the same, an overwhelming buzz as you enter the large main bar and you are hit with the sight of two floors of psychobillies who are all probably soaking up the party atmosphere just as much as you. Add to that the various stalls of clothing and records in the same room and you know you are home at last. (Brackenridge 2014a, 20)

These descriptions attest to the significance of finding oneself in a community of other nonnormative people, contributing to important feelings of belonging "to a tribe," as Tawney suggested. The relationships that are formed at these international festivals and continuously fostered through virtual interaction online result in feeling part of a "family," as Greener and Hollands note in their study (2006, 414). As one member of an English psychobilly band told me:

The last three years, we've played all over the world, and I think my favorite thing would be meeting so many brilliant people. Really brilliant people. You can walk into a psychobilly event like this anywhere and everyone's friendly, everyone knows each other. I could go to a gig in L.A. and within seconds be like: "Oh, there's Dave and Danny from the Gamblers Mark," or whatever. You feel like part of a big family really. If you see someone you don't know, but you know who they're with, you are quickly introduced to them, and now you know this person. That's probably my favorite thing.

This powerful desire to find one's tribe, especially if that tribe is particularly unique, hard to find, and shunned and rejected by "normals," motivates psychobillies to attend performances and events so that they do not have to feel so alone and can identify as participants in a social network of others like them. Paul Hodkinson notes that "as important as a sense of affiliation with perceived insiders, here, are feelings of distinction from those regarded as outsiders" (2002, 31). As Simon Reynolds puts it, "A noise band in Manchester can have more in common with a peer group in Austin, Texas than with one of its 'neighbours' two blocks away" (quoted in Kruse 1993, 34). Hodkinson finds that goths "hold a perception that they are involved in a distinct cultural grouping and share feelings of identity with one another" (2002, 30–31), a trait recognized in subcultural groups since the Chicago School. As we have seen, psychobillies derive feelings of confidence, acceptance, and pleasure from interacting with other "freaks" who identify more with each other than with "normal" people.

As Hodkinson notes, a strong identification with a subculture usually results in long-lasting commitment, participation over a number of years, rather than a fleeting pastime. Many psychobillies I met in Europe had been participating in the subculture since it developed there in the 1980s because they derived satisfaction from the social networks, which improved their general quality of life and offered them lasting friendships. When I talked to Fergus, for example, he could not imagine what his life would be like if he had not discovered psychobilly:

Fergus: I'm not gonna change now. I can't see any point where'd I wake up and say: "Oh, I'm forty-eight now—." I think we were one of the first generations that'll keep doing it [participating in a subculture] until we die. You're not gonna change your friends. Everything, almost everything I'm involved with is through the psychobilly scene—

Kim: Like, your community is—

Fergus: I don't know any rocker people. I only know psychos. There's (*sic*) people that I see more from Finland in a year than I see my neighbors, and I'm pretty happy with that. And it's a funny feeling, especially when you go to a lot of [psychobilly] festivals, there's far more time with people, you're spending seventy-two hours with people, whereas even if you went out every Friday

night with your neighbors, you probably wouldn't have spent
that much time—you're living with them, you're staying in a
hotel room, you get up, you're having breakfast, lunch, stay up
'til three, four in the morning—

Kim: That's what I noticed in Pineda—

Fergus: So you're closer to those people than to Joe Schmo—I don't
know if it's the same for punks, or other subcultures. Again, I
genuinely have more friends in Europe, that I would genuinely
call friends, from the scene, than I have outside. And if anything
happened to that, I—

At that point, he laughed and threw his hands up in the air, as if to suggest
that he did not want to imagine what he would do if he did not have his
friends and his subcultural life.

Social and Economic Networks of Support

The powerful sense of belonging that results from socializing with others
with unique shared interests is an important aspect of social capital; it
improves people's lives by providing "mutual sympathy and social inter-
course" (Hanifan 1916, 130–131). But L. J. Hanifan goes further, suggesting
that social capital can—and should—"bear a social potentiality sufficient to
the substantial improvement of living conditions in the whole community"
and confer upon individuals the "advantages of the help, the sympathy, and
the fellowship of his neighbors." As illustrated previously, this is particularly
important in a scene that flies below the radar of commercial interests in
music. We have already seen that band members rely on the "help, the
sympathy, and the fellowship" of members of their own community to get
out on the road and play performances. Not only do they "crash" frequently
with friends or with mates in other bands, but they also depend on the
support of members of the subcultures when faced with hard times. Several
bands have been devastated, both emotionally and financially, when their
vans broke down on tour (often multiple times on one tour), their gear was
stolen, they were robbed, or everything was destroyed in a trailer fire. Bands
usually cannot afford to stay in hotels that have guarded or well-protected
parking for their vehicles loaded with gear; they often only have a simple
lock from a hardware store to protect their precious instruments; and they
sometimes have no other choice than to drive a beat-up van, often decades
old, that probably has not been serviced recently and is likely to malfunction
on the road.

Psychobilly band Loveless was touring when their trailer caught fire and they lost most of their gear: all their guitars, amps, drums, and bass equipment. The news of their setback quickly spread throughout the community, both in person and through social media. One fan posted a picture of the burned trailer on the Austin Psychobillies Facebook group page and encouraged the community to come to Loveless's aid: "Hey everyone, life sucks sometimes, we all know this. Well it comes times when we need a little support from our friends and fans in this case. The Loveless need some love right now. Any little bit would help." Their GoFundMe page raised almost $8,000 in just a couple of days (their goal was $5,000), mostly in increments of $5–$20. For the rest of the tour (they were on their way to the Long Beach Psyclone weekender), they got by through borrowing gear from local psychobilly fans and bands until they could buy replacements. When I checked their Facebook page for updates several months after the festival, I saw they were paying it forward by collecting clothes and money for medical bills for a friend in another band whose house had burned down and who was facing outrageous costs after staying in an intensive care unit. A community whose members themselves struggle financially pulled together an incredible amount of money to help the struggling band.

Stellar Corpses also lost all of their gear on tour when their trailer was broken into; everything was stolen. When fans and other bands created and shared a GoFundMe page to raise money for the band, over $10,000 was raised in just seventeen days. They thanked everyone through social media in addition to thanking each Facebook poster personally and sending supporters free merchandise:

> We would like to express our gratitude for all of your support during the worst and best tour of Stellar Corpses' history. As many of you know, our equipment was stolen on Halloween morning in San Antonio, TX. We were devastated. . . . People offering their condolences, musicians offering to lend us their gear, and others offering to donate money. That was enough to inspire us to continue the tour, and each night we were greeted by the immense outpouring of love from everyone at the shows. . . . There are no words to express the gratitude we feel for everyone that donated their hard-earned dollars to help us replace our stolen equipment. Not only has this experience shown us the strength and compassion of this community, but it has also brought us closer together as a band.

Fans have also supported bands when promoters outside of the scene have tried to get out of paying performers. Steve Whitehouse remembered when Frenzy played a show and the promoter tried to back out of the contract. The audience witnessed the heated discussion on the patio, hearing the promoter say that she was not going to pay the band. Fans went down to the ATM downstairs, pooled their money, and came up with several hundred dollars to pay the band out of their own pockets. Steve did not want to take their hard-earned money—after all, they had already each paid the entrance fee— but the fans insisted, saying that they did not want the band, who had come all the way from England, to never perform in their city again. Steve concluded, "That's what makes the scene so great—how the crowd itself supports the performers."

I remember a particular promoter in Southern California who was notorious for stiffing bands, even ones that had flown in from out of the country. Several fans took it upon themselves to file a lawsuit, set up a website to "out" the promoter for leaving the bands high and dry, and raised money from the psychobilly community to pay back all the bands who had been cheated. Everyone knew they had paid quite a high entrance fee for many of that promoter's events, but they were willing to pay more to make sure the bands would be willing to return to the United States, knowing that at least their fans would support them financially. As L. J. Hanifan argues, the community as a whole is strengthened when individual members' living conditions are improved.

Psychobillies also pool their money to support members of the local community. Because local scenes are rather small, almost everyone who attends shows knows everyone else or can at least recognize others from having seen them at psychobilly events. As a result, when something devastating happens to a member of the local community—whether a performer or a fan—regular attendees immediately know about it. Promoters such as Mason use events to raise money or resources to help those in need directly, alleviating the financial costs of funerals, medical treatments, disaster relief, and unemployment. One event I attended was organized to memorialize the life of a member of the Southern California community who had died of cancer at a young age. All of the proceeds of the event went to the family to help pay for funeral costs and to alleviate the financial burden of losing a working member of the family. Mason booked the bands he knew the woman had loved, and the venue ran a special on her favorite drinks. As news of the memorial show spread throughout social media, comments illustrated the importance of social capital in the local community. Members comforted each other, shared memories of going to psychobilly shows together, posted photos, and grieved together, first online through Facebook and then in person at the show. After the memorial show, one of her family members posted a comment on the Facebook event page thanking everyone for their emotional and financial support.

Benefit concerts and online fund-raisers are common throughout the local and global communities. Psychobillies know what it feels like to be at an economic disadvantage, to have a hard time surviving due to their low status on the socioeconomic ladder of society. They often do not have economically successful family members on whom they can rely. They are used to having to make do. As a result, they are particularly generous when one of their own is experiencing especially tough times. When members of the community face expensive medical costs, fund-raisers (both online and at local events) are organized to lend a hand; monetary donations are collected and local community members help out in any way they can with babysitting, grocery shopping, and driving the affected members to and from doctor's appointments. These are the important benefits of social capital that contribute to the "substantial improvement of living conditions in the whole community" and bestow upon its members "the advantages of the help, the sympathy, and the fellowship" of one's peers (Hanifan 1916, 130–131).

Given their own experiences of social and economic marginalization, psychobillies are also invested in improving the conditions of those outside their own community who have also faced extraordinary challenges. They recognize that they are part of a larger community of individuals, outside of the psychobilly scene, who have not had it easy. At a "Support the Troops" event at Fort Hood near Killeen, Texas, pinup girls posed for a calendar; the calendars—and profits from local sales—were shipped overseas to provide both financial assistance and delight to war-weary soldiers. At a "Fighting Hunger, Giving Hope" event, cans of food and 100 percent of the money collected through ticket sales were donated to The Los Angeles Food Bank. Southern California psychobillies also generated proceeds for the Susan G. Komen for the Cure foundation. The organizers established a website to advertise the benefit event and express their personal connections to the cause: "We've lost a few friends over the years including a male friend to breast cancer. We want to do our part to make this world awesome, so [we] present the Pinup Car Wash and Bake Sale at American Vintage Tattoo." They raised over $500 to be donated to the foundation, but the event also testified to the importance of social capital, as participants shared stories of loss and survival and distributed information about early detection and treatments on the website and at the event. When Hurricane Harvey struck Texas, Mason hosted a benefit event so that Southern Californians could donate supplies and money. Several members of the SoCal psychobilly scene then drove the donations to Texas and helped with hurricane relief efforts, drawing on their skills in construction and demolition. Among the other causes that psychobilly benefit events have raised awareness of, or money for, are domestic violence and abuse, cancer, hunger, veterans suffering from

injuries or PTSD, animal abuse, wildlife sanctuaries, and children's education. More than 30 percent of the shows I have attended were benefit concerts—whether for specific psychobillies in times of need or for more general
charities—demonstrating just how important it is to psychobillies to give
what small resources they have to someone in even greater need, offering to
share the economic and social capital that flows through their community.

Concluding Thoughts: The Autonomy of a DIY Approach

L. J. Hanifan was not the only one to consider the development and impact
of capital within a group; Pierre Bourdieu, James Coleman, and Robert
Putnam have all written about the importance of social relationships in
sustaining a community:

> Social capital is the aggregate of the actual or potential resources
> which are linked to possession of a durable network of more or less
> institutionalized relationships of mutual acquaintance and recog-
> nition—or in other words, to membership in a group—which pro-
> vides each of its members with the backing of collectivity-owned
> capital. (Bourdieu 1986, 248)

> Like other forms of capital, social capital is productive, making
> possible the achievement of certain ends that in its absence would
> not be possible. (Coleman 1988, 98)

> Community connectedness is not just about warm fuzzy tales of
> civic triumph. In measurable and well-documented ways, social
> capital makes an enormous difference to our lives. The networks
> that constitute social capital also serve as conduits for the flow of
> helpful information that facilitates achieving our goals. . . . Social
> capital operates through psychological and biological processes to
> improve individual lives. (Putnam 2001, 290)

As the stories that I have related in this chapter demonstrate, socially
subjugated and economically disadvantaged psychobillies pool their
aggregate assets to help those both within and outside of their communities.
They derive an important sense of belonging by connecting with others who
share their nonnormative identity; they cultivate a sense of communitas
that encourages equality among all members, whether performers or fans;
and the strong personal relationships that are fostered, both in person and
online, act as a conduit for the flow of important emotional and economic
resources and support for each other.

The flow of social and economic capital within the psychobilly community reflects and enacts the DIY approach of the subculture. Having not signed with major labels, bands rely on the economic assistance of their fans, who pay to see shows, buy merchandise, and contribute extra money when things go horribly wrong. They often produce their own albums or record in the studios of established psychobilly musicians, such as P. Paul Fenech (from The Meteors), Alan Wilson (from The Sharks), and Gator McMurder (from Coffin Draggers). Fanzines are printed and distributed, paid for by the fans who make them. I have often been told that event organizers and promoters "do it not for the money, but for the love of the scene." The crew that organizes the Bedlam Breakout festival has been described as "gig-going billies who work their butts off . . . and tirelessly help advertise bands and all the other psychobilly gigs going on up and down the country" (Bedlam Breakout History 2012). Sometimes event organizers and performers actually lose money. As a member of a psychobilly band once said to me: "You know how you make a million dollars playing psychobilly? Start with two million!" The organizers of Bedlam Breakout lost so much money on their third attempt to host the festival that they took a ten-year break before working up the nerve to try again (Bedlam Breakout History 2012). In short, this community exists independently of the commercial music industry. As Craig Brackenridge points out, "as a genre to milk for huge stacks of cash then move on, psychobilly is a pretty poor bet" (2007, 206). The support comes from within the community; the participants feel invested in keeping the subculture alive because it is the source of their happiness and well-being: "Being a psychobilly has never been an easy option, but for the faithful the rewards are too damn great to ignore" (Brackenridge 2007, 56).

I close by returning to the psychobilly fetishization of zombies described in Chapter 3. The 2007 movie *Aaah! Zombies!!* (Kohnen 2010), is a comedy told from the perspective of the undead themselves as they begin to grasp the implications of their existence. They feel rejected, hated, ugly, and alone, just like psychobillies. The lead zombie gives a triumphant speech to his fellow undead, raising their spirits with the promise of an ideal zombie society: "You see, they hate us. Whatever happened between us in the past is over. We're part of a larger struggle. A fight for our very survival. . . . Can't you see? This is our chance to start anew. No more career worries. No more rent. No more car payments. . . . We could have a zombie society where everyone is equal, separate from the intolerance and hatred of the outside world" (Kohnen 2010). The speech at once evokes a state of liminality (as the zombies exist outside of structural norms and are rejected by the elite), the hope for communitas (a society in which everyone is equal), and a preference for a world without the problems that working-class individuals face (no more financial or career worries). This scene alludes to the ways in which psychobillies' obsession with zombies and their construction of tight-knit social networks are interrelated. Both zombie fantasies and social networks provide psychobillies with an alternative to a broken-down infra-structure, a support system that ultimately gives them a sense of optimism and the hope of survival in the tenuous present. They do not need to look elsewhere, to the institutions of power that have failed them; they take care of themselves. This, for Alexis de Toqueville, was one of the benefits of small societies or tiny publics: "If some obstacle blocks the public road halting the circulation of traffic, the neighbors at once form a deliberative body; this improvised assembly produces an executive authority which remedies the trouble before anyone has thought of the possibility of some previously con-stituted authority beyond that of those concerned" ([1835] 1966, 232). The psychobilly subculture survives because of the dedication and commitment of its members; *they* keep *it* alive. But also, *it* keeps *them* alive. More than thirty-five years after the birth of psychobilly, the subculture is still going because its participants, people who are on the outskirts of society and have not thrived in mainstream contexts, benefit from the social, emotional, and economic resources that circulate within the community.

At the same time, it is important to recognize that this goal of commu-nitarianism and equality within the subculture is not always achieved. Of course there are tensions between groups or people within the community, and certain levels of status are observed and maintained. After all, as Susanne Schröter notes, "Turner recognized that, despite all their inten-tions, after a while structure appeared within the so-called anti-structure, hierarchy emerged and the community of equals changed into a stratified organization. Thus, according to Turner, every attempt to endure and pro-long the liminal phase is doomed to fail: the rebellion reveals itself to be just a ritual" (2004, 46).[2] It is not surprising that the most friction revolves around the issue of "selling out" to corporate interests and how the interest of outsiders has changed the community. Because they feel that the capital-ist economy has contributed to their economic disadvantages, psychobillies are suspicious of corporate interests and prefer that the subculture remain entirely supported from within, by its most dedicated and committed par-ticipants. They worry that newcomers or outsiders might not be "doing it all just for the love of psychobilly." I wrap up this book by turning to these issues in the afterword.

Gatekeeping a Subculture, or Are
the Psychobilly Police Killing the Scene?

Subcultures no longer excite or rebel. . . . I wonder if we have
moved on from subcultures? Are they dead? . . . Perhaps we
have transcended from the necessity of subcultures.

—EVE MAIR, "The Death of the Subculture," 2016

What you might call the 20th-century idea of a youth subculture is
now just outmoded. The internet doesn't spawn mass movements,
bonded together by a shared taste in music, fashion and ownership
of subcultural capital: it spawns brief, microcosmic ones.

—ALEXIS PETRIDIS, "Youth Subcultures: What Are They Now?," 2014

E ver since punk fashion of the late 1970s began to be sold in stores,
people have lamented the loss of subculture. As Dylan Clark explains,
rebellion was commodified and sold back to the people who were
convinced that they were rebelling:

> The image of rebellion has become one of the most dominant
> narratives of the corporate capitalist landscape: the "bad boy" has
> been reconfigured as a prototypical consumer. And so it was a new
> culture in the 1970s, the punk subculture, which emerged to fight
> even the normalization of subculture itself, with brilliant new forms
> of social critique and style. But even punk was caught, caged, and
> placed in the subcultural zoo, on display for all to see. Torn from its
> societal jungle and safely taunted by viewers behind barcodes, punk,
> the last subculture, was dead. The classical subculture "died" when
> it became the object of social inspection and nostalgia, and when it
> became so amenable to commodification. (2003, 223)

This is exactly what many of the CCCS subcultural theorists were concerned
about. Hebdige believed that media and commerce would inevitably incor-

porate the style of subcultures, and its resistant potential along with it (1979, 86). Later, the postmodern subculturalists also believed that commercialization and globalization precipitated the end of distinctive subcultures, but for a different reason. They theorized that the endless glut of options to choose from meant that consumers were saturated with simulacra, "elective, build-your-own, consumer identities" that were detached from substantive meaning (Muggleton 1997, 189). As Hodkinson summarizes:

> Although [mass culture theories] lament the manipulative power of big business and the [postmodern approaches] seem more prone to celebrate the endless choice of fluid postmodern consumers, they both describe a de-differentiation of society as a result of saturation by media and commerce. . . . Both theories regard media and commercial saturation as incompatible with substantive or distinctive cultural groupings and hence, are liable either to exclude or to misrepresent the relative stability and boundedness of groupings such as the goth scene. (2002, 19).

Several critical observers, like those quoted at the beginning of this chapter, have written extensively about the loss of subcultures. Many are convinced that the Internet is to blame for the loss of unique and distinct subcultural identities that can be recognized by sartorial and behavioral expressions (e.g., J. Gill 2017). Like postmodernists, they posit that people are more interested in making hyperindividualized choices, which they use to construct an identity for themselves and express that identity online.

These arguments suggest that subcultures have in fact died, that there are no longer "groups of people that have something in common with each other . . . which distinguishes them in a significant way from the members of other social groups" (Thornton 1997, 1), expressed through shared beliefs, tastes, behaviors, or sartorial choices that represent their nonnormative or marginal identity and interests (Gelder 2005, 1). Yet Clark makes clear that he does not in fact believe that subculture in this sense is dead:

> Yet still they come: goths, neo-hippies, and '77-ish mohawked punk rockers. And still people find solidarity, revolt, and individuality by inhabiting a shared costume marking their membership in a subculture. And still parents get upset, people gawk, peers shudder, and selves are recreated. Perhaps it is cruel or inaccurate to call these classical motifs dead, because they can be so very alive and real to the people who occupy them. (2003, 223)

We could add psychobillies to this list of people who still clearly express a meaningful subcultural identity. They still are (almost always) recognizable through the expressive and performative choices they make. As noted throughout this book, psychobillies still shock "the squares," and they delight in doing so through their excessive and outrageous hair; body modifications; and eclectic mishmash of rockabilly, Teddy Boy, punk, and macabre fashion. They still feel a need to find a nonnormative community to relate to and identify with. Returning to Paul Hodkinson's indicators of subcultural substance (2002), discussed in the Introduction, psychobilly fits the bill: the values and styles expressed by participants across the subculture are relatively consistent and distinct, participants identify themselves as members of this particular subcultural group, they are committed to their identity and not likely to pass through only momentarily, and they remain relatively autonomous and independent from large-scale corporate interests.

It is the last of these parameters of subcultural substance that causes the most tension. Acknowledging that the subculture will be "inevitably connected to the society and politico-economic system of which it is a part," Hodkinson notes that subcultures exhibit "a *relatively* high level of autonomy" through the development and distribution of goods and services within the subculture (2002, 32). He distinguishes between "internal or *subcultural* forms of media and commerce—which operated mostly within the networks of a particular grouping—and external or *non-subcultural* products and services, produced by larger-scale commercial interests for a broader consumer base" (33). Psychobilly is an interesting case study because of its very high degrees of autonomy from commercial marketplaces; other subcultural musics, such as goth and punk, circulate in the nonsubcultural economy as well as the subcultural one. In psychobilly, the production and distribution of both goods (such as music, fanzines, and band merchandise) and services (graphic artists, music producers, venue owners, deejays, and event promoters) is overwhelmingly subcultural. Major labels have no interest in psychobilly given its small fanbase. Even Hellcat Records, a label that includes some psychobilly bands that have arguably the largest distribution potential, is a small, independent label in comparison to any "major" record company. Most psychobilly albums are released independently by the band or are issued on labels run by psychobilly fans and musicians. Production occurs subculturally as well: bands record and master their own music in home studios or work with psychobilly producers. Consumption of these products is also mostly subcultural: fans buy merchandise directly from bands at shows or online, not primarily through third-party vendors. With the exception of perhaps one group, Tiger Army, which has experienced some crossover success outside the subculture, one would not expect to find psychobilly music or a band T-shirt for sale in a corporate "big box" store.

Like punk (Hannerz 2015; Haenfler 2016), psychobilly is marked by an "authenticity" crisis: fans debate endlessly over whether a band has "sold out" and is therefore no longer "real" psychobilly. However, a few excerpts from a discussion on a psychobilly Facebook group about "mainstream" psychobilly bands serve to underscore the "undergroundness" of even the most successful psychobilly bands:

> Are mainstream psychobilly bands actually a thing? I know a few individual songs have gone mainstream, but I'm not sure the average person listening to Top 40 radio could even name a psychobilly band. Even the most "mainstream" psychobilly songs I can think of aren't going to get play on pop radio, commercials, shopping malls, or anywhere else you'd expect to hear mainstream music.

> Most people still don't even know that there is a thing called psychobilly, so even the "mainstream" is still quite underground.

> Mainstream psychobilly seems like an oxymoron.

> It's never been cool or fashionable enough to sell out anyway.

Psychobilly's continued undergroundness stems from a refusal among some to engage with commercial interests, a self-filling prophecy reproduced by subcultural discourse that equates selling out with inauthenticity. Psychobillies are self-consciously aware of the fine line they walk between maintaining their subcultural distinctiveness and autonomy on the one hand and allowing the subculture to grow, expand, and evolve on the other. To remain completely autonomous and independent from outside influences could contribute to the stagnation of the scene, while too much involvement with corporate entities could jeopardize the "authenticity" and "undergroundness" of the subculture.

Here at the end of this book, I briefly consider the debates on subcultural authenticity that psychobillies routinely engage with. Some cling desperately to narrowly defined ideas about what constitutes the community's beloved music, fashion, and beliefs. Others acknowledge the general characteristics that are relevant to the music and people they consider to be "psychobilly" while allowing the particulars to change over time. Some are extremely suspicious of outsiders or commercial interests who discover psychobilly music or fashion through "gateway" bands such as Tiger Army, Nekromantix, HorrorPops, Koffin Kats, and Reverend Horton Heat, while others are excited to share the subculture they love with others who might enjoy it too.

OTMAPP versus Tiger Army

Only The Meteors Are Pure Psychobilly (OTMAPP) is frequently conjured up on social media sites whenever the origins of the genre are discussed. OTMAPP patches adorn the vests of fans at shows, and some members of the World Wide Wrecking Crew (WWWC), also known as The Kattle, express their permanent devotion to their subcultural heroes with an OTMAPP tattoo. OTMAPP followers at Meteors events have even attacked people who dare to wear anything other than a Meteors shirt. The OTMAPP rallying cry has been aggressively spewed at anyone who dares criticize psychobilly's founding fathers. On a Facebook discussion about whether The Cramps could be characterized as "psychobilly," one WWWC member, offended that anyone other than The Meteors might be credited with the birth of the genre, posted a meme that read: "If you don't like The Meteors, go fuck thyself." When a member of a prominent band observed that psychobilly resembles the diverse "Psychobilly Cadillac" described in the song "One Piece at a Time," because both are aggregates of many different parts and styles, one offended WWWC member replied, "You are trying hard to justify the roots of psychobilly, but we all know where it started." Some of the performers who were directly involved in the development of the first wave of psychobilly have attempted to shut down OTMAPP fans with comments like, "Psychobilly is a hybrid style of music so it's impossible for it to be pure. It's like saying only a mule is pure donkey!" or "Would anyone say that *only* The Ramones are pure punk? That's just silly."

Nevertheless, OTMAPP believers continue to aggressively attack bands that take a diverse approach to psychobilly's musical style. The band that probably most disgusts many WWWC members is Tiger Army, a band largely credited with generating the "third wave" of psychobilly by introducing the genre to a broad spectrum of American youth as a result of their relatively mainstream exposure vis-à-vis Hellcat Records and their appearance on the Vans Warped Tour. One journalist summed up the Tiger Army controversy as follows:

> With the rise of Psychobilly however, came the backlash from hardcore fans. This rampant elitism throughout the scene has come to be known as the genre's most unpleasant feature. The scene has been divided between the rise of Psychobilly and the will to keep it underground; a particular example of this would be issue of Tiger Army. Some fans condemn the band for bringing Psycho into the forefront of the music scene and for including emotional lyrics, even going so far as to calling them "Emobilly." (Hellcat 2009)

I often found that people on both sides of this debate were eager to talk about their love—or hate—for Tiger Army. I struck up a conversation once with a fan at a show who showed me a blurry self-made "TAND" tattoo on one of her fingers. She explained that it stood for "Tiger Army Never Dies," a slogan the band cries out at shows to suggest that their community of fans will survive the hard times they have experienced. She told me: "A lot of people talk shit about how Tiger Army isn't really psychobilly. But that doesn't matter to me. It was because of them that I first heard about psychobilly. I don't care what other people think. I still like them." On the other hand, I have heard many psychobillies call the members of Tiger Army and their fans "gay," another example of how authenticity is coded as masculine, while commercial success is femininized or homosexualized, as demonstrated in Chapter 5 (Baulch 2007; Hutcherson and Haenfler 2010).

Because Tiger Army achieved some commercial success and brought fans into the subculture who did not know much (or anything) about the decades-old history of the genre, many longtime fans reacted by privileging their own authenticity and rejecting the uninitiated. Some of these gatekeeping psychobillies believe that newcomers who have found the scene through mainstream exposure want to "look the look" but do not really understand what the subculture is all about. These "wannabes," "fashionbillies," and "poseurs," as they are called, are not taken seriously by some who have participated in the subculture for much longer. Those who feel that Tiger Army ruined the subculture by exposing it to these "fashionbillies" have posted vitriolic comments online about the way the scene has changed—for the worse, as evidenced by the following three statements.

> No one could ever bring that '80s spirit, that fun, that pure and distinctive sound and the Clarendon back again. Most bands today play metal, hardcore, punk, anything but not psychobilly. This recent boom is caused by america's [sic] interest in the scene but they're too far from the real stuff and they are killing whatever's left. I began listening to psychobilly at the end of the '80s (and it was fantastic cause [sic] there was no internet and only a few people knew about the scene—in and out of the uk, and naturally, harder out of the uk, as you can imagine—and even today, whenever I listen I always get the same records from the same bands from that specific era.

> Tiger Army—this is why psychobilly should never have gone to the states [sic]. Bullshit flakey fans and ex emos running their mouths acting like they know shit.

Could someone please name the exact date when psychobilly stopped to be a subculture and became a bucket full of fashion-wankers hipster-sperm? I'd like to design a tombstone.

The last of these three comments may have consciously referenced the 1988 Meteors album *Only The Meteors Are Pure Psychobilly*, the cover of which depicts the names of other psychobilly bands on tombstones, insinuating that they sold out and "died" while only The Meteors remained "pure psychobilly." In short, some psychobillies have held hard and fast to their own ideas of what defines psychobilly as a consistent and distinct set of aesthetic values; have identified strongly as psychobilly (according to their definition) and have committed to that identity; and have been particularly insistent that the subculture remain independent and autonomous, sheltering itself from those who, in their minds, have not proven themselves worthy participants in the community. Summing up this insistence on protecting the scene from poseurs, one Psychobilly Worldwide member circulated a cartoon in which the man chooses Peggy Sue because she "knows that good old psychobilly" and rejects Lucille "who didn't even know the fucking Frantic Flintstones," a prolific band that has remained an instrumental part of the scene since the 1980s.[1]

On the other hand, many psychobillies have openly criticized "the psychobilly police," calling them narrow-minded and chastising them for not wanting the genre to be enjoyed by others. They argue that if Tiger Army, Nekromantix, and HorrorPops, who each achieved crossover appeal and a modicum of mainstream success, had not introduced new fans to the subculture, there might not still be a subculture. And how would that do anyone any good, they wonder? Comments on Facebook defending Tiger Army's potential for bringing new people into the subculture have included the following:

"If it weren't for these popsters and Tiger Army, there would be no new blood getting into psychobilly."

"Even if a lot of us here in North America didn't get into psychobilly directly because of those bands, they opened the doors way wider and got the discussion going. I never would have heard of The Meteors if I hadn't heard Tiger Army first. And I'd bet quite a few others who now slag those bands probably would say the same if they were honest with themselves."

"Tiger Army will always have a special place in my heart. I saw the music video for 'Cupid's Victim' when I was 12, and [one of the performers in the video] was wearing a Mad Sin shirt, and that's how I discovered Mad Sin. I will always love them for that."

As Nick 13, the lead singer and guitarist of Tiger Army, reflects: "Some people say the psychobilly scene has gotten too big. The funny thing is that none of the maybe 200 Americans who were into before it grew are complaining. Back then, people wished there was a scene so they could find records and the European bands could afford to tour the States. The people complaining got into *after* it started growing" (quoted in Downey 2004, 80).

Many of the bands I interviewed agreed with this assessment and felt that the community should embrace anyone who takes a legitimate interest in the music. I often end interviews with the open-ended question: "Is there anything else you want to add; anything you think is particularly important to understand about this subculture?" The most common response has been to underscore the need for established fans to embrace newcomers, as the following interview excerpt demonstrates:

Kim: Anything else you want to add?
Member 1: Help your scene, grow the scene. Don't stick to one band, you know. Buy merch from the bands because that's what really helps. And if your friend's in a band, help 'em push their band and then, you know, don't knock on somebody that's at the show and they're new and they don't know what they're listening to, because at one point, everybody was there.
Member 2: *Show* them.
Member 1: Yeah, exactly. Don't talk shit because they don't know who the Guana Batz or The Meteors are, and they're wearing a certain band shirt, you know, or they have grease in their hair but they're at a psychobilly show, you know.[2] Don't. That's how it stays stagnant, you know. If they look like they're lost, you know, show them what bands are cool. Because nobody grew up, like, already being a full-fledged psychobilly. You weren't born with a quiff listening to The Meteors and have a whole T-shirt collection already. You have to start somewhere.
Member 2: Yeah, someone's gotta expose you to it. So help them out.

Similarly, a concert promoter in Southern California summed up his philosophy during one of our conversations as "Don't hate! Educate!" He recently posted additional thoughts on Facebook: "Encourage new people to get into [psychobilly]. This is not a competition. Who cares if you know some really obscure band from wherever. Old heads need to be more welcoming. Shit.

Everyone needs to be more welcoming. We're a small scene but we don't have to be. Psychobilly kicks ass too much for it to be listened to just by a few people."

Reflecting a similar desire to share the music with those who want to listen to it, another Psychobilly Worldwide user added: "I still after 15 years of playing music and recording bands and booking shows in this scene can't understand why people are still so worried about street cred, and the holier than thou crap. If punk is a single swiming [sic] pool on Africa, psychobilly is a shot glass. Be happy somebody besides yourself listens to good bands." As these comments indicate, there is a contingent that wants the scene not only to be discovered by more people, but to grow and evolve in new musical directions.

One of the reasons psychobilly gatekeepers dislike Tiger Army in particular is that they have drawn on a variety of influences and have refused to follow a template. Lead singer and guitarist Nick 13 was clearly informed by the genre's innovators. He has spoken publicly about discovering The Meteors and traveling to a psychobilly festival in Germany in the early 1990s; since psychobilly was a rare underground secret in the United States at the time, this was the only way he could have personally experienced the legends who had invented the genre. But he did not want to merely imitate something that had been done before. He pushed the boundaries of the genre and experimented with a myriad of influences. In actuality, he did what the first psychobilly musicians did, as demonstrated in Chapter 1. First-wavers pushed against the clichés of rockabilly and punk, drawing on things that interested them specifically, such as gore and horror, and daring to insult and offend anyone who was not ready for a "bastardized" mutation of rockabilly and punk. The Meteors, The Sharks, Guana Batz, and King Kurt all sound very different from one another. They each explored their love for rockabilly and punk but had a unique vision of what that fusion could sound like.

Some observant psychobillies have noted the irony of the contemporary debate: Why are the fans of The Meteors and other bands from that initial creative period of psychobilly, bands who rebelled against conventionality, predictability, and stagnation, so insistent on only legitimizing that "old school" sound? The following posts from Psychobilly Worldwide criticize OTMAPP fans and other gatekeepers for their narrow-mindedness, given the subculture's diverse beginnings:

Psychobilly should be, and is, a music style that has its innovators. The reason behind the 80s movement was to take the music to a different place and a lot of today's groups are experimenting with

new stuff. The history will always be there but it has to keep rollin'
or it will just stagnate.

Isn't psychobilly intrinsically supposed to be expanding the boundaries of "billy" music? Tiger Army did that, as did lots of others.

The UK scene died almost completely out [in the late 1980s] and
moved to mainland Europe. When the European psychobilly scene
stagnated in the late '90s it was rediscovered by the Americans. Up
through the 2000s, that actually yet again blew life into the European
scene, bringing out old bands that had been defunct for years.
Unfortunately we have reached another point of stagnation in the
scene worldwide but I assure you that bitching does not help. We
desperately need some young blood (both on and off stage) to carry
on the heritage and I don't care if that means bands not up to par
with the psycho police's standards or not.

When I talked to a performer at the Pineda Festival, he observed that some
people were upset to find bands on the bill who did not play "authentic"
psychobilly. He felt that his own band, which he considered "neo-rockabilly,"
did not conform to certain stereotypes about the "old school" psychobilly
sound. For him, nothing should conform to stereotypes, because the subculture was built on rebellion:

Lucas: That's what it's all about. The '50s people rebelled against
what was happening.
Kim: Yeah, that's what it was. Yes.
Lucas: It happened again in the very late '70s, early '80s. Now people
say, "You can't listen outside psychobilly. You can't do that. Why
are The Toy Dolls [a punk band] on a psychobilly festival?" and
all that, you know. It's like, come on.
Kim: Keep rebelling.
Lucas: We were always pushing the envelope, and people go, "Oh,
you can't do that." Why? We want to rebel.

Another interviewee, who has participated in the subculture since the
early 1980s, agreed. He noted that psychobilly started precisely because
youth wanted to experiment: "Older people were telling us teens what we
could or couldn't do or wear or listen to. This scene was created to rebel
against all that." I asked him how he felt about those who embraced only a
very strict type of psychobilly as "authentic" and wanted to "protect" the
scene from diverse influences. He expressed his concern: "To think this

scene I love so much is tolerating idiots like that pisses me off. They have missed the point completely!"

Concluding Thoughts: Stagnation or Change?

What happens when a subculture that originally valued nonconformity begins to reject anything that does not conform to one particular set of aesthetic guidelines? Is it against the philosophy of the original psychobilly movement to shut down innovation and privilege only one way of being and sounding "psychobilly"? Dylan Clark notes that punk never really died, "it faked its own death": "By slipping free of its orthodoxies—its costumes, musical regulations, behaviors, and thoughts—punk embodied the anarchism it aspired to" (2003, 231). He argues that punk survived by escaping the limelight of mainstream interest: "The do-it-yourself culture had spawned independent record labels, specialty record stores, and music venues: in these places culture could be produced with less capitalism, more autonomy, and more anonymity" (231). For him, punk is sustained outside the grasp of corporate culture.

Psychobilly, on the other hand, may only survive if it comes out of its protected shell a bit. Like its fans, I do not want to see the genre become ever more commodified, but I believe the history of psychobilly's development demonstrates that the subculture has only survived when it has embraced change. What would have happened to the subculture in the 1980s as it faced its first possible extinction if the "second wave" bands such as Demented Are Go, Mad Sin, and Nekromantix had not experimented with a different interpretation of the style that found new fans? As Craig Brackenridge argues, these bands warded off the extinction of the community in part because they "attracted followers outside the psychobilly fraternity particularly amongst many punks" (2007, 40). One member of a band that was particularly influential in the 1980s told me, "Bands are trying too hard today to be certain way, whether it's 'old school' or whatever. They are missing the boat completely. We never wanted to be the king of the subgenre. We wanted our music to appeal to people in the scene and other people outside the scene." What would have happened to the subculture in the 1990s as it faced its second possible extinction had not Hellcat Records exposed Tiger Army, Nekromantix, and HorrorPops to alternative music audiences? Kim Nekroman, among others, believes that the development of that third wave was "the only reason overseas bands were able to keep coming back," supported by a whole new generation of enthusiastic and energetic fans and performers (Downey 2004). Psychobilly fan Ken Partridge suggests that as long as some bands are content to produce derivative reinventions of old-school psychobilly clichés, then the gatekeepers should be content to let others do as they please: "Bands that distinguish themselves by pushing boundaries do so at the risk of alienating scenesters, though maybe they ought to stop worrying about such things. After all, if only The Meteors are pure psychobilly, everyone else is free to experiment" (2015).

By definition, subcultures occupy a liminal space. In order to remain "sub," participants attempt to remain relatively autonomous, rejecting mainstream tastes and norms as they pursue the expression of their own distinct identity. As with most subcultures, there is an overwhelming belief throughout the psychobilly community that mainstream success is inherently at odds with an authentic subcultural status (see Moore 2005; Spracklen 2014; Hannerz 2015; Haenfler 2016). At the same time, as demonstrated by the elitist impulses within the community that have been described here, remaining too closed-minded can jeopardize the very principles that a creative subculture such as psychobilly was initially based on. In addition, some fans, like Craig Brackenridge, would actually love to see psychobilly artists achieve recognition, particularly in economic terms: "If I had my way the British pioneers of psychobilly would be sunning themselves by the pools of LA mansions, thumbing their way through wads of royalty cheques, sipping Merrydown from crystal glasses and blasting out enough psychobilly on the hi-fi to piss off their neighbours. They deserve it" (2003, 93). Ultimately, the survival of a subculture comes down to a fine balance between maintaining a distinct and autonomous identity and attracting new fans.

In psychobilly's case, I imagine there will always be young people who are looking for the particular combination of elements that defines this subculture: loud, fast music with some rockabilly and some punk that has a sense of humor, rejects politics, and embraces horror and gore in a tongue-and-cheek way. There will always be some who will be intrigued by the campy yet dark leisure that psychobilly offers. There will be those who continue to search for nondominant, nonmainstream communities in which they can express countercultural values and resist hegemonic values and norms. There will be those "young people, the working classes and others bereft of power, jobs and status, who find in the collective resistance of alternative leisure solace and communicative satisfaction," as Karl Spracklen puts it (2014, 253–254). There will be those frustrated, marginalized, and stigmatized members of society who benefit from subcultural participation, deriving satisfaction, social capital, and economic support by identifying as part of a community of other nonnormative individuals. There will be those who seek to disrupt hegemonic structures, to "under-fuck the system," as Shane Greene argues, all while having fun: breaking taboos, defying institutional attempts to control them and their bodies, refusing to "play the game," expressing nonnormative ways of being, and calling attention to the constructedness of ideas about normativity. Ultimately, I hope that debates about authenticity are rendered moot when all the benefits of participation are taken into account. What really matters are the meaningful ways in which subcultural participation improves the daily lived experience of psychobillies who have found this community. I hope this book helps to shine light on the ways that subcultural participation and identification helps these fans survive.

When did you first hear psychobilly? Can you describe your first memory of it?

What did you listen to before psychobilly?

Do you still listen to other types of music?

What do you like about psychobilly? What attracted you to it?

How do you define psychobilly? How would you describe it to someone who isn't a psychobilly?

What's "billy" about it?

What does the "psycho" in psychobilly mean?

Is it important to you that the music be "underground" and not widely popular in the mainstream?

Do you think that psychobilly is a "politics-free" space? If so, is that partly why you are interested in it?

Do you think horror or science fiction is an important part of psychobilly? If so, are you interested in those themes, and why?

Do you like to wreck? If so, what's fun about wrecking?

What do you like about going to psychobilly events ("shows")?

What are some of your favorite psychobilly songs, and why?

Do you identify first and foremost as a member of this particular subculture? Is your everyday life largely informed by your participation in this subculture?

How do you express yourself through your fashion choices? Do you think that you dress "like a psychobilly"?

Would you classify psychobilly as a primarily working-class subculture?

What do you like most about being part of the psychobilly community?

What do you have in common with other psychobillies other than the music?

Do you hang out mostly with other psychobillies?

Do you think psychobilly celebrates rebellion, nonconformity, and taboo-breaking? If so, is psychobilly's "undergroundness," rebelliousness, or unconventionality something that appealed to you when you discovered it, and does that continue to appeal to you now?

Have you tended to identify as different from the "norm," as rebellious, or as not interested in "mainstream" trends and culture? If so, do you see your rejection of "the mainstream" as a choice you made, or do you feel that you were stigmatized, marginalized, or excluded from mainstream society?

Do you feel that there are an equal number of female and male musicians?

Do you feel that there is any difference in the way that women and men are treated in the scene?

How/where would you like to see the psychobilly subculture continue to grow/go from here?

What excites you about something that's happening in the psychobilly scene today?

What do you really want people to know about psychobilly? What do you think is really important for me to represent and convey about the scene?

DISCOGRAPHY

Batmobile. *Batmobile*. Kix 4 U Records. 1985.

Citizen Fish. *Millennia Madness (Selected Notes from the Late 20th Century)*. Bluurg Records. 1995.

The Creepshow. *Run for Your Life*. Stomp Records. 2008.

Demented Are Go. *In Sickness and in Health*. I.D. Records. 1986.

Dypsomaniaxe. *One Too Many*. Tombstone Records. 1993.

Frantic Flintstones. *Take a Hike*. Kix 4 U Records. 1991.

HorrorPops. *Hell Yeah!* Hellcat Records. 2004.

———. *Kiss Kiss Kill Kill*. Hellcat Records. 2008.

King Kurt. *Banana Banana*. Stiff Records. 1984.

The Meteors. *Hell Ain't Hot Enough for Me*. Sonovabitch Records. 1994.

———. *In Heaven*. Lost Soul Records. 1981.

———. *Johnny Remember Me*. I.D. Records. 1983.

———. *Meteor Madness*. Ace. 1981.

———. *Only The Meteors Are Pure Psychobilly*. Anagram Records. 1988.

———. *Teenagers from Outer Space*. Big Beat Records. 1986.

———. *Undead, Unfriendly and Unstoppable*. Anagram Records. 1989.

———. *Wreckin' Crew*. I.D. Records. 1983.

The Mutilators. *She Put the Baby in the Microwave*. Stroked and Bored Records. 2009.

Nekromantix. *Brought Back to Life*. Intermusic. 1992.

———. *Curse of the Coffin*. Nervous Records. 1991.

———. *Dead Girls Don't Cry*. Hellcat Records. 2004.

———. *Demons Are a Girl's Best Friend*. Kick Music. 1996.

———. *Hellbound*. Tombstone. 1989.

Norm and the Nightmarez. *Psychobilly D.N.A.* Western Star. 2016

The Quakes. *The Quakes*. Nervous Records. 1988.
The Rocketz. *Rise of the Undead*. Hairball8 Records. 2005.
The Sharks. *Phantom Rockers*. Nervous Records. 1983.
———. *Sir Psycho*. Fury Records. 1996.
The Surfin' Wombatz. *Menagerie of Abominations*. Western Star. 2017.
Torment. *Hypnosis*. Nervous Records. 1990.
Various Artists. *Psycho Attack over Europe*. Kix 4 U. 1985.
Various Artists. *Psycho Vixens*. Raucous Records. 2007.

ENDNOTES

INTRODUCTION: SUBCULTURAL PARTICIPATION
AS A SURVIVAL STRATEGY

1. A work boot that quickly gained popularity among working-class subcultures in the 1960s, predominantly among skinheads and punks.

2. Snakebite, equal parts cider and lager, became popular at psychobilly clubs in the United Kingdom.

3. I unpack the term "mainstream" later in the book. For now, I use it as my interlocutors did and as many members of subcultures do: "to denote an imaginary hegemonic center of corporatized culture. . . . It serves to conveniently outline a dominant culture for purposes of cultural critique and identity formation" (Clark 2003, 233).

4. Paul Hodkinson observes that most contemporary theories agree that subcultures are represented by a *distinct* set of values, behaviors, and style, but not all scholars agree that the distinct characteristics of the group are necessarily representative of "difference from the mainstream." He notes "the continued utilisation of subculture as useful academic currency for distinctive youth groupings with a clear collective character and, *usually*, a discernable sense of difference vis-à-vis a perceived broader society" (2016, 633; emphasis added).

5. I borrow Ross Haenfler's (2006) term "subculturalist" to refer to participants in a subculture.

6. Throughout this manuscript, I have opted to use "they" (and its inflected and derivative forms, such as "their" and "themself") as an epicene (gender-neutral) singular pronoun. This was done to avoid reducing the diversity and fluidity of gender identities.

7. Nancy MacDonald also makes this distinction in her understanding of subculture: "A subculture may be defined as that which *constructs, perceives and portrays itself as standing apart from others* as an isolated, defined and boundaried group" (2001, 152; emphasis added).

8. Having established that "the dominant culture," "the mainstream," "the normative," and "the conventional" are imaginary constructions and seeking to convey the realness of these terms to those psychobillies who meaningfully define themselves against such categories, I hereafter discontinue the use of quotation marks around these terms.

9. This is by no means an exhaustive or comprehensive evaluation of subcultural and post-subcultural theory. For general summaries of key theories, see Bennett 1999; Blackman 2005, 2014; Gelder 2005; Williams 2011; Haenfler 2014, 2016; and Hodkinson 2016.

10. An early critique of the CCCS's portrayal of homogeneous working-class subcultures and its romanticization of collective and symbolic "resistance" came from within the CCCS, in Gary Clarke's essay "Defending Ski-Jumpers: A Critique of Theories of Youth Subcultures" ([1981] 1990). Influential post-subcultural studies that emerged in the 1990s and 2000s include Redhead 1993; Melechi 1993; Chaney 1996; Redhead, Wynne, and O'Connor 1997; Polhemus 1997; Bennett 1999, 2000; Malbon 1999; Hetherington 2000; Miles 2000; Muggleton 2000; Muggleton and Weinzierl 2003; Bennett and Kahn-Harris 2004; and Huq 2006.

11. Reflecting on the "post-subcultural turn," Bennett notes that Polhemus's often-cited description has actually done a disservice to post-subcultural theory by implying that youth do not attribute any meaning to the styles and commodities they choose to consume (2011, 498).

12. Many journalists have also proclaimed the death of subcultures, either lamenting the demise of stylistically unified social groups or celebrating hyperindividualism. Consider this quote from an article in *The Guardian*, "Youth Subcultures: What Are They Now?": "Mods, punks, soulboys, metallers, goths, hippies: there was a time when young people made it clear what tribe and music they were into by the way they dressed. Not any more" (Petridis 2014). See also the eight-part series "The Death of Subculture," written by digital marketing company Further (J. Gill 2017); the *Huffington Post* piece "Is Subculture Dead?" (Mallory 2014); and the *Telegraph* article "Why Don't Young People Want to Be Part of a Tribe Any More?" (Moss 2015).

13. In "The Post-subcultural Turn: Some Reflections Ten Years On" (2011), Bennett responds to some of these critiques.

14. See Bennett 1999, 2011; Stahl 1999; Muggleton and Weinzierl 2003; Bennett and Kahn-Harris 2004; Blackman 2005; Hesmondhalgh 2005; Shildrick and MacDonald 2006; and Hodkinson 2016.

15. Shane Blackman also notes that "the postmodernist understanding of youth subculture . . . denies the immense diversity in the CCCS theorization" (2005, 1).

16. For instance, Andy Bennett (1999) and Ben Malbon (1999) tend to emphasize "taste, aesthetics and affectivity as primary drivers for participation in forms of collective youth cultural activity" (Bennett 2011, 495). Subcultural scholars such as Blackman (2005) and Shildrick and MacDonald (2006) criticize post-subculturalists for not paying adequate attention to how structural inequalities affected youth's consumption of style: "This new 'postmodern' work on subculture has been criticized . . . as creating problems for sociology because of the apparent reluctance to integrate social structures into the analysis and instead promote an individualistic understanding of the social" (Blackman 2005, 8–9). Bennett (2011) responds to this critique in the article previously cited in this note.

17. Ross Haenfler's sections "Why Do People Participate?" and "Subcultures as Strategies" (2014, 33–40) provide a helpful exploration of subcultural theories and ethnographic studies on this subject. Here he adapts and updates some of the strategies discussed in Brake's comparative work on youth cultures (1985, 24) but adds relevant perspectives

from more recent studies of subcultures. In addition, I draw on a variety of works that seek to understand what subculturalists derive from identifying with and participating in "alternative" communities, including Leblanc 1999; Fikentscher 2000; Halnon 2004; Holland 2004; Williams and Copes 2005; Haenfler 2006; Greener and Hollands 2006; Kahn-Harris 2007; Brill 2008; G. St. John 2009; Riley, Griffin, and Morley 2010; P. Greene 2011; Spracklen and Spracklen 2012; Winge 2012; Thompson 2015; and Dimou and Ilan 2018.

18. See Clarke (1981) 1990; Kruse 1993; Thornton 1996; Muggleton 2000; Kahn-Harris 2007; and Berger 2008, among others, for this critique. Shane Blackman (2014, 505) argues, however, that Phil Cohen and Dick Hebdige both engaged in grounded ethnographic fieldwork, and suggests that this criticism is not entirely warranted.

19. Stephen Baron (1989) also discusses the value of participant observation over surveys, particularly for subcultural studies, noting that subculturalists may not be likely to complete questionaires without having first built trusting relationships with the ethnographer (211).

20. Historically also called "informants," "consultants," "teachers," or "translators."

21. This is because the subculture developed in England in the 1980s and only arrived in America about a decade later. Generally, then, there are older psychobilly fans in England. Thus while I was in England and Ireland, I focused on interviewing people who had participated in the psychobilly subculture in the 1980s, since that was my only opportunity to do so. But I also interviewed younger participants there.

22. Only one interview lasted under an hour (because the interviewee needed to leave), and several interviews took more than three hours.

23. My choices are influenced by Melanie Lowe's description of transcribing speech from group interviews (2004).

24. I began interviews with an explanation of my purpose and explained (and reminded them throughout) that they could specify anything that they wished to remain "off the record." Interviews concluded with the signing of IRB (institutional review board) paperwork, which confirmed their consent to include any material from the interview that they had not specified as off the record.

25. An early and influential example of a reflexive ethnography is Clifford Geertz's *The Interpretation of Cultures* (1973). In his chapter "Notes on the Balinese Cockfight," he describes how hiding from the police with villagers allowed him to establish rapport with his interlocutors.

26. For instance, many assumed I must be from a privileged, upper-class background, given that I had attended a four-year university and then gone on to graduate school. Many of my interviewees talked to me extensively about their desire to pursue higher education but felt that they did not have the financial luxury or the educational background to do so.

27. For a detailed history of psychobilly, see Craig Brackenridge's *Hell's Bent on Rockin': A History of Psychobilly* (2007).

CHAPTER 1: THE DEVELOPMENT OF PSYCHOBILLY

1. "Loud Fast Rules!," the title of a 1979 song by punk band Stimulators, became a catchphrase to describe punk's aesthetic approach in general.

2. The Ted subculture was interpreted by the CCCS as a working-class reaction to the unfulfilled promise of a more classless and egalitarian society after World War II (Jefferson 1976). Working-class youth appropriated the Edwardian look of the upper class, "lending an aura of dignity, grace and elegance to young men whose fathers had gone

through life flat cap in hand, stylistically uninhibited, knowing their place" (Polhemus 1994, 34). Although the sound track to the style in the immediate postwar period was big band, rock 'n' roll became synonymous with Ted culture by the mid-1950s.

3. Platform shoes with a crinkled sole several inches high. The Teddy Boys adopted them in the 1950s, pairing them with drainpipe trousers. Punks caught on to the trend when Malcolm McLaren started selling them in his "Let It Rock" shop, and they have continued to be popular within the Teddy Boy, rockabilly, punk, and psychobilly subcultures.

4. Angela McRobbie (1988) provides a case study of the subcultural use of anti-fashion in her exploration of the secondhand clothes stalls that punks operated in London flea markets.

5. Roy Williams, a lifelong Teddy Boy and the founder of neo-rockabilly and psychobilly label Nervous Records, underscored to me that rockabilly is a subset of rock 'n' roll: "All rockabilly is rock 'n' roll, but not all rock 'n' roll is rockabilly."

6. Punk developed first in New York clubs such as CBGB, with bands such as Television, the Ramones, Patti Smith, and the New York Dolls, around 1974. Instrumental to the development of punk in the United Kingdom was Malcolm McLaren's return in 1975 from the United States, where he had been involved in the punk scene and had managed the New York Dolls. Upon his return, he formed and managed the Sex Pistols, who drew mainstream attention to the subculture.

7. How the word "psychobilly" came to be associated with this subculture is complex and not entirely clear. As the subculture began to develop, different people called it different things. Nigel Lewis of The Meteors remembers calling the music "psychebilly" in the early 1980s to convey the psychedelic—or "anything goes"—nature of the music (Decay 2004). In another interview, Lewis recalls being at a party where he called an erratic drunk person a "psychobilly," referencing the song "One Piece at a Time" specifically, and then realizing that the word could also be used to describe the type of music he performed (Dipple 2015, 97). The Meteors referred to their own music in various interviews as "punk hillbilly" (Wall 1981), "punkabilly" (*No Class Fanzine* 1981), "mutant rockabilly" (*News Beat* 1982), and "psycho rockabilly" (Mark Robertson, in interview with author). Then in 1981, *Sounds* magazine (Wall 1981) issued a story on The Meteors that featured a cover photo of Fenech captioned "The Psychobilly Kid," and the term stuck. In short, the subculture was associated with a number of different names until it settled on "psychobilly."

8. They also produced covers of some of the more twisted examples of rock 'n' roll they could find, such as "Johnny Remember Me" (recorded originally by John Leyton in 1961), a "death ditty" of a man haunted by his dead lover (*Johnny Remember Me*, 1983).

9. Pogo dancing refers to the way punks would jump up and down to the music, often knocking their bodies into one another due to their uncontrolled movements.

10. As discussed in the Introduction, wrecking is the style of dancing associated with psychobilly.

11. The 100 Club played an important role in the history of punk, as it was the location of the first punk festival in 1976. The event brought attention to the underground movement and helped the subculture move into the mainstream.

12. Plaid textile common in rockabilly fashion.

CHAPTER 2: CARNIVALESQUE EVENTS AND TRANSGRESSIVE PERFORMANCE

1. At the beginning of the first wave of psychobilly's development, there was sometimes little difference between a "neo-rockabilly" and a "psychobilly" band. They had

in common a desire to break free from the clichés and restrictions of the rockabilly scene by playing faster, singing about unconventional subjects, and drawing from other popular music styles. Accordingly, neo-rockabilly bands shared the Klub Foot's stage with bands that were a little more "psycho," and Klub Foot regulars enjoyed both styles. First-wave neo-rockabilly and psychobilly bands who played at the Klub Foot include (dates indicate the year that the band was formed) Restless (1978—Ipswich, Suffolk), The Meteors (1980—South London), The Sharks (1980—Bristol), King Kurt (1981—London), The Stingrays (1981—Couch End, North London), Guana Batz (1982—Feltham, West London), The Krewmen (1982—Surrey), Demented Are Go (1982—Cardiff, Wales), The Caravans (1983—Portsmouth, Hampshire), Frenzy (1983—Bristol), Batmobile (1983—Rotterdam, Netherlands), The Pharaohs (1983—Harlow, Essex), Torment (1985—Bristol), Long Tall Texans (1985—Brighton, East Sussex), Coffin Nails (1985—Reading), Skitzo (1985—South London), and The Quakes (1986—New York, then London).

2. ABC Records released the first volume in 1984. The fifth and final volume was released in 1988, the year that the Clarendon Hotel was demolished.

3. My interlocutors pointed out that one only needed to be sixteen years old to get into the club, and that younger teenagers who could "pass" as sixteen often were able to get in. Accordingly, many psychobillies were already seasoned club-goers by the age of eighteen.

4. Drawing on Pierre Bourdieu's definition of social capital, Sarah Thornton describes "subcultural capital" as the knowledge and cultural commodities that individuals acquire in order to gain status within the subcultural group and identify themselves as knowledgeable members (1996).

5. When my interlocutors used "tribe" they meant a community of like-minded alternative individuals. Their use of the word did not convey the partial and temporary nature of post-subcultural "neo-tribes" as that term is used by Bennett (1999).

6. Hall 1988, 58.

7. Although the moderator deleted posts that took political "sides" or conveyed a specific political agenda, posts were allowed that expressed a disdainful or humorous approach to politics. For instance, one graphic artist designed a series of images that transformed Bill Clinton, George W. Bush, Barack Obama, Donald Trump, Vladimir Putin, and Kim Jong-un into psychobillies by adding quiffs and distinctive markers of the subcultural fashion style. Since these images were not endorsements of a political persuasion but rather a comical way of poking fun at politics and representing the subculture's general antiauthoritarian attitude, they received great reviews from the users of the Facebook group.

8. There are many parallels between Bakhtin's understanding of the "grotesque body" and Julia Kristeva's (1982) concept of the "abject" in terms of how subcultures may transgress certain norms (see Kahn-Harris 2007, 29–30).

9. GG Allin (1956–1993) was a shock punk rocker known for his notorious stage antics, including the consumption of feces, violence, and self-injury, which resulted in many venues banning him for the damage he caused.

10. Of course, psychobillies are not the first subculture to engage in wildly carnivalesque behavior in their countercultural spaces. Indeed, first-wavers were influenced by the transgressive behaviors of the original rockabillies, who shuddered and shook their limbs in ways that horrified conservatives. They were aware of the over-the-top performances by shock rockers such as Screamin' Jay Hawkins, Screaming Lord Sutch, Ozzy Osbourne, and Alice Cooper, and punk rebels such as Iggy Pop and Sid Vicious. Many of these artists also broke taboos, cutting themselves on stage (e.g., Sid Vicious),

smearing themselves with food (famously, Iggy Pop with peanut butter), incorporating dead animals in their performances (Ozzy Osbourne biting the head off a bat), and wildly theatrical performances that featured lots of fake blood and simulated beheadings (Alice Cooper).

11. This collaborative behavior, in which participants assist those who need help, is similar in heavy metal (Berger 1999, 71) and punk (Tsitsos 1999, 406).

12. I had to ask what "baloobas" meant. As *Urban Dictionary* (Shenaniganz00 2006) defines it, "to get baloobas or go baloobas is a set of behaviour occurring when a person has a consumed a large amount of drink or drugs and behaves wildly, erratically, but all the while having fun."

13. In rare cases, a particularly angry or assertive individual may disrupt the supportive nature of the pit. Typically, antagonistic individuals are encouraged to leave or are removed from the pit by other psychobillies, or in some cases, by security guards.

14. The title of The Meteors' 1983 album, *Wreckin' Crew*, pays tribute to the wrecking fans of the foundational psychobilly band.

15. This is so in part because it is readily accessible and relatively cheap, and those using it illegally are rarely arrested (unless they're caught driving under the influence, of course) (see Thornton 1996, 21).

16. Psychobilly's unique style has been briefly documented in a variety of books, including Ted Polhemus's *Street Style: From Sidewalk to Catwalk* (1994), Gavin Baddeley's *Street Culture: 50 Years of Subculture Style* (2015), and Martin Roach's *Dr. Martens: A History of Rebellious Self-Expression* (2015).

CHAPTER 3: THE POWER AND PLEASURE OF FANTASIZING ABOUT MONSTERS, MURDERERS, AND MADNESS

1. The band's name reflected the members' witty and subversive humor: Demented Are Go was based on the phrase "Demon Teds Are Go!," itself a reference to the "Thunderbirds Are Go!" catchphrase of *Thunderbirds*, a British science fiction television show that aired in the mid-1960s. True to their name, they were a demonic version of Teddy Boy rock 'n' roll music and fashion.

2. The movies in *The Purge* series also depict this carnivalesque abandonment of rules and law, to an extreme.

3. Consider the variety of video games (*Resident Evil*, *Plants vs. Zombies*), television shows (*The Walking Dead*), movies (*Night of the Living Dead*, *Zombieland*), books (*The Zombie Survival Guide: Complete Protection from the Living Dead*, *Pride and Prejudice and Zombies*), and events (humans versus zombies live action role-playing games on college campuses, walk-through horror mazes in which people run from zombies) that root for human victory over the evil zombies.

CHAPTER 4: MALE DOMINANCE AND FEMALE EMPOWERMENT

1. One psychobilly-related female band released an album in the 1980s: The Shillelagh Sisters (in 1984). While they played a punk-tinged version of rockabilly and new wave, they considered themselves more "neo-rockabilly" than "psychobilly."

2. Mad Marge and the Stonecutters, Silver Shine, The Hatchet Wounds, and The Formaldebrides.

3. HorrorPops (Denmark/United States), 13 Black Coffins (United States), Klax (United States), Devil Doll (United States), Nekromantix (United States), Mad Marge and

the Stonecutters (United States), The Creepshow (Canada), The Hellfreaks (Hungary), and Night Nurse (Finland).

4. The Creepshow (Canada), Eve Hell and the Razors (Canada), Klax (United States), Thee Merry Widows (United States), Termin-acks (United States), Mad Skeletons (Mexico), As Diabatz (Brazil), Trix or Treat (Thailand), Silver Shine (Hungary), The Wolfgangs (Hungary), The Hellfreaks (Hungary), Clockwork Psycho (Slovenia), Kitty in a Kasket (Germany), Retarded Rats (Germany), Night Nurse (Finland), and Zombina and the Skeletones (United Kingdom).

5. Obviously not every psychobilly song written by a male fantasizes about sexual control over women. In fact, one songwriter pointed out to me that many of his songs place women in control: "Try my 'Kiss of the Spider Woman' from when I was in Mickey & the Mutants. She killed her sexual encounters after sleeping with them. There's also my previous band's song 'Widow, Widow Maker' (by The Bionic Krugerrands). That's about a girl who grew up with abusive stepfathers. She marries guys then kills them."

6. This issue has been discussed in detail by female anthropologists and ethno-musicologists such as Carol Babiracki (2008) and several authors in the edited volume *Sex, Sexuality, and the Anthropologist* (Markowitz and Ashkenazi 1999). Female eth-nographers often have a hard time making it clear that they are serious researchers, as male members of the culture assume that their interest in them is primarily sexual or romantic.

7. *Pleasantville* features a scene in which the housewife masturbates and experi-ences her first orgasm. This causes the movie to change from black-and-white to color, symbolizing the radical leap forward this represented for feminism and the possibility of fulfilled sexual desire for women.

CHAPTER 5: THE POWER, JOY, AND PURPOSE OF SOCIAL AND ECONOMIC CAPITAL

1. Many fans will use online discussion groups to share stories about the friendli-ness—or unfriendliness—of certain psychobilly bands, leading fans to eventually boy-cott some musicians who have a reputation for being rude to their fans.

2. Similarly, Sarah Thornton recognized that club cultures established their own forms of exclusion and hierarchy (1996).

AFTERWORD

1. The cartoon references Little Richard's song "Lucille," in which the narrator is torn between his feelings for Lucille and Peggy Sue.

2. Rockabillies use grease or pomade, while psychobillies use hairspray, to stiffen their quiffs.

REFERENCES

Abu-Lughod, Lila. 1990. "Can There Be a Feminist Ethnography?" *Women and Performance: A Journal of Feminist Theory* 5 (1): 7–27.

Adorno, Theodor. (1941) 1990. "On Popular Music." In *On Record: Rock, Pop and the Written Word*, edited by Simon Frith and Andrew Goodwin, 301–314. London: Routledge.

———. (1967) 1981. *Prisms*. Translated by Samuel Weber and Shierry Weber. Cambridge, MA: MIT Press.

Adorno, T. W., and Max Horkheimer. (1947) 2002. *Dialectic of Enlightenment: Philosophical Fragments*. Edited by Gunzelin Schmid Noerr. Translated by Edmund Jephcott. Stanford, CA: Stanford University Press.

Anderson, Tammy L. 2009. *Rave Culture: The Alteration and Decline of a Philadelphia Music Scene*. Philadelphia: Temple University Press.

Babcock, Barbara. 1978. *The Reversible World: Symbolic Inversion in Art and Society*. Oxford: Clarendon Press.

Babiracki, Carol. 2008. "What's the Difference? Reflections on Gender and Research in Village India." In *Shadows in the Field*, edited by Gregory Barz and Timothy Cooley, 167–182. 2nd ed. New York: Oxford University Press.

Baddeley, Gavin. 2015. *Street Culture: 50 Years of Subculture Style*. London: Plexus.

Bakhtin, Mikhail. (1936) 1984. *Rabelais and His World*. Translated by H. Iswolsky. Bloomington: Indiana University Press.

Baron, Stephen W. 1989. "Resistance and Its Consequences: The Street Culture of Punks." *Youth and Society* 21 (2): 207–237.

Barz, Gregory, and Timothy Cooley. 2008. *Shadows in the Field*. 2nd ed. New York: Oxford University Press.

Baulch, Emma. 2007. *Making Scenes: Reggae, Punk, and Death Metal in 1990s Bali*. Durham, NC: Duke University Press, 2007.

Bayton, Mavis. 1997. "Women and the Electric Guitar." In *Sexing the Groove: Popular Music and Gender*, edited by Sheila Whitely, 37–49. New York: Routledge.

BBC. 2013. "The Thatcher Years in Statistics." *BBC News*, April 9. Accessed August 20, 2018. https://www.bbc.com/news/uk-politics-22070491.

Becker, Howard. 1963. *Outsiders: Studies in the Sociology of Deviance*. New York: Free Press.

Bedlam Breakout History. 2012. "Bedlam Breakout History." *Alcoholic Rats UK Psychobilly Guide*, September 11. Accessed July 20, 2018. http://alcoholicrats.proboards.com/thread/598/bedlam-breakout-history.

Beem, Christopher. 1999. *The Necessity of Politics: Reclaiming American Public Life*. Chicago: University of Chicago Press.

Benjamin, Walter. 1968. "The Work of Art in the Age of Mechanical Reproduction." In *Illuminations*, edited by Hannah Arendt and translated by Harry Zohn, 217–251. New York: Schocken Books.

Bennett, Andy. 1999. "Subcultures or Neo-tribes? Rethinking the Relationship between Youth, Style and Musical Taste." *Sociology* 33 (3): 599–617.

———. 2000. *Popular Music and Youth Culture: Music, Idetity and Place*. New York: Palgrave Macmillan.

———. 2005. "In Defence of Neo-tribes: A Response to Blackman and Hesmondhalgh." *Journal of Youth Studies* 8 (2): 255–259.

———. 2011. "The Post-subcultural Turn: Some Reflections Ten Years On." *Journal of Youth Studies* 14 (5): 493–506.

Bennett, Andy, and Keith Kahn-Harris, eds. 2004. *After Subculture: Critical Studies in Contemporary Youth Culture*. London: Palgrave.

Berger, Harris. 1999. *Metal, Rock, and Jazz: Perception and the Phenomenology of Musical Experience*. Hanover, NH: University Press of New England.

———. 2008. "Phenomenology and the Ethnography of Popular Music: Ethnomusicology at the Juncture of Cultural Studies and Folklore." In *Shadows in the Field*, edited by Gregory Barz and Timothy Cooley, 62–75. 2nd ed. New York: Oxford University Press.

Bettie Page Clothing. n.d. "Vintage and Retro Clothing for the Modern Woman." Accessed December 1, 2010. http://www.bettiepageclothing.com/.

Biernacki, Patrick, and Dan Waldorf. 1981. "Snowball Sampling." *Sociological Research and Methods* 10: 141–163.

Bishop, Kyle William. 2010. *American Zombie Gothic: The Rise and Fall (and Rise) of the Walking Dead in Popular Culture*. Jefferson, NC: McFarland.

Blackman, Shane. 2005. "Youth Subcultural Theory: A Critical Engagement with the Concept, Its Origins and Politics, from the Chicago School to Postmodernism." *Journal of Youth Studies* 8 (1): 1–20.

———. 2014. "Subculture Theory: An Historical and Contemporary Assessment of the Concept for Understanding Deviance." *Deviant Behavior* 35: 496–512.

Blair, Eric. 2009. "HorrorPops Patricia Talks to Eric Blair at Hootenanny 2009." *Blairing Out with Eric Blair*. YouTube. Accessed January 12, 2011. http://www.youtube.com/watch?v=tjrXJuhDzYM.

Böse, Martina. 2003. "Race and Class in the 'Post-subcultural' Economy." In *The Post-subcultures Reader*, edited by David Muggleton and Rupert Weinzierl, 167–180. Oxford: Berg.

Bourdieu, Pierre. 1986. "Forms of Capital." In *Handbook of Theory and Research for the Sociology of Education*, edited by J. C. Richards, 241–258. New York: Greenwood Press.

Brackenridge, Craig. 2003. *Let's Wreck: Psychobilly Flashbacks from the Eighties and Beyond*. 2nd ed. Nottinghamshire, U.K.: Stormscreen Productions.

———. 2007. *Hell's Bent on Rockin': A History of Psychobilly*. London: Cherry Red Books.

———. 2008. "Interview with As Diabatz." *Old School Psychobilly*. June. Accessed June 15, 2019. http://www.oldschool-psychobilly.de/as_diabatz.htm.

———. 2014a. "Bedlam Breakout Psychobilly Festival #16: Review by Craig Brackenridge." *DogEatRobot Fanzine*, no. 6, 19–22.

———. 2014b. "Pompey Rumble #4: Review by Craig Brackenridge." *DogEatRobot Fanzine*, no. 7, 14–15.

Brake, Michael. 1985. *Comparative Youth Culture: The Sociology of Youth Cultures and Youth Subcultures in America, Britain, and Canada*. New York: Routledge.

Brill, Dunja. 2008. *Goth Culture: Gender, Sexuality and Style*. London: Berg.

Brooks, Daphne. 2008. "The Write to Rock: Racial Mythologies, Feminist Theory, and the Pleasures of Rock Music Criticism." *Women and Music: A Journal of Gender and Culture* 12: 54–62.

Butler, Judith. (1990) 2007. *Gender Trouble: Feminism and the Subversion of Gender*. New York: Routledge.

———. 1990. "Performative Acts and Gender Constitution: An Essay in Phenomenology and Feminist Theory." *Theatre Journal* 40 (4): 519–531.

Cavicchi, Daniel. 2011. *Listening and Longing: Music Lovers in the Age of Barnum*. Middletown, CT: Wesleyan University Press.

Chambers, Iain. 1985. *Urban Rhythms: Pop Music and Popular Culture*. London: Macmillan.

Chaney, David. 1996. *Lifestyles*. London: Routledge.

———. 2004. "Fragmented Culture and Subcultures." In *After Subculture*, edited by Andy Bennett and Keith Kahn-Harris, 36–48. London: Palgrave.

Chatabox, Jerry. 2011. Foreword to *Rockin': The Rockabilly Scene*, by Andrew Shaylor, 9–15. London: Merrell.

Clark, Dylan. 2003. "The Death and Life of Punk, the Last Subculture." In *The Post-Subcultures Reader*, edited by David Muggleton and Rupert Weinzierl, 223–236. Oxford: Berg.

Clarke, Gary. (1981) 1990. "Defending Ski-Jumpers: A Critique of Theories of Youth Subcultures." In *On Record: Rock, Pop and the Written Word*, edited by Simon Frith and Andrew Goodwin, 81–96. London: Routledge.

Clarke, John, Stuart Hall, Tony Jefferson, and Brian Roberts. 1976. "Subcultures, Cultures and Class: A Theoretical Overview." In *Resistance Through Rituals: Youth Subcultures in Post-War Britain*, edited by Stuart Hall and Tony Jefferson, 9–74. London: Routledge.

Clifford, James, and George E. Marcus, eds. 1986. *Writing Culture: The Poetics and Politics of Ethnography*. Berkeley: University of California Press.

Cohen, Albert. 1955. *Delinquent Boys*. New York: Free Press.

Cohen, Sara. 1991. *Rock Culture in Liverpool: Popular Music in the Making*. New York: Oxford University Press.

———. 1993. "Ethnography and Popular Music Studies." *Popular Music* 12 (2): 123–138.

———. 1997. "Men Making a Scene: Rock Music and the Production of Gender." In *Sexing the Groove: Popular Music and Gender*, edited by Sheila Whitely, 17–36. New York: Routledge.

Cohen, Stanley. 1972. *Folk Devils and Moral Panics: The Creation of the Mods and the Rockers*. Cambridge, MA: Blackwell.

Coleman, John. 1988. "Social Capital in the Creation of Human Capital." *American Journal of Sociology* 94: 95–120.

Cranston, Maurice. 1968. Introduction to *The Social Contract*, by Jean-Jacques Rousseau, 9–43. Baltimore, MD: Penguin Books.

Cray, Jen. 2009. "HorrorPops Concert Review." *Ink19*, May 6. Accessed January 5, 2011. http://www.ink19.com/issues/june2009/eventReviews/horrorpops.html.

Dargis, Manohla. 2008. "Always Comfortable in Her Own Skin." *The New York Times*, December 12. Accessed October 20, 2010. http://www.nytimes.com/2008/12/13/movies/13page.html.

Dean, Malcolm. 2013. "Margaret Thatcher's Policies Hit the Poor Hardest—and It's Happening Again." *The Guardian*, April 9. Accessed August 20, 2018. https://www.theguardian.com/society/2013/apr/09/margaret-thatcher-policies-poor-society.

Decay, Mike, dir. 2004. *Psychobilly: A Cancer on Rock'n'Roll*. Produced by Mike Decay and Ronni Thomas. Zombilly Productions. YouTube. Accessed January 15, 2017. https://www.youtube.com/watch?v=Nsd0MqDZUYQ.

Décharné, Max. 2010. *A Rocket in My Pocket: The Hipster's Guide to Rockabilly*. London: Serpent's Tail.

Dimou, Eleni, and Jonathan Ilan. 2018. "Taking Pleasure Seriously: The Political Significance of Subcultural Practice." *Journal of Youth Studies* 21 (1): 1–18.

Dipple, Jane. 2015. "Rockin with the Undead: How Zombies Infected the Psychobilly Subculture." In *The Zombie Renaissance in Popular Culture*, edited by Laura Hubner, Marcus Leaning, and Paul Manning, 91–106. New York: Palgrave Macmillan.

DJ Trash. 2010. "Fujiyama Mamas: Women in Psychobilly." *That Cat Named Johnny Trash* (blog), April 1. Accessed August 4, 2017. http://thatcatcalledjohnnytrash.blogspot.com/2010/04/fujiyama-mamas-women-in-psychobilly-and.html.

DogEatRobot Fanzine. 2013a. "The Blue Cats: Interview with Clint Bradley." No. 4, 2–8.

———. 2013b. "Interview with Mark 'MadDog' Cole." No. 4, 12.

———. 2013c. "Interview with the Legendary Bang Bang Bazooka!!" No. 5, 9–12.

———. 2013d. "7th Psychomania Rumble." No. 5, 23–26.

———. 2014. "Interview: Retarded Rats." No. 7, 23–26.

Donovan, Carrie. 1998. "Psychobilly, Creeping into the Culture." *Washington Post*, December 20. Accessed August 5, 2018. http://www.hayridetohell.com/press/wpost.html.

Downey, Ryan. 2004. "Psyched to Be Here." *Alternative Press* 196 (November): 76–82.

Eagleton, Terry. 1981. *Walter Benjamin: Towards a Revolutionary Criticism*. London: Verso.

Farley, Helen. 2009. "Demons, Devils and Witches: The Occult in Heavy Metal Music." In *Heavy Metal Music in Britain*, edited by Gerd Bayer, 73–88. Burlington, VT: Ashgate.

Fast, Susan. 2008. "Calling Ellen Willis: Quarreling with the 'Radicals,' Loving Consumer Culture, and Hearing Women's Voices." *Women and Music: A Journal of Gender and Culture* 12: 44–53.

Fenech, Marc. 1995. "The Meteors . . . and BEFORE . . . and the Birth of Psychobilly (1976–1982)." *Southern & Rocking Music*, no. 5 (January/February), 5–7.

Field, John. 2003. *Social Capital*. London: Routledge.

Fikentscher, Kai. 2000. *"You Better Work!": Underground Dance Music in New York City*. Hanover, NH: Wesleyan University Press.

Fine, Gary A. 2003. "Towards a Peopled Ethnography: Developing a Theory from Group Life." *Ethnography* 4 (1): 41–60.

Fine, Gary Alan, and Brooke Harrington. 2004. "Tiny Publics: Small Groups and Civil Society." *Sociological Theory* 22 (3): 341–356.

Fischer, Nancy. 2015. "Vintage, the First 40 Years: The Emergence and Persistence of Vintage Style in the United States." *Culture Unbound: Journal of Current Cultural Research* 6: 45–66.

Fiske, John. 1989. *Understanding Popular Culture*. Boston: Unwin Hyman.

Flint, David. 2009. *Zombie Holocaust: How the Living Dead Devoured Pop Culture*. London: Plexus.

Foucault, Michael. 1978. *The History of Sexuality*. Vol. 1, *An Introduction*, translated by Robert Hurley. New York: Pantheon Books.

Freeland, Cynthia. 2000. *The Naked and the Undead: Evil and the Appeal of Horror*. Boulder, CO: Westview Press.

Friedan, Betty. 1963. *The Feminine Mystique*. New York: Norton.

Frith, Simon. 1981. *Sound Effects: Youth, Leisure, and the Politics of Rock 'n' Roll*. New York: Pantheon.

———. 1988. *Music for Pleasure: Essays in the Sociology of Pop*. New York: Routledge.

———. 1996. *Performing Rites: On the Value of Popular Music*. Cambridge, MA: Harvard University Press.

———. 2004. Afterword to *After Subculture: Critical Studies in Contemporary Youth Culture*, edited by Andy Bennett and Keith Kahn-Harris, 173–178. London: Palgrave.

Gardner, Robert Owen. 2010. "Introduction: Spaces of Musical Interaction: Scenes, Subcultures, and Communities." *Studies in Symbolic Interaction* 35: 71–77.

Geertz, Clifford. 1973. *The Interpretation of Cultures: Selected Essays*. New York: Basic Books, 1973.

Gelder, Ken, ed. 2005. *The Subcultures Reader*. 2nd ed. New York: Routledge.

Gelder, Ken, and Sarah Thornton, eds. 1997. *The Subcultures Reader*. New York: Routledge.

Gill, James. 2017. "The Death of Subculture." *Further* (blog), October 25–December 12. Accessed August 18, 2018. https://www.further.co.uk/blog/death-subculture-part-1-changing-role-subculture-21st-century-britain/.

Gill, Pat. 1997. "Technonostalgia: Making the Future Past Perfect." *Camera Obscura* 40–41: 163–179.

Goffman, Erving. 1963. *Stigma: Notes on the Management of Spoiled Identity*. New York: Simon and Schuster.

Goodlad, Lauren M. E., and Michael Bibby, eds. 2007. *Goth: Undead Subculture*. Durham, NC: Duke University Press.

Gramsci, Antonio. 1971. *Selections from the Prison Notebooks*. London: Lawrence and Wishart.

Greene, Paul D. 2011. "Electronic and Affective Overdrive: Tropes of Transgression in Nepal's Heavy Metal Scene." In *Metal Rules the Globe: Heavy Metal Music around the World*, edited by Jeremy Wallach, Harris M. Berger, and Paul D. Greene, 109–134. Durham, NC: Duke University Press.

Greene, Richard. 2006. "The Badness of Undeath." In *The Undead and Philosophy: Chicken Soup for the Soulless*, edited by Richard Greene and K. Silem Mohammad, 3–14. Chicago: Open Court.

Greene, Richard, and K. Silem Mohammad. 2006. "(Un)dead (Un)certainties." In *The Undead and Philosophy: Chicken Soup for the Soulless*, edited by Richard Greene and K. Silem Mohammad, xiii–xvi. Chicago: Open Court.

Greene, Shane. 2012. "The Problem of Peru's Punk Underground: An Approach to Under-Fuck the System." *Journal of Popular Music Studies* 24 (4): 578–589.

Greener, Tracey, and Robert Hollands. 2006. "Beyond Subculture and Post-subculture? The Case of Virtual Psytrance." *Journal of Youth Studies* 9 (4): 393–418.

Greer, Germaine. 1970. *The Female Eunuch*. New York: Farrar, Straus and Giroux.

Grodal, Torben. 1997. *Moving Pictures: A New Theory of Film Genres, Feelings, and Cognition*. Oxford: Clarendon Press.

Guffey, Elizabeth E. 2006. *Retro: The Culture of Revival*. London: Reaktion Books.

Haenfler, Ross. 2006. *Straight Edge: Clean-Living Youth, Hardcore Punk, and Social Change*. New Brunswick, NJ: Rutgers University Press.

———. 2014. *Subcultures: The Basics*. New York: Routledge.

———. 2016. *Goths, Gamers, and Grrrls: Deviance and Youth Subcultures*. 3rd ed. London: Oxford University Press.

Halberstam, Jack. 1998. *Female Masculinity*. Durham, NC: Duke University Press.

Hall, Stuart. 1981. "Notes on Deconstructing 'The Popular.'" In *People's History and Socialist Theory*, edited by Raphael Samuel, 227–240. London: Routledge.

———. 1988. *The Hard Road to Renewal—Thatcherism and the Crisis of the Left*. London: Verso.

Hall, Stuart, and Tony Jefferson, eds. 1976. *Resistance Through Rituals: Youth Subcultures in Post-War Britain*. London: Routledge.

Halnon, Karen Bettez. 2004. "Inside Shock Music Carnival: Spectacle as Contested Terrain." *Critical Sociology* 30 (3): 743–779.

———. 2006a. "Alienation Incorporated: 'F— the Mainstream Music' in the Mainstream." In *The Evolution of Alienation: Trauma, Promise, and the Millennium*, edited by Lauren Langman and Devorah Kalekin-Fishman, 201–226. London: Rowman and Littlefield.

———. 2006b. "Heavy Metal Carnival and Dis-alienation: The Politics of Grotesque Realism." *Symbolic Interaction* 29 (1): 33–48.

Handelman, Don. 1990. *Models and Mirrors: Towards an Anthropology of Public Events*. New York: Cambridge University Press.

Hanifan, Lyda Judson. 1916. "The Rural School Community Center." *Annals of the American Academy of Political and Social Science* 67: 130–138.

Hannerz, Erik. 2015. *Performing Punk*. New York: Palgrave Macmillan.

Hebdige, Dick. 1979. *Subculture: The Meaning of Style*. London: Routledge.

Hellcat. 2009. "It's a Psychobilly Freakout!" *Mibba*. http://www.mibba.com/Articles/Entertainment/2097/Its-a-Psychobilly-Freakout/.

Hesmondhalgh, David. 2005. "Scenes, Subcultures and Tribes: None of the Above." *Journal of Youth Studies* 8 (1): 21–40.

Hetherington, Kevin. 2000. *New Age Travellers*. London: Cassells.

Hodkinson, Paul. 2002. *Goth: Identity, Style and Subculture*. Oxford: Berg.

———. 2016. "Youth Cultures and the Rest of Life: Subcultures, Post-subcultures and Beyond." *Journal of Youth Studies* 19 (5): 629–645.

Holland, Samantha. 2004. *Alternative Femininities: Body, Age and Identity*. London: Berg.

Hollands, Robert. 2002. "Divisions in the Dark: Youth Cultures, Transitions and Segmented Consumption Spaces in the Night-Time Economy." *Journal of Youth Studies* 5: 153–171.

Hutcherson, Ben, and Ross Haenfler. 2010. "Musical Genre as a Gendered Process: Authenticity in Extreme Metal." *Studies in Symbolic Interaction* 35: 101–121.

Huq, Rupa. 2006. *Beyond Subculture: Pop, Youth and Identity in a Postcolonial World*. London: Routledge.

Jackson, Nate. 2017. "Camp Psycho Brings a Spirit of Togetherness to the Psychobilly Scene." *OC Weekly*, June 6. Accessed October 12, 2017. https://ocweekly.com/camp-psycho-brings-a-spirit-of-togetherness-to-the-psychobilly-scene.

Jameson, Fredric. 1991. *Postmodernism, or, the Cultural Logic of Late Capitalism*. Durham, NC: Duke University Press.

Jefferson, Tony. 1976. "Cultural Responses of the Teds: The Defence of Space and Status." In *Resistance through Rituals: Youth Subcultures in Post-War Britain*, edited by Stuart Hall and Tony Jefferson, 81–86. London: Routledge.

Jenss, Heike. 2015. *Fashioning Memory: Vintage Style and Youth Culture*. New York: Bloomsbury Publishing.

Jervis, John. 1999. *Transgressing the Modern*. London: Blackwell.

Kahn-Harris, Keith. 2007. *Extreme Metal: Music and Culture on the Edge*. Oxford: New York.

Kattari, Kimberly. 2009. "Sexual Desire in Psychobilly—Bettie Page, Hot Zombie Chicks, and S/M Sex Slaves." *Examiner.com*, November 9. Accessed December 22, 2010. www.examiner.com/article/sexual-desire-in-psychobilly.

Kattari, Kimberly. 2011. "Psychobilly: Imagining and Realizing a 'Culture of Survival' through Mutant Rockabilly." Ph.D. diss., Butler School of Music, University of Texas at Austin. Katz, Nate. 2012. "The Dawn of Psychobilly." *Perfect Sound Forever*, February. Accessed August 20, 2018. http://www.furious.com/perfect/psychobilly.html.

Kelley, Robin K. 1992. Notes on Deconstructing 'The Folk.'" *American Historical Review* 97 (5): 1400–1408.

Kohnen, Matthew, dir. 2010. *Aaah! Zombies!!* DVD. Los Angeles: Wasted Pictures.

Komara, Edward M., ed. 2006. *Encyclopedia of the Blues: A–J*. New York: Routledge.

Krenske, Leigh, and Jim McKay. 2000. "Hard and Heavy: Gender and Power in a Heavy Metal Subculture." *Gender, Place and Culture: A Journal of Feminist Geography* 7 (3): 287–304.

Kristeva, Julia. 1982. *Powers of Horror: An Essay on Abjection*. New York: Columbia University Press.

Kruse, Holly. 1993. "Subcultural Identity in Alternative Music Culture." *Popular Music* 12 (1): 33–41.

Lamb, Sharon. 2001. *The Secret Lives of Girls: What Good Girls Really Do—Sex Play, Aggression, and Their Guilt*. New York: Free Press.

Leblanc, Lauraine. 1999. *Pretty in Punk: Girl's Gender Resistance in a Boy's Subculture*. New Brunswick, NJ: Rutgers University Press.

Lewis, Nigel. 2010. "Interview with Nigel Lewis." By Wildhank. *Old School Psychobilly*, November. Accessed August 20, 2018. http://www.oldschool-psychobilly.de/nigel_lewis.htm.

Limón, José. 1994. *Dancing with the Devil: Society and Cultural Poetics in Mexican-American South Texas*. Madison: University of Wisconsin Press.

Livingston, Tamara E. 1999. "Music Revivals: Towards a General Theory." *Ethnomusicology* 43 (1): 66–85.

Lowe, Melanie. 2004. "'Tween' Scene: Resistance within the Mainstream." In *Music Scenes: Local, Translocal, and Global*, edited by Andy Bennett and Richard A. Peterson, 80–95. Nashville, TN: Vanderbilt University Press.

Lumb, Berni. 2007. "Interview with Berni Lumb (Front Man of Sgt. Bilko's Krazy Combo)." By Wildhank. *Old School Psychobilly*, October. Accessed August 20, 2018. http://www .oldschool-psychobilly.de/berni_lumb.htm.

Maat, Roy. 2003. "FAQ of Psychobilly." *Wrecking Pit*. Accessed December 22, 2010. http:// www.wreckingpit.com/psycho/faq.php3.

MacDonald, Nancy. 2001. *The Graffiti Subculture: Youth, Masculinity and Identity in London and New York*. London: Palgrave.

Maffesoli, Michel. 1996. *The Time of the Tribes: The Decline of Individualism in Mass Society*. Translated by Don Smith. Thousand Oaks, CA: Sage Publications.

Mair, Eve. 2016. "The Death of the Subculture." *The Cambridge Tab*, October 12. https:// thetab.com/uk/cambridge/2016/10/12/the-death-of-the-subculture-81567.

Malbon, Ben. 1999. *Clubbing*. London: Routledge.

Mallory, Charlotte. 2014. "Is Subculture Dead?" *Huffington Post*, May 23. Accessed August 20, 2018. https://www.huffingtonpost.co.uk/charlotte-mallory/is-subculture-dead_b _5359046.html?guccounter=1&guce_referrer_us=aHR0cHM6Ly93d3cuZ29vZ2xlLmN vbS88&guce_referrer_cs=M8PLclNVq6VajFroqd6vTA.

Marcus, Greil. 1989. *Lipstick Traces: A Secret History of the Twentieth Century*. Cambridge, MA: Harvard University Press.

Marcuse, Herbert. 1964. *One Dimensional Man*. Boston: Beacon Press.

Markowitz, Fran, and Michael Ashkenazi, eds. 1999. *Sex, Sexuality, and the Anthropologist*. Chicago: University of Illinois Press.

McDonnell, Evelyn, and Ann Powers, eds. 1999. *Rock She Wrote: Women Write about Rock, Pop, and Rap*. New York: Delta.

McIntosh, Shawn. 2008. "The Evolution of the Zombie: The Monster That Keeps Coming Back." In *Zombie Culture: Autopsies of the Living Dead*, edited by Shawn McIntosh and Marc Leverette, 1–17. Lanham, MD: Scarecrow Press.

McRobbie, Angela. 1988. "Second-Hand Dresses and the Role of the Ragmarket." In *Zoot Suits and Second-Hand Dresses: An Anthology of Fashion and Music*, edited by Angela McRobbie, 23–49. Boston: Unwin Hyman.

———. (1991) 2000. "Settling Accounts with Subcultures: A Feminist Critique." In *Feminism and Youth Culture: From Jackie to Just Seventeen*, edited by Angela McRobbie, 26–43. 2nd ed. London: Macmillan.

McRobbie, Angela, and Jenny Garber. (1991) 2000. "Girls and Subcultures." In *Feminism and Youth Culture: From Jackie to Just Seventeen*, edited by Angela McRobbie, 12–25. 2nd ed. London: Macmillan.

Mead, Margaret, and Frances Balgely Kaplan, eds. 1965. *American Women: The Report of the President's Commission on the Status of Women and Other Publications of the Commission*. New York: Scribner.

Melechi, Antonio. 1993. "The Ecstasy of Disappearance." In *Rave Off: Politics and Deviance in Contemporary Youth Culture*, edited by Steve Redhead, 7–28. Aldershot, U.K.: Avebury Press.

Merton, Robert K. 1957. *Social Theory and Social Structure*. Glencoe, IL: Free Press.

Miles, Steven 2000. *Youth Lifestyles in a Changing World*. Buckingham, U.K.: Open University Press.

Minh-ha, Trinh T. 1989. *Woman, Native, Other: Writing Postcoloniality and Feminism*. Bloomington: Indiana University Press.

Moore, Ryan. 2005. "Alternative to What? Subcultural Capital and the Commercialization of a Music Scene." *Deviant Behavior* 26: 229–252.

———. 2009. "The Unmaking of the English Working Class: Deindustrialization, Reification and the Origins of Heavy Metal." In *Heavy Metal Music in Britain*, edited by Gerd Bayer, 143–160. Burlington, VT: Ashgate.

Morrison, Craig. 1996. *Go Cat Go! Rockabilly Music and Its Makers*. Urbana: University of Illinois Press.

Moss, Chris. 2015. "Why Don't Young People Want to Be Part of a Tribe Any More?" *The Telegraph*, May 26. Accessed August 20, 2018. https://www.telegraph.co.uk/men /fashion-and-style/11624401/Why-dont-young-people-want-to-be-part-of-a-tribe -any-more.html.

Muggleton, David. 1997. "The Post-subculturalist." In *The Club Cultures Reader: Readings in Popular Cultural Studies*, edited by Steve Redhead, D. Wynne, and J. O. Connor, 185–203. Oxford: Blackwell.

———. 2000. *Inside Subculture: The Postmodern Meaning of Style*. Oxford: Berg.

Muggleton, David, and Robert Weinzierl, eds. 2003. *The Post-subcultures Reader*. Oxford: Berg.

Mullen, Patrick. 1984. "Hillbilly Hipsters of the 1950s: The Romance of Rockabilly." *Southern Quarterly* 22 (3): 79–92.

Myers, Helen, ed. 1992. *Ethnomusicology: Historical and Regional Studies*. New York: W.W. Norton.

Nayak, Anoop. 2003. *Race, Place and Globalisation: Youth Cultures in a Changing World*. Oxford: Berg.

"Nekromantix." n.d. *Wrecking Pit*. Accessed August 20, 2018. http://www.wreckingpit .com/psycho/bands/nekromantix2.php3.

Nettl, Bruno. 2005. *The Study of Ethnomusicology: Thirty-one Issues and Concepts*. Urbana: University of Illinois Press.

Newitz, Annalee. 2008. "War and Social Upheaval Cause Spikes in Zombie Movie Production." *io9.com*, October 29. Accessed October 12, 2010. http://io9.com/5070243 /war-and-social-upheaval-cause-spikes-in-zombie-movie-production.

News Beat. 1982. "Can We Have the 'Billy' Please?"

No Class Fanzine. 1981. "The Meteors—1981 Interview at the Marquee." *No Class*, no. 2. Accessed July 2, 2016. http://www.noclass.co.uk/meteors.html.

Nurse, Keith. 1999. "Globalisation and Trinidad Carnival: Diaspora, Hybridity and Identity in Global Culture." *Cultural Studies* 13: 661–690.

Office for National Statistics (GB). n.d. "Unemployment Rate (Aged 16 and Over, Seasonally Adjusted)." Accessed August 20, 2018. https://www.ons.gov.uk/employmentand labourmarket/peoplenotinwork/unemployment/timeseries/mgsx/lms.

Ortner, Sherry B. 1974. "Is Female to Male as Nature Is to Culture?" In *Woman, Culture, and Society*, edited by Michelle Rosaldo and Louise Lamphere, 68–87. Stanford, CA: Stanford University Press.

Owen, Frank. 1991. "Antihero." *Spin*, March, 68–70.

Page, Bettie. 2010. The Official Site of Bettie Page. Accessed December 1, 2010. http:// www.bettiepage.com/.

Partridge, Kenneth. 2015. "Where to Start with Psychobilly." *The A.V. Club*, April 20. Accessed January 1, 2017. http://www.avclub.com/article/where-start-psychobilly-217841.

Paul, William. 1994. *Laughing Screaming: Modern Hollywood Horror and Comedy*. New York: Columbia University Press.

Peacock, Tim. 2015. "Psycho Killers." *Record Collector*, no. 446 (November): 32–39.

Pershing, Linda. 1996. *The Ribbon around the Pentagon: Peace by Piecemakers*. Knoxville: University of Tennessee Press.

Petridis, Alexis. 2014. "Youth Subcultures: What Are They Now?" *The Guardian*, March 20. Accessed August 20, 2018. https://www.theguardian.com/culture/2014/mar/20/youth -subcultures-where-have-they-gone.

Pilkington, Heather. 2004. "Youth Strategies for Global Living: Space, Power and Communication in Everyday Cultural Practice." In *After Subculture: Critical Studies in Contemporary Youth Culture*, edited by Andy Bennett and Keith Kahn-Harris, 119–134. London: Palgrave.

Polhemus, Ted. 1994. *Street Style: From Sidewalk to Catwalk*. New York: Thames and Hudson.

———. 1997. "In the Supermarket of Style." In *The Club Cultures Reader: Readings in Popular Cultural Studies*, edited by Steve Redhead, D. Wynne, and J. O. Connor, 148–151. Oxford: Blackwell.

Presdee, Mike. 2000. *Cultural Criminology and the Carnival of Crime*. London: Routledge.

Pryce, Lois. 2015. "My First Psychobilly Gig: The Klub Foot, the Meteors, and a Thousand DMs." *Independent*, August 24. Accessed January 11, 2017. http://www.independent. co.uk/arts-entertainment/music/features/my-first-psychobilly-gig-the-klub-foot-the -meteors-and-a-thousand-dms-10469857.html.

Psychobilly Worldwide. n.d. Public Facebook Group. https://www.facebook.com/groups /psychobillyworldwide/.

Psychomania TV. 2016. "Interview Batmobile—Bremen 2015." YouTube. Accessed June 15, 2019. https://www.youtube.com/watch?v=nb6cqx-71cI.

Purcell, Natalie J. 2003. *Death Metal Music: The Passion and Politics of a Subculture*. Jefferson, NC: McFarland.

Putnam, Robert. 2001. *Bowling Alone: The Collapse and Revival of American Community*. New York: Touchstone.

Redhead, Steve, ed. 1993. *Rave Off: Politics and Deviance in Contemporary Youth Culture*. Aldershot, U.K.: Avebury Press.

Redhead, Steve, Derek Wynne, and Justin O'Connor, eds. 1997. *The Club Cultures Reader: Readings in Popular Cultural Studies*. Oxford: Blackwell.

Reynolds, Simon. 1997. "Rave Culture: Living Dream or Living Death?" In *The Club Cultures Reader: Readings in Popular Cultural Studies*, edited by Steve Redhead, D. Wynne, and J. O. Connor, 102–111. Oxford: Blackwell.

———. 2011a. *Retromania: Pop Culture's Addiction to Its Own Past*. London: Faber and Faber.

———. 2011b. "Total Recall: Why Retromania Is All the Rage." *The Guardian*, June 2. Accessed January 20, 2018. https://www.theguardian.com/music/2011/jun/02/total-recall retromania-all-rage.

Rietveld, Hillegonda. 1993. "Living the Dream." In *Rave Off: Politics and Deviance in Contemporary Youth Culture*, edited by Steve Redhead, 41–78. Aldershot, U.K.: Avebury Press.

———. 1998. *This Is Our House*. Aldershot, U.K.: Ashgate.

Riley, Sarah C. E., Christine Griffin, and Yvette Morey. 2010. "The Case for 'Everyday Politics': Evaluating Neo-tribal Theory as a Way to Understand Alternative Forms of Political Participation, Using Electronic Dance Music Culture as an Example." *Sociology* 44 (2): 345–363.

Roach, Martin. 2015. *Dr. Martens: A History of Rebellious Self-Expression*. Northamptonshire, U.K.: AirWair.

Robertson, Sandy. 1981. "The Meteors: 'Radioactive Kid.'" *Sounds*, May 30.

Rosaldo, Michelle, and Louise Lamphere, eds. 1974, *Woman, Culture, and Society*. Stanford, CA: Stanford University Press.

Russo, Mary. 1994. *The Female Grotesque: Risk, Excess and Modernity*. New York: Routledge.

———. 1997. "Female Grotesques: Carnival and Theory." In *Writing on the Body: Female Embodiment and Feminist Theory*, edited by Katie Conboy, Nadia Medina, and Sarah Stanbury, 318–336. New York: Columbia University Press.

Ruthren, Brer. 1981. "Review: Levi Dexter, the Ripchords, the Meteors at Dingwalls." *New Musical Express*, October 18.

Sahagun, Louis. 2008. "Pin-up Queen Bettie Page Dies at 85." *Los Angeles Times*, December 12. Accessed November 9, 2010. https://www.latimes.com/local/obituaries/la-me-page12-2008dec12-story.html.

Santino, Jack. 2011. "The Carnivalesque and the Ritualesque." *Journal of American Folklore* 124 (491): 61–73.

Savage, Jon. 2002. *England's Dreaming: Anarchy, Sex Pistols, Punk Rock, and Beyond*. 2nd ed. New York: St. Martin's Press.

Schröter, Susanne. 2004. "Rituals of Rebellion—Rebellion as Ritual: A Theory Reconsidered." In *The Dynamics of Changing Rituals: The Transformation of Religious Rituals within Their Social and Cultural Context*, edited by J. Kreinath, C. Hartung, and A. Deschner, 41–57. New York: Peter Lang.

Shank, Barry. 1994. *Dissonant Identities: The Rock'n'Roll Scene in Austin, Texas*. Hanover: Wesleyan University Press.

Shenaniganz00. 2006. "Baloobas." *Urban Dictionary*, August 18. Accessed June 15, 2019. https://www.urbandictionary.com/define.php?term=Baloobas.

Shields, Rob. 1992. *Lifestyle Shopping: The Subject of Consumption*. London: Routledge.

Shildrick, Tracy. 2006. "Youth Culture, Subculture and the Importance of Neighbourhood." *Young* 14 (1): 61–74.

Shildrick, Tracy, and Robert MacDonald. 2006. "In Defence of Subculture: Young People, Leisure and Social Divisions." *Journal of Youth Studies* 9 (2): 125–140.

Shugart, Helene A., and Catherine Egley Waggoner. 2005. "A Bit Much: Spectacle as Discursive Resistance." *Feminist Media Studies* 5 (1): 65–81.

Sicko, Dan. 2010. *Techno Rebels: The Renegades of Electronic Funk*. 2nd ed., rev. and updated. Detroit: Wayne State University Press.

Sklar, Annelise. 2008. "Can't Sleep When You're Dead: Sex, Drugs, Rock and Roll, and the Undead in Psychobilly." In *Zombie Culture: Autopsies of the Living Dead*, edited by Shawn McIntosh and Marc Leverette, 135–152. Lanham, MD: Scarecrow Press.

Slobin, Mark. 1993. *Subcultural Sounds: Micromusics of the West*. Hanover, NH: Wesleyan University Press.

Spitz, Marc, and Brendan Mullen. 2001. *We Got the Neutron Bomb: The Untold Story of L.A. Punk*. New York: Three Rivers Press.

Spracklen, Karl. 2014. "There Is (Almost) No Alternative: The Slow 'Heat Death' of Music Cubcultures and the Instrumentalization of Contemporary Leisure." *Annals of Leisure Research* 17 (3): 252–266.

———. 2018. "Sex, Drugs, Satan and Rock and Roll: Re-thinking Dark Leisure, from Theoretical Framework to an Exploration of Pop-Rock-Metal Music Norms." *Annals of Leisure Research* 21 (4): 407–423.

Spracklen, Karl, and Beverley Spracklen. 2012. "Pagans and Satan and Goths, Oh My: Dark Leisure as Communicative Agency and Communal Identity on the Fringes of the Modern Goth Scene." *World Leisure Journal* 54 (4): 350–362.

St. John, Graham. 2009. *Technomad: Global Raving Countercultures*. London: Equinox.

St. John, Warren. 2006. "Market for Zombies? It's Undead (Aaahhh!)." *New York Times*, March 26. Accessed October 12, 2010. http://www.nytimes.com/2006/03/26/fashion/sundaystyles/26ZOMBIES.html?_r=1&ref=warren_st_john.

Stahl, Geoff. 1999. "'Still Winning Space?' Updating Subcultural Theory." *Invisible Culture* 2: 4.

———. 2003. "Tastefully Renovating Subcultural Theory: Making Space for a New Model." In *The Post-subcultures Reader*, edited by David Muggleton and Rupert Weinzeirl, 27–40. Oxford: Berg.

Stallybrass, Peter, and Allon White. 1986. *The Politics and Poetics of Transgression*. London: Methuen.

———. 1997. "From Carnival to Transgression." In *The Subcultures Reader*, edited by Ken Gelder and Sarah Thornton, 293–301. New York: Routledge.

Straw, Will. 1991. "Systems of Articulation, Logics of Change: Scenes and Communities in Popular Music." *Cultural Studies* 5 (3): 361–375.

———. 1997. "Sizing up Record Collections: Gender and Connoisseurship in Rock Music Culture." In *Sexing the Groove: Popular Music and Gender*, edited by Sheila Whitely, 3–16. New York: Routledge.

Taussig, Michael. 2006. *Walter Benjamin's Grave*. Chicago: University of Chicago Press.

Thompson, Beverly Yuen. 2015. *Covered in Ink: Tattoos, Women, and the Politics of the Body*. New York: New York University Press.

Thornton, Sarah. 1996. *Club Cultures: Music, Media, and Subcultural Capital*. Middletown, CT: Wesleyan University Press.

———. 1997. General Introduction to *The Subcultures Reader*, edited by Ken Gelder and Sarah Thornton, 1–7. London: Routledge.

———. 2005. "The Social Logic of Subcultural Capital." In *The Subcultures Reader*, edited by Ken Gelder, 184–192. 2nd ed. London: Routledge.

Tocqueville, Alexis de. (1835) 1966. *Democracy in America*. New York: Harper and Row.

Tsitsos, William. 1999. "Rules of Rebellion: Slamdancing, Moshing, and the American Alternative Scene." *Popular Music* 18 (3): 397–414.

Tudor, Andrew. 1997. "Why Horror? The Peculiar Pleasures of a Popular Genre." *Cultural Studies* 11 (3): 443–463.

Turino, Thomas. 1993. *Moving Away from Silence: Music of the Peruvian Altiplano and the Experience of Urban Migration*. Chicago: University of Chicago Press.

———. 2008. *Music as Social Life: The Politics of Participation*. Chicago: University of Chicago Press.

Turner, Victor. 1969. *The Ritual Process: Structure and Anti-Structure*. Chicago: Aldine Publishing.

Ustinova, Yulia. 2017. *Divine Mania: Alteration of Consciousness in Ancient Greece*. New York: Routledge.

Vitos, Botond. 2010. "DemenCZe: Psychedelic Madhouse in the Czech Republic." In *The Local Scenes and Global Culture of Psytrance*, edited by Graham St. John, 151–169. New York: Routledge.

Wall, Mick. 1981. "The Psychobilly Kid." *Sounds*, April 18.

Walser, Robert. 1993. *Running with the Devil: Power, Gender and Madness in Heavy Metal Music*. Hanover, NH: University Press of New England.

Warwick, Jacqueline. 2007. *Girl Groups, Girl Culture: Popular Music and Identity in the 1960s*. New York: Routledge.

Weinraub, Judith. 1971. "Germaine Greer—Opinions That May Shock the Faithful." *New York Times*, March 21. Accessed June 15, 2019. https://archive.nytimes.com/www.ny times.com/books/99/05/09/specials/greer-shock.html.

Weinstein, Deena. 2000. *Heavy Metal: The Music and Its Cultures*. New York: Da Capo Press.

Whiteley, Sheila, ed. 1997. *Sexing the Groove: Popular Music and Gender*. New York: Routledge.

Wilkins, Amy. 2004. "'So Full of Myself as a Chick': Goth Women, Sexual Independence, and Gender Egalitarianism." *Gender and Society* 18 (3): 238–249.

Williams, J. Patrick. 2011. *Subcultural Theory: Traditions and Concepts*. Cambridge, U.K.: Polity.

Williams, J. Patrick, and Heith Copes. 2005. "'How Edge Are You?' Constructing Authentic Identities and Subcultural Boundaries in a Straitedge Internet Forum." *Symbolic Interaction* 28 (1): 67–89.

Williams, J. Patrick, and Erik Hannerz. 2014. "Articulating the 'Counter' in Subculture Studies." *M/C Journal* 17 (6). http://journal.media-culture.org.au/index.php/mcjour nal/article/view/912.

Willis, Paul. 1972. "Pop Music and Youth Groups." Ph.D. diss., Centre for Contemporary Cultural Studies, University of Birmingham.

———. 1977. *Learning to Labour: How Working Class Kids Get Working Class Jobs*. Farnborough, U.K.: Saxon House.

Wilson, Brian. 2006. *Fight, Fight, or Chill: Subcultures, Youth, and Rave into the Twenty-First Century*. Montreal: McGill-Queen's University Press.

Winge, Therèsa M. 2012. *Body Style*. London: Berg.

Wong, Deborah. 2004. *Speak It Louder: Asian Americans Making Music*. New York: Routledge.

Wood, Robin. (1979) 2004. "An Introduction to the American Horror Film." In *Planks of Reason: Essays on the Horror Film*, edited by Barry Keith Grant and Christopher Sharrett, 107–141. Lanham, MD: Scarecrow Press.

Wrecking Pit. n.d. The Psychobilly Homepage. http://www.wreckingpit.com/index.php3.

Yavuz, M. Selim, Samantha Holland, and Karl Spracklen. 2018. "A Descent into Dark Leisure in Music." *Annals of Leisure Research* 21 (4): 391–394.

Young, Jock. (1971) 2005. "The Subterranean World of Play." In *The Subcultures Reader*, edited by Ken Gelder, 148–156. 2nd ed. London: Routledge.

Zemon Davis, Natalie. 1975. *Society and Culture in Early Modern France: Eight Essays*. Stanford, CA: Stanford University Press.

Kimberly Kattari is an Assistant Professor of Ethnomusicology in the Department of Performance Studies at Texas A&M University.